1839-1908 Ouida

Cecil Castlemaine's gage and other novelettes

1839-1908 Ouida

Cecil Castlemaine's gage and other novelettes

ISBN/EAN: 9783742844019

Manufactured in Europe, USA, Canada, Australia, Japa

Cover: Foto ©Thomas Meinert / pixelio.de

Manufactured and distributed by brebook publishing software (www.brebook.com)

1839-1908 Ouida

Cecil Castlemaine's gage and other novelettes

COLLECTION
OF
BRITISH AUTHORS

TAUCHNITZ EDITION.

VOL. 1247.

CECIL CASTLEMAINE'S GAGE BY OUIDA.

IN ONE VOLUME.

TAUCHNITZ EDITION.

By the same Author,

IDALIA	2 vols.
TRICOTRIN	2 vols.
PUCK	2 vols.
CHANDOS	2 vols.
STRATHMORE	2 vols.
UNDER TWO FLAGS	2 vols.
FOLLE-FARINE	2 vols.
A LEAF IN THE STORM, ETC.	1 vol.
MADAME LA MARQUISE	1 vol.
PASCARÈL	2 vols.
HELD IN BONDAGE	2 vols.
TWO LITTLE WOODEN SHOES	1 vol.
SIGNA (WITH PORTRAIT)	3 vols.
IN A WINTER CITY	1 vol.
ARIADNÊ	2 vols.
FRIENDSHIP	2 vols.
MOTHS	3 vols.
PIPISTRELLO	1 vol.
A VILLAGE COMMUNE	2 vols.
IN MAREMMA	3 vols.
BIMBI	1 vol.
WANDA	3 vols.
FRESCOES AND OTHER STORIES	1 vol.
PRINCESS NAPRAXINE	3 vols.
OTHMAR	3 vols.
A HOUSE PARTY	1 vol.
A RAINY JUNE	ℳ 0,60.
DON GESUALDO	ℳ 0,60.

CECIL CASTLEMAINE'S GAGE,

AND OTHER NOVELETTES.

BY

OUIDA,

AUTHOR OF "IDALIA," "TRICOTRIN," ETC.

COPYRIGHT EDITION.

LEIPZIG

BERNHARD TAUCHNITZ

1872.

The Right of Translation is reserved.

CONTENTS.

	Page
Cecil Castlemaine's Gage; or, The Story of a Broidered Shield	7
Little Grand and the Marchioness; or, Our Maltese Peerage	37
Lady Marabout's Troubles; or, The Worries of a Chaperone	91
A Study à la Louis Quinze; or, Pendant to a Pastel by La Tour	237
"Deadly Dash." A Story told on the Off Day	263

CECIL CASTLEMAINE'S GAGE;

OR,

THE STORY OF A BROIDERED SHIELD.

CECIL CASTLEMAINE was the beauty of her county and her line, the handsomest of all the handsome women that had graced her race, when she moved a century and a half ago down the stately staircase and through the gilded and tapestried halls of Lilliesford. The Town had run mad after her, and her face levelled politics, and was cited as admiringly by the Whigs at St. James's as by the Tories at the Cocoa-tree, by the beaux and Mohocks at Garraway's as by the alumni at the Grecian, by the wits at Will's as by the fops at Ozinda's.

Wherever she went, whether to the Haymarket or the Opera, to the 'Change for a fan or the palace for a state ball, to Drury Lane to see Pastoral Philips's dreary dilution of Racine, or to some fair chief of her faction for basset and ombre, she was surrounded by the best men of her time, and hated by Whig beauties with virulent wrath, for she was a Tory to the backbone, indeed a Jacobite at heart; worshipped Bolingbroke, detested Marlborough and Eugene, believed in all the horrors of the programme said to have been plotted by the Whigs for the anniversary show of 1711, and was thought to have prompted the satire on those fair politicians who are disguised as *Rosalinda* and *Nigranilla* in the 81st paper of the *Spectator*.

Cecil Castlemaine was the greatest beauty of her day, lovelier still at four-and-twenty than she had been at seventeen, unwedded, though the highest coronets in the land had been offered to her; far above the coquetries and minauderies of her friends, far above imitation of the affectations of "Lady Betty Modley's skuttle," or need of practising the Fan exercise; haughty, peerless, radiant, unwon—nay, more—untouched; for the finest gentleman on the town could not flatter himself that he had ever stirred the slightest trace of interest in her, nor boast, as he stood in the inner circle at the Chocolate-house (unless, indeed, he lied more impudently than Tom Wharton himself), that he had ever been honoured by a glance of encouragement from the Earl's daughter. She was too proud to cheapen herself with coquetry, too fastidious to care for her conquests over those who whispered to her through Nicolini's song, vied to have the privilege of carrying her fan, drove past her windows in Soho-square, crowded about her in St. James's Park, paid court even to her little spaniel Indamara, and, to catch but a glimpse of her brocaded train as it swept a ball-room floor, would leave even their play at the Groom Porter's, Mrs. Oldfield in the green-room, a night hunt with Mohun and their brother Mohocks, a circle of wits gathered "within the steam of the coffee-pot" at Will's, a dinner at Halifax's, a supper at Bolingbroke's —whatever, according to their several tastes, made their best entertainment and was hardest to quit.

The highest suitors of the day sought her smile

and sued for her hand; men left the Court and the Mall to join the Flanders army before the lines at Bouchain less for loyal love of England than hopeless love of Cecil Castlemaine. Her father vainly urged her not to fling away offers that all the women at St. James's envied her. She was untouched and unwon, and when her friends, the court beauties, the fine ladies, the coquettes of quality, rallied her on her coldness (envying her her conquests), she would smile her slight proud smile and bow her stately head. "Perhaps she was cold; she might be; they were personable men? Oh yes! she had nothing to say against them. His Grace of Belamour?—A pretty wit, without doubt. Lord Millamont?—Diverting, but a coxcomb. He had beautiful hands; it was a pity he was always thinking of them! Sir Gage Rivers?—As obsequious a lover as the man in the 'Way of the World,' but she had heard he was very boastful and facetious at women over his chocolate at Ozinda's. The Earl of Argent?— A gallant soldier, surely, but whatever he might protest, no mistress would ever rival with him the dice at the Groom Porter's. Lord Philip Bellairs?—A proper gentleman; no fault in him; a bel esprit and an elegant courtier; pleased many, no doubt, but he did not please her overmuch. Perhaps her taste was too finical, or her character too cold, as they said. She preferred it should be so. When you were content it were folly to seek a change. For her part, she failed to comprehend how women could stoop to flutter their fans and choose their ribbons, and rack their tirewomen's brains for new pulvillios, and lappets, and devices, and practise their curtsey and recovery before their pier-glass, for no better aim or stake than to draw the glance and win the praise of men for whom they cared nothing. A woman who had the eloquence of beauty and a true pride should be above heed for such affectations, pleasure in such applause!"

So she would put them all aside and turn the tables on her friends, and go on her own way, proud, peerless, Cecil Castlemaine, conquering and unconquered; and Steele must have had her name in his thoughts, and honoured it heartily and sincerely, when he wrote one Tuesday, on the 21st of October, under the domino of his Church Coquette, "I say I do honour to those who *can be coquettes and are not such*, but I despise all who would be so, and, in despair of arriving at it themselves, hate and villify all those who can." A definition justly drawn by his keen, quick graver, though doubtless it only excited the ire of, and was entirely lost upon, those who read the paper over their dish of bohea, or over their toilette, while they shifted a patch for an hour before they could determine it, or regretted the loss of ten guineas at crimp.

Cecil Castlemaine was the beauty of the Town: when she sat at Drury Lane on the Tory side of the house the devoutest admirer of Oldfield or Mrs. Porter scarcely heard a word of the *Heroic Daughter* or the *Amorous Widow*, and the "beau fullest of his own dear self" forgot his silver-fringed gloves, his medallion snuff-box, his knotted cravat, his clouded cane, the slaughter that he planned to do, from gazing at her where she sat, as though she were reigning sovereign at St. James's, the Castlemaine diamonds flashing crescent-like above her brow. At church and court, at park and assembly, there were none who could eclipse that haughty gentlewoman; therefore her fond women friends, who had caressed her so warmly and so gracefully, and pulled her to pieces behind her back, if they could, so eagerly over their dainty cups of tea in an afternoon visit, were glad, one and all, when on "Barnaby-bright," Anglicè, the 22nd (then the 11th) of June, the great Castlemaine chariot, with its three herons blazoned on its coronetted panels, its laced liveries and gilded harness, rolled over the heavy, ill-made roads down into the country in almost princely pomp, the peasants pouring out from the wayside cottages to stare at my lord's coach.

It was said in the town that a portly divine, who wore his scarf as one of the chaplains to the Earl of Castlemaine, had prattled somewhat indiscreetly at Child's of his patron's politics; that certain cypher letters had passed the Channel enclosed in chocolate cakes as soon as French goods were again imported after the peace of Utrecht; that gentlemen in high places were strongly suspected of mischievous designs against the tranquillity of the country and government; that the Earl had, among others, received a friendly hint from a relative in power to absent himself for a while from the court where he was not best trusted, and the town where an incautious word might be picked up and lead to Tower-hill, and amuse himself at his goodly castle of Lilliesford, where the red deer would not spy upon him, and the dark beech-woods would tell no tales. And the ladies of quality, her dear friends and sisters, were glad when they heard it as they punted at basset and fluttered their fans complacently. They would have the field for themselves, for a season, while Cecil Castlemaine was immured in her manor of Lilliesford; would be free of her beauty to eclipse them at the next birthday, be quit of their most dreaded rival, their most omnipotent leader of fashion: and they rejoiced at the whisper of the cypher letter, the damaging gossipry of the Whig coffee-houses, the bad repute into which my Lord Earl had grown at St. James's, at the misfortune of their friend, in a word, as human nature, masculine or feminine, will ever do—to its shame be it spoken—unless the *fomes peccati* be more completely wrung out of it than it ever has been since the angel Gabriel performed that work of purification on the infant Mahomet.

It was the June of the year '15, and the coming disaffection was seething and boiling secretly among the Tories; the impeachment of Ormond and Bolingbroke had strengthened the distaste to the new-come Hanoverian pack, their attainder had been the blast of air needed to excite the smouldering wood to flame, the gentlemen of that party in the South began to grow impatient of the intrusion of the distant German branch, to think lovingly of the old legitimate line, and to feel something of the chafing irritation of the gentlemen of the North, who were fretting like staghounds held in leash.

Envoys passed to and fro between St. Germain, and Jacobite nobles, priests of the church that had fallen out of favour and were typified as the Scarlet Woman by a rival who, though successful, was still bitter, plotted with ecclesiastical relish in the task; letters were conveyed in rolls of innocent lace, plans were forwarded in frosted confections, messages were passed in invisible cypher that defied investigation. The times were dangerous; full of plot and counter-plot, of risk and danger, of fomenting projects and hidden disaffection—times in which men, living habitually over mines, learned to like the uncertainty, and to think life flavourless without the chance of losing it any hour; and things being in this state, the Earl of Castlemaine deemed it prudent to take the counsel of his friend in power, and retire from London for a while, perhaps for the safety of his own person, perhaps for the advancement of his cause, either of which were easier ensured at his seat in the western counties than amidst the Whigs of the capital.

The castle of Lilliesford was bowered in the thick woods of the western counties, a giant pile built by Norman masons. Troops of deer herded under the gold-green beechen-boughs, the sunlight glistened through the aisles of the trees, and quivered down on to the thick moss, and ferns, and tangled grass that grew under the park woodlands; the water-lilies clustered on the river, and the swans "floated double, swan and shadow," under the leaves that swept into the water; then, when Cecil Castlemaine came down to share her father's retirement, as now, when her name and titles on the gold plate of a coffin that lies with others of her race in the mausoleum across the park, where winter snows and summer sun-rays are alike to those who sleep within, is all that tells at Lilliesford of the loveliest woman of her time who once reigned there as mistress.

The country was in its glad green midsummer beauty, and the musk-rosebuds bloomed in profuse luxuriance over the chill marble of the terraces, and scattered their delicate odorous petals in fragrant showers on the sward of the lawns, when Cecil Castlemaine came down to what she termed her exile. The morning was fair and cloudless, its sunbeams piercing through the darkest glades in the woodlands, the thickest shroud of the ivy, the deepest-hued pane of the mullioned windows, as she passed down the great staircase where lords and gentlewomen of her race gazed on her from the canvas of Lely and Jamesone, Bourdain and Vandyke, crossed the hall with her dainty step, so stately yet so light, and standing by the window of her own bower-room, was lured out on to the terrace overlooking the west side of the park.

She made such a picture as Vandyke would have liked to paint, with her golden glow upon her, and the musk-roses clustering about her round the pilasters of marble—the white chill marble to which Belamour and many other of her lovers of the court and town had often likened her. Vandyke would have lingered lovingly on the hand that rested on her staghound's head, would have caught her air of court-like grace and dignity, would have painted with delighted fidelity her deep azure eyes, her proud brow, her delicate lips arched haughtily like a Cupid's bow, would have picked out every fold of her sweeping train, every play of light on her silken skirts, every dainty tracery of her point-lace. Yet even painted by Sir Anthony, that perfect master of art and of elegance, though more finished, it could have hardly been more faithful, more instinct with grace, and life, and dignity, than a sketch drawn of her shortly after that time by one who loved her well, which is still hanging in the gallery at Lilliesford, lighted up by the afternoon sun when it streams in through the western windows.

Cecil Castlemaine stood on the terrace looking over the lawns and gardens through the opening vistas of meeting boughs and interlaced leaves to the woods and hills beyond, fused in a soft mist of green and purple, with her hand lying carelessly on her hound's broad head. She was a zealous Tory, a skilled politician, and her thoughts were busy with the hopes and fears, the chances for and against, of a cause that lay near her heart, but whose plans were yet immature, whose first blow was yet unstruck, and whose well-wishers were sanguine of a success they had not yet hazarded, though they hardly ventured to whisper to each other their previous designs and desires. Her thoughts were far away, and she hardly heeded the beauty round her, musing on schemes and projects dear to her party, that would imperil the Castlemaine coronet, but would serve the only royal house the Castlemaine line had ever in their hearts acknowledged.

She had regretted leaving the Town, moreover; a leader of the mode, a wit, a woman of the world, she missed her accustomed sphere; she was no pastoral Phyllis, no country-born Mistress Fiddy, to pass her time in provincial pleasures, in making cordial waters, in tending her beau-pots, in preserving her fallen rose-leaves, and inspecting the confections in the still-room; as little was she able, like many fine ladies when in similar exile, to while it away by scolding her tirewomen, and sorting a suit of ribbons, in ordering a set of gilded leather hangings from Chelsea for the state chambers, and yawning over chocolate in her bed till mid-day. She regretted leaving the Town, not for Belamour, nor Argent, nor any of those who vainly hoped, as they glanced at the little mirror in the lids of their snuff-boxes that they might have graven themselves, were it ever so faintly, in her thoughts; but for the wits, the pleasures, the choice clique, the accustomed circle to which she was so used, the courtly, brilliant town-life where she was wont to reign.

So she stood on the terrace the first morning of her exile, her thoughts far away, with the loyal gentlemen of the North, and the banished court of St. Germain, the lids drooping proudly over her haughty eyes, and her lips half parted with a faint smile of triumph in the visions limned by ambition and imagination, while the wind softly stirred the rich lace of her bodice, and her fingers lay, lightly yet firmly, on the head of her staghound. She looked up at last as she heard the ring of a horse's hoofs, and saw a sorrel, covered with dust and foam, spurred up the avenue, which, rounding past the terrace, swept on to the front entrance; the sorrel looked well-nigh spent, and his rider somewhat worn and languid, as a man might do with justice who had been in boot and saddle twenty-four hours at the stretch, scarce stopping for a stoup of wine; but he lifted his hat, and bowed down to his saddle-bow as he passed her.

"Was it the long-looked-for messenger with definite news from St. Germain?" wondered Lady Cecil, as her hound gave out a deep-tongued bay of anger at the stranger. She went back into her bower-room, and toyed absently with her flowered handkerchief, broidering a stalk to a violet-leaf, and wondering what additional hope the horseman might have brought to strengthen the good Cause, till her servants brought word that his Lordship prayed the pleasure of her presence in the octagon-room. Whereat she rose and swept through the long corridors, entered the octagon-room, the sunbeams gathering about her rich dress as they passed through the stained glass oriels, and saluted the new comer, when her father presented him to her as their trusty and welcome friend and envoy, Sir Fulke Ravensworth, with her careless dignity, and queenly grace, that nameless air which was too highly bred to be condescension, but markedly and proudly repelled familiarity, and signed a pale of distance beyond which none must intrude.

The new comer was a tall and handsome man, of noble presence, bronzed by foreign suns, pale and jaded just now with hard riding, while his dark silver-laced suit was splashed and covered with dust; but as he bowed low to her, critical Cecil Castlemaine saw that not Belamour himself could have better grace, not my Lord Millamont courtlier mien nor whiter hands, and listened with gracious air to what her father unfolded to her of his mission from St. Germain, whence he had come, at great personal risk, in many disguises, and at breathless speed, to place in their hands a precious letter in cypher from James Stuart to his well-beloved and loyal subject Herbert George, Earl of Castlemaine. A letter spoken of with closed doors and in low whispers, loyal as was the household, supreme as the Earl ruled over his domains of Lilliesford, for these were times when men mistrusted those of their own blood, and when the very figures on the tapestry seemed instinct with life to spy and to betray —when they almost feared the silk that tied a missive should babble of its contents, and the hound that slept beside them should read and tell their thoughts.

To leave Lilliesford would be danger to the Envoy and danger to the Cause; to stay as guest was to disarm suspicion. The messenger who had brought such priceless news must rest within the shelter of his roof; too much were risked by returning to the French coast yet awhile, or even by joining Mar or Derwentwater, so the Earl enforced his will upon the Envoy, and the Envoy thanked him, and accepted.

Perchance the beauty, whose eyes he had seen lighten and proud brow flush as she read the royal greeting and injunction, made a sojourn near her presence not distasteful; perchance he cared little where he stayed till the dawning time of action and of rising should arrive, when he should take the field and fight till life or death for the "White Rose and the long heads of hair." He was a soldier of fortune, a poor gentleman with no patrimony but his name, no chance of distinction save by his sword; sworn to a cause whose star was set for ever; for many years his life had been of changing adventure and shifting chances, now fighting with Berwick at Almanza, now risking his life in some delicate and dangerous errand for James Stuart that could not have been trusted so well to any other officer about St. Germain; gallant to rashness, yet with much of the acumen of the diplomatist, he was invaluable to his Court and Cause, but, Stuart-like, men-like, they hastened to employ, but ever forgot to reward!

Lady Cecil missed her town-life, and did not over-favour her exile in the western counties. To note down on her Mather's tablets the drowsy homilies droned out by the chaplain on a Sabbath noon, to play at crambo, to talk with her tirewomen of new washes for the skin, to pass her hours away in knotting?—she, whom Steele might have writ of when he drew his character of *Eudoxia*, could while her exile with none of these inanities; neither could she consort with gentry who seemed to her little better than the boors of a country wake, who had never heard of Mr. Spectator and knew nothing of Mr. Cowley, countrywomen whose ambition was in their cowslip wines, fox-hunters more ignorant and uncouth than the dumb brutes they followed.

Who was there for miles around with whom she could stoop to associate, with whom she cared to exchange a word? Madam from the vicarage, in her grogram, learned in syrups, salves, and possets? Country Lady Bountifuls, with gossip of the village and the poultry-yard? Provincial Peeresses, who had never been to London since Queen Anne's coronation? A squirearchy, who knew of no music save the concert of their stop-hounds, no court save the court of the county assize, no literature unless by miracle 'twere Tarleton's Jests? None such as these could cross the inlaid oak parquet of Lilliesford, and be ushered into the presence of Cecil Castlemaine.

So the presence of the Chevalier's messenger was not altogether unwelcome and distasteful to her. She saw him but little, merely conversing at table with him with that distant and dignified courtesy which marked her out from the light, free, inconsequent manners in vogue with other women of quality of her time; the air which had chilled half the softest things even on Belamour's lips, and kept the vainest coxcomb hesitating and abashed.

But by degrees she observed that the Envoy was a man who had lived in many countries and in many courts, was well versed in the tongues of France and Italy and Spain—in their belles lettres too, moreover—

and had served his apprenticeship to good company
in the salons of Versailles, in the audience-room of the
Vatican, at the receptions of the Duchess du Maine,
and with the banished family at St. Germain. He
spoke with a high and sanguine spirit of the troublous
times approaching and the beloved Cause whose crisis
was at hand, which chimed in with her humour better
than the flippancies of Belamour, the airy nothings of
Millamont. He was but a soldier of fortune, a poor
gentleman who, named to her in the town, would have
had never a word, and would have been unnoted
amidst the crowding beaux who clustered round to
hold her fan and hear how she had been pleasured
with the drolleries of *Grief à la Mode*. But down in
the western counties she deigned to listen to the
Prince's officer, to smile—a smile beautiful when it
came on her proud lips, as the play of light on the
opals of her jewelled stomacher—nay, even to be
amused when he spoke of the women of foreign courts,
to be interested when he told, which was but reluctantly,
of his own perils, escapes, and adventures, to discourse
with him, riding home under the beech avenues from
hawking, or standing on the western terrace at curfew
to watch the sunset, of many things on which the
nobles of the Mall and the gentlemen about St. James's
had never been allowed to share her opinions. For
Lady Cecil was deeply read (unusually deeply for her
day, since fine ladies of her rank and fashion mostly
contented themselves with skimming a romance of
Scuderi's, or an act of *Aurungzebe*); but she rarely
spoke of those things, save perchance now and then
to Mr. Addison, who, though a Whig, was certainly
an elegant scholar.

Fulke Ravensworth never flattered her, moreover, and flattery was a honeyed confection of which she had long been cloyed; he even praised boldly before her other women of beauty and grace whom he had seen at Versailles, at Sceaux, and at St. Germain; neither did he defer to her perpetually, but where he differed would combat her sentiments courteously but firmly. Though a soldier and a man of action, he had an admirable skill at the limner's art; could read to her the Divina Commedia, or the comedies of Lope da' Vega, and transfer crabbed Latin and abstruse Greek into elegant English for her pleasure; and though a beggared gentleman of most precarious fortunes, he would speak of life and its chances, of the Cause and its perils, with a daring which she found preferable to the lisped languor of the men of the town, who had no better campaigns than laying siege to a prude, cared for no other weapons than their toilettes and snuff-boxes, and sought no other excitement than a *coup d'éclat* with the lion-tumblers.

On the whole, through these long midsummer days, Lady Cecil found the Envoy from St. Germain a companion that did not suit her ill, sought less the solitude of her bower-room, and listened graciously to him in the long twilight hours, while the evening dew gathered in the cups of the musk-roses, and the star-rays began to quiver on the water-lilies floating on the river below, that murmured along, with endless song, under the beechen-boughs. A certain softness stole over her, relaxing the cold hauteur of which Belamour had so often complained, giving a nameless charm, supplying a nameless something, lacking before, in the beauty of The Castlemaine.

She would stroke, half sadly, the smooth feathers of her tartaret falcon Gabrielle when Fulke Ravensworth brought her the bird from the ostreger's wrist, with its azure velvet hood, and silver bells and jesses. She would wonder, as she glanced through Corneille or Congreve, Philips, or Petrarca, what it was, this passion of love, of which they all treated, on which they all turned, no matter how different their strain. And now and then would come over her cheek and brow a faint fitful wavering flush, delicate and changing as the flush from the rose-hued reflexions of western clouds on a statue of Pharos marble, and then she would start and rouse herself, and wonder what she ailed, and grow once more haughty, calm, stately, dazzling, but chill as the Castlemaine diamonds that she wore.

So the summer-time passed, and the autumn came, the corn-lands brown with harvest, the hazel-copses strewn with fallen nuts, the beech-leaves turning into reddened gold. As the wheat ripened but to meet the sickle, as the nuts grew but to fall, as the leaves turned to gold but to wither, so the sanguine hopes, the fond ambitions of men, strengthened and matured only to fade into disappointment and destruction! Four months had sped by since the Prince's messenger had come to Lilliesford—months that had gone swiftly with him as some sweet delicious dream; and the time had come when he had orders to ride north, secretly and swiftly, speak with Mr. Forster and other gentlemen concerned in the meditated rising, and convey despatches and instructions to the Earl of Mar; for Prince James was projecting soon to join his loyal adherents in Scotland, and the critical moment was close at hand, the moment when, to Fulke Ravensworth's high and sanguine courage, victory seemed certain; failure, if no treachery marred, no dissension weakened, impossible; the moment to which he looked for honour, success, distinction, that should give him claim and title to aspire—*where?* Strong man, cool soldier though he was, he shrank from drawing his fancied future out from the golden haze of immature hope, lest he should see it wither upon closer sight. He was but a landless adventurer, with nothing but his sword and his honour, and kings he knew were slow to pay back benefits, or recollect the hands that hewed them free passage to their thrones.

Cecil Castlemaine stood within the window of her bower-room, the red light of the October sun glittering on her gold-broidered skirt and her corsage sewn with opals and emeralds; her hand was pressed lightly on her bosom, as though some pain were throbbing there; it was new this unrest, this weariness, this vague weight that hung upon her; it was the perils of their Cause, she told herself; the risks her father ran: it was weak, childish, unworthy a Castlemaine! Still the pain throbbed there.

Her hound, asleep beside her, raised his head with a low growl as a step intruded on the sanctity of the bower-room, then composed himself again to slumber, satisfied it was no foe. His mistress turned slowly; she knew the horses waited; she had shunned this ceremony of farewell, and never thought any would be bold enough to venture here without permission sought and gained.

"Lady Cecil, I could not go upon my way without

one word of parting. Pardon me if I have been too rash to seek it here."

Why was it that his brief frank words ever pleased her better than Belamour's most honeyed phrases, Millamont's suavest periods? She scarcely could have told, save that there were in them an earnestness and truth new and rare to her ear and to her heart.

She pressed her hand closer on the opals—the jewels of calamity—and smiled:

"Assuredly I wish you God speed, Sir Fulke, and safe issue from all perils."

He bowed low; then raised himself to his fullest height, and stood beside her, watching the light play upon the opals:

"That is all you vouchsafe me?"

"*All?* It is as much as you would claim, sir, is it not? It is more than I would say to many."

"Your pardon—it *is* more than I should claim if prudence were ever by, if reason always ruled! I have no right to ask for, seek for, even wish for, more; such petitions may only be addressed by men of wealth and of high title: a landless soldier should have no pride to sting, no heart to wound; they are the prerogative of a happier fortune."

Her lips turned white, but she answered haughtily; the crimson light flashing in her jewels, heirlooms priceless and hereditary, like her beauty and her pride:

"This is strange language, sir! I fail to apprehend you."

"You have never thought that I ran a danger deadlier than that which I have ever risked on any field? You have never guessed that I have had the madness, the presumption, the crime—it may be in your eyes—to love you."

The colour flushed to her face, crimsoning even her brow, and then fled back. Her first instinct was insulted pride—a beggared gentleman, a landless soldier, spoke to her of love!—of love!—which Belamour had barely had courage to whisper of; which none had dared to sue of her in return. He had ventured to feel this for her! he had ventured to speak of this to her!

The Envoy saw the rising resentment, the pride spoken in every line of her delicate face, and stopped her as she would have spoken.

"Wait! I know all you would reply. You think it infinite daring, presumption that merits highest reproof——"

"Since you divined so justly, it were pity you subjected yourself and me to this most useless, most unexpected interview. Why——"

"*Why?* Because, perchance, in this life you will see my face no more, and you will think gently, mercifully of my offence (if offence it be to love you more than life, and only less than honour), when you know that I have fallen for the Cause, with your name in my heart, held only the dearer because never on my lips! Sincere love can be no insult to whomsoever proffered; Elizabeth Stuart saw no shame to her in the devotion of William Craven!"

Cecil Castlemaine stood in the crimson glory of the autumn sunset, her head erect, her pride unshaken, but her heart stirred strangely and unwontedly. It smote the one with bitter pain, to think a penniless exile should thus dare to speak of what Princes and

Dukes had almost feared to whisper; what had she done—what had she said, to give him license for such liberty? It stirred the other with a tremulous warmth, a vague, sweet pleasure, that were never visitants there before; but that she scouted instantly as weakness, folly, debasement, in the Last of the Castlemaines.

He saw well enough what passed within her, what made her eyes so troubled, yet her brow and lips so proudly set, and he bent nearer towards her, the great love that was in him trembling in his voice:

"Lady Cecil, hear me! If in the coming struggle I win distinction, honour, rank—if victory come to us, and the King we serve remember me in his prosperity as he does now in his adversity—if I can meet you hereafter with tidings of triumph and success, my name made one which England breathes with praise and pride, honours gained such as even you will deem worthy of your line—then—then—will you let me speak of what you refuse to hearken to now—then may I come to you, and seek a gentler answer?"

She looked for a moment upon his face, as it bent towards her in the radiance of the sunset light, the hope that hopes all things glistening in his eyes, the high-souled daring of a gallant and sanguine spirit flushing his forehead, the loud throbs of his heart audible in the stillness around; and her proud eyes grew softer, her lips quivered for an instant.

Then she turned towards him with queenly grace:
"*Yes!*"

It was spoken with stately dignity, though scarce above her breath; but the hue that wavered in her cheek was but the lovelier, for the pride that would not let her eyes droop nor her tears rise; would not let her utter one softer word. That one word cost her much. That single utterance was much from Cecil Castlemaine.

Her handkerchief lay at her feet, a delicate costly toy of lace, embroidered with her shield and chiffre; he stooped and raised it, and thrust it in his breast to treasure it there.

"If I fail, I send this back in token that I renounce all hope; if I can come to you with honour and with fame, this shall be my gage that I may speak, that you will listen?"

She bowed her noble head, ever held haughtily, as though every crown of Europe had a right to circle it; his hot lips lingered for a moment on her hand; then Cecil Castlemaine stood alone in the window of her bower-room, her hand pressed again upon the opals under which her heart was beating with a dull, weary pain, looking out over the landscape, where the golden leaves were falling fast, and the river, tossing sadly dead branches on its waves, was bemoaning in plaintive language the summer days gone by.

Two months came and went, the beech-boughs, black and sear, creaked in the bleak December winds that sighed through frozen ferns and over the couches of shivering deer, the snow drifted up on the marble terrace, and ice-drops clung where the warm rosy petals of the musk-rosebuds had nestled. Across the country came terrible whispers that struck the hearts of men of loyal faith to the White Rose with a bolt of ice-cold terror and despair. Messengers riding in hot haste, open-mouthed peasants gossiping by the village forge, horsemen who tarried for a breathless rest at alehouse doors, Whig divines who returned thanks for God's most gracious mercy in vouchsafing victory to the strong, all told the tale, all spread the news of the drawn battle of Sheriff-Muir, of the surrender under Preston walls, of the flight of Prince James. The tidings came one by one to Lilliesford, where my Lord Earl was holding himself in readiness to co-operate with the gentlemen of the North to set up the royal standard, broidered by his daughter's hands, in the western counties, and proclaim James III. "sovereign lord and king of the realms of Great Britain and Ireland." The tidings came to Lilliesford, and Cecil Castlemaine clenched her white jewelled hands in passionate anguish that a Stuart should have fled before the traitor of Argyll, instead of dying with his face towards the rebel crew; that men had lived who could choose surrender instead of heroic death; that *she* had not been there, at Preston, to shame them with a woman's reading of courage and of loyalty, and show them how to fall with a doomed city rather than yield captive to a foe!

Perhaps amidst her grief for her Prince and for his Cause mingled—as the deadliest thought of all—a memory of a bright proud face, that had bent towards her with tender love and touching grace a month before, and that might now be lying pale and cold, turned upwards to the winter stars, on the field of Sheriff-Muir.

A year rolled by. Twelve months had fled since the gilded carriage of the Castlemaines, with the lordly blazonment upon its panels, its princely retinue and stately pomp, had come down into the western counties. The bones were crumbling white in the coffins in the

Tower, and the skulls over Temple-bar had bleached white in winter snows and spring-tide suns; Kenmuir had gone to a sleep that knew no wakening, and Derwentwater had laid his fair young head down for a thankless cause; the heather bloomed over the mounds of dead on the plains of Sheriff-Muir, and the yellow gorse blossomed under the city walls of Preston.

Another summer had dawned, bright and laughing, over England; none the less fair for human lives laid down, for human hopes crushed out; daisies powdering the turf sodden with human blood, birds carolling their song over graves of heaped-up dead. The musk-roses tossed their delicate heads again amidst the marble pilasters, and the hawthorn boughs shook their fragrant buds into the river of Lilliesford, the purple hills lay wrapped in sunny mist, and hyacinth bells mingled with the tangled grass and fern under the woodland shades, where the red deer nestled happily. Herons plumed their silvery wings down by the water-side, swallows circled in sultry air above the great bell-tower, and wood-pigeons cooed with soft love-notes among the leafy branches. Yet the Countess of Castlemaine, last of her race, sole owner of the lands that spread around her, stood on the rose-terrace, finding no joy in the sunlight about her, no melody in the song of the birds.

She was the last of her name; her father, broken-hearted at the news from Dumblain and Preston, had died the very day after his lodgment in the Tower. There was no heir male of his line, and the title had passed to his daughter; there had been thoughts of confiscation and attainder, but others, unknown to her, solicited what she scorned to ask for herself, and the greed of the hungry "Hanoverian pack" spared the lands and the revenues of Lilliesford. In haughty pride, in lonely mourning, the fairest beauty of the Court and Town withdrew again to the solitude of her western counties, and tarried there, dwelling amidst her women and her almost regal household, in the sacred solitude of grief, wherein none might intrude. Proud Cecil Castlemaine was yet prouder than of yore; alone sorrowing for her ruined Cause and exiled King, she would hold converse with none of those who had had a hand in drawing down the disastrous fate she mourned, and only her staghound could have seen the weariness upon her face when she bent down to him, or Gabrielle the falcon felt her hand tremble when it stroked her folded wings. She stood on the terrace, looking over her spreading lands, not the water-lilies on the river below whiter than her lips, pressed painfully together. Perhaps she repented of certain words, spoken to one whom now she would never again behold—perhaps she thought of that delicate toy that was to have been brought back in victory and hope, that now might lie stained and stiffened with blood next a lifeless heart, for never a word in the twelve months gone by had there come to Lilliesford as tidings of Fulke Ravensworth.

Her pride was dear to her, dearer than aught else; she had spoken as was her right to speak, she had done what became a Castlemaine; it would have been weakness to have acted otherwise; what was he—a landless soldier—that he should have dared as he had dared? Yet the sables she wore were not solely for the dead Earl, not solely for the lost Stuarts the hot mist that would blind the eyes of Cecil Castlemaine, as hours swelled to days, and days to months, and she —the flattered beauty of the Court and Town—stayed in self-chosen solitude in her halls of Lilliesford, still unwedded und unwon.

The noon hours chimed from the bell-tower, and the sunny beauty of the morning but weighed with heavier sadness on her heart; the song of the birds, the busy hum of the gnats, the joyous ring of the silver bell round her pet fawn's neck, as it darted from her side under the drooping boughs—none touched an answering chord of gladness in her. She stood looking over her stretching woodlands in deep thought, so deep that she heard no step over the lawn beneath, nor saw the frightened rush of the deer, as a boy, crouching among the tangled ferns, sprang up from his hiding-place under the beechen branches, and stood on the terrace before her, craving her pardon in childish, yet fearless tones. She turned, bending on him that glance which had made the over-bold glance of Princes fall abashed. The boy was but a little tatterdemalion to have ventured thus abruptly into the presence of the Countess of Castlemaine; still it was with some touch of a page's grace that he bowed before her.

"Lady, I crave your pardon, but my master bade me watch for you, though I watched till midnight."

"Your master!"

A flush, warm as that on the leaves of the musk-roses, rose to her face for an instant, then faded as suddenly. The boy did not notice her words, but went on in an eager whisper, glancing anxiously round, as a hare would glance fearing the hunters.

"And told me when I saw you not to speak his

name, but only to give you this as his gage, that though all else is lost he has not forgot *his* honour nor *your* will."

Cecil Castlemaine spoke no word, but she stretched out her hand and took it—her own costly toy of cambric and lace, with her broidered shield and coronet.

"Your master! Then—he lives?"

"Lady, he bade me say no more. You have his message; I must tell no further."

She laid her hand upon his shoulder, a light, snow-white hand, yet one that held him now in a clasp of steel.

"Child! answer me at your peril! Tell me of him whom you call your master. Tell me all—quick—quick!"

"You are his friend?"

"His friend? My Heaven! Speak on!"

"He bade me tell no more on peril of his heaviest anger! but if you *are* his friend I sure may speak what you should know without me. It is a poor friend, lady, who has need to ask whether another be dead or living!"

The scarlet blood flamed in the Countess's blanched face, she signed him on with impetuous command; she was unused to disobedience, and the child's words cut her to the quick.

"Sir Fulke sails for the French coast to-morrow night," the boy went on, in tremulous haste. "He was left for dead—our men ran one way, and Argyll's men the other—on the field of Sheriff-Muir; and sure if he had not been strong indeed, he would have died that awful night, untended, on the bleak moor, with the wind roaring round him, and his life ebbing away. He was not one of those who *fled;* you know that of him if you know aught. We got him away before dawn, Donald and I, and hid him in a shieling; he was in the fever then, and knew nothing that was done to him, only he kept that bit of lace in his hand for weeks and weeks, and would not let us stir it from his grasp. What magic there was in it we wondered often, but 'twas a magic, mayhap, that got him well at last; it was an even chance but that he'd died, God bless him! though we did what best we could. We've been wandering in the Highlands all the year, hiding here and tarrying there. Sir Fulke sets no count upon his life. Sure I think he thanks us little for getting him through the fever of the wounds, but he could not have borne to be pinioned, you know, lady, like a thief, and hung up by the brutes of Whigs, as a butcher hangs sheep in the shambles! The worst of the danger's over—they've had their fill of the slaughter; but we sail to-morrow night for the French coast—England's no place for my master."

Cecil Castlemaine let go her hold upon the boy, and her hand closed convulsively upon the dainty handkerchief—her gage sent so faithfully back to her!

The child looked upon her face; perchance, in his master's delirium, he had caught some knowledge of the story that hung to that broidered toy.

"If you *are* his friend, Madam, doubtless you have some last word to send him?"

Cecil Castlemaine, whom nothing moved, whom nothing softened, bowed her head at the simple question, her heart wrestling sorely, her lips set together in unswerving pride, a mist before her haughty eyes, the broidered shield upon her handkerchief—the shield of her stately and unyielding race—pressed close against her breast.

"You have no word for him, lady?"

Her lips parted; she signed him away. Was this child to see her yielding to such weakness? Had she, Countess of Castlemaine, no better pride, no better strength, no better power of resolve, than this?"

The boy lingered.

"I will tell Sir Fulke then, lady, that the ruined have no friends?"

Whiter and prouder still grew the delicate beauty of her face; then she raised her stately head, haughtily as she had used to glance over a glittering Court, where each voice murmured praise of her loveliness and reproach of her coldness; and placed the fragile toy of lace back in the boy's hands.

"Go, seek your master, and give him this in gage that their calamity makes friends more dear to us than their success. Go, he will know its meaning!"

In place of the noon chimes the curfew was ringing from the bell-tower, the swallows were gone to roost amidst the ivy, and the herons slept with their heads under their silvery wings among the rushes by the river-side, the ferns and wild hyacinths were damp with evening dew, and the summer starlight glistened amidst the quivering woodland leaves. There was the silence of coming night over the vast forest glades, and no sound broke the stillness, save the song of the grasshopper stirring the tangled grasses, or the sweet low sigh of the west wind fanning the bells of the flowers. Cecil Castlemaine stood once more on the rose-terrace, shrouded in the dense twilight shade flung from above by the beech-boughs, waiting, listening, catching every rustle of the leaves, every tremor of the heads of the roses, yet hearing nothing in the stillness around but the quick, uncertain throbs of her heart beating like the wing of a caged bird under its costly lace. Pride was forgotten at length, and she only remembered—fear and love.

In the silence and the solitude came a step that she knew, came a presence that she felt. She bowed her head upon her hands; it was new to her this weakness, this terror, this anguish of joy; she sought to calm herself, to steel herself, to summon back her pride, her strength; she scorned herself for it all!

His hand touched her, his voice fell on her ear once more, eager, breathless, broken.

"Cecil! Cecil! is this true? Is my ruin thrice blessed, or am I mad, and dream of heaven?"

She lifted her head and looked at him with her old proud glance, her lips trembling with words that all her pride could not summon into speech; then her eyes filled with warm, blinding tears, and softened to new beauty;—scarce louder than the sigh of the wind among the flower-bells came her words to Fulke Ravensworth's ear, as her royal head bowed on his breast:

"Stay, stay! Or, if you fly, your exile shall be my exile, your danger my danger!"

The kerchief is a treasured heirloom to her descendants now, and fair women of her race, who inherit from her her azure eyes and her queenly grace, will recal how the proudest Countess of their Line loved a ruined gentleman so well that she was wedded to him at even, in her private chapel, at the hour of his greatest peril, his lowest fortune, and went with him across the seas till friendly intercession in high places gained them royal permission to dwell again at Lilliesford unmolested. And how it was ever noticeable to those who murmured at her coldness and her pride, that Cecil Castlemaine, cold and negligent as of yore to all the world beside, would seek her husband's smile, and love to meet his eyes, and cherish her beauty for his sake, and be restless in his absence even for the short span of a day, with a softer and more clinging tenderness than was found in many weaker, many humbler women.

They are gone now the men and women of that generation, and their voices come only to us through the faint echo of their written words. In summer nights the old beech-trees toss their leaves in the silvery light of the stars, and the river flows on unchanged, with the ceaseless, mournful burden of its mystic song, the same now as in the midsummer of a century and a half ago. The cobweb handkerchief lies before me with its broidered shield; the same now as long years since, when it was treasured close in a soldier's breast, and held by him dearer than all save his honour and his word. So, things pulseless and passionless endure, and human life passes away as swiftly as a song dies off from the air—as quickly succeeded, and as quickly forgot! Ronsard's refrain is the refrain of our lives:

> Le temps s'en va, le temps s'en va, ma dame!
> Las! le temps, non; mais *nous* nous, en allons!

LITTLE GRAND AND THE MARCHIONESS;

OR,

OUR MALTESE PEERAGE.

ALL first things are voted the best: first kisses, first *toga virilis*, first hair of the first whisker; first speeches are often so superior that members subside after making them, fearful of eclipsing themselves; first money won at play must always be best, as it is always the dearest bought; and first wives are always so super-excellent, that, if a man lose one, he is generally as fearful of hazarding a second as a trout of biting twice.

But of all first things commend me to one's first uniform. No matter that we get sick of harness, and get into mufti as soon as we can now; there is no more exquisite pleasure than the first sight of oneself in shako and sabretasche. How we survey ourselves in the glass, and ring for hot water, that the handsome housemaid may see us in all our glory, and lounge accidentally into our sister's schoolroom, that the governess, who is nice-looking and rather flirty, may go down on the spot before us and our scarlet and gold, chains and buttons! One's first uniform! Oh! the exquisite sensation locked up for us in that first box from Sagnarelli, or Bond-street!

I remember *my* first uniform. I was eighteen—as raw a young cub as you could want to see. I had not been licked into shape by a public school, whose tongue may be rough, but cleans off grievances and nonsense better than anything else. I had been in that hotbed of effeminacy, Church principles and weak tea, a Private Tutor's, where mamma's darlings are wrapped up, and stuffed with a little Terence and Horace to show grand at home; and upon my life I do believe my sister Julia, aged thirteen, was more wide awake and up to life than I was, when the governor, an old rector, who always put me in mind of the Vicar of Wakefield, got me gazetted to as crack a corps as any in the Line.

The —th (familiarly known in the Service as the "Dare Devils," from old Peninsular deeds) were just then at Malta, and with, among other trifles, a chest protector from my father, and a recipe for milk-arrow-root from my Aunt Matilda who lived in a constant state of catarrh and of cure for the same, I tumbled across the Bay of Biscay, and found myself in Byron's confounded "little military hot-house," where most military men, some time or other, have roasted themselves to death, climbing its hilly streets, flirting with its Valetta belles, drinking Bass in its hot verandahs, yawning with ennui in its palace, cursing its sirocco, and being done by its Jew sharpers.

From a private tutor's to a crack mess at Malta!—from a convent to a casino could hardly be a greater change. Just at first I was as much astray as a young pup taken into a stubble-field, and wondering what the deuce he is to do there; but as it is a pup's nature to sniff at birds and start them, so is it a boy's nature to snatch at the champagne of life as soon as he catches sight of it, though you may have brought him up on water from his cradle. I took to it, at least, like a retriever to water-ducks, though I was green enough to be a first-rate butt for many a day, and the practical jokes I had passed on me would have furnished the *Times* with food for crushers on "The Shocking State of the Army" for a twelvemonth. My chief friend and ally, tormentor and initiator, was a little fellow, Cosmo Grandison; in Ours he was "Little Grand" to everybody, from the Colonel to the baggage-women. He was seventeen, and had joined about a year. What a pretty boy he was, too! All the fair ones in Valetta, from his Excellency's wife to our washerwomen, admired that boy, and spoilt him and petted him, and I do not believe there was a man of Ours who would have had heart to sit in court-martial on Little Grand if he had broken every one of the Queen's regulations, and set every General Order at defiance. I think I see him now—he was new to Malta as I, having just landed with the Dare Devils, *en route* from India to Portsmouth —as he sat one day on the table in the mess-room as cool as a cucumber, in spite of the broiling sun, smoking, and swinging his legs, and settling his forage-cap on one side of his head, as pretty-looking, plucky, impudent a young monkey as ever piqued himself on being an old hand, and a knowing bird not to be caught by any chaff however ingeniously prepared.

"Simon," began Little Grand (my "St. John," first barbarised by Mr. Pope for the convenience of his dactyles and hexameters into Sinjin, being further barbarised by this little imp into Simon)—"Simon, do you want to see the finest woman in this confounded little pepper-box? You're no judge of a woman, though, you muff—taste been warped, perhaps, by constant contemplation of that virgin Aunt Minerva—Matilda, is it? all the same."

"Hang your chaff," said I; "you'd make one out a fool."

"Precisely, my dear Simon; just what you are!" responded Little Grand, pleasantly. "Bless your heart, I've been engaged to half a dozen women since I joined. A man can hardly help it, you see; they've such a way of drawing you on, you don't like to disappoint them, poor little dears, and so you compromise yourself out of sheer benevolence. There's such a run on a handsome man—it's a great bore. Sometimes I think I shall shave my head, or do something to disfigure myself, as Spurina did. Poor fellow, I feel for him! Well, Simon, you don't seem curious to know who my beauty is?"

"One of those Mitchell girls of the Twenty-first? You waltzed with 'em all night; but they're too tall for you, Grand."

"The Mitchell girls!" ejaculated he, with supreme scorn. "Great maypoles! they go about with the Fusiliers, like a pair of colours. On every ball-room battle-field one's safe to see *them* flaunting away, and as everybody has a shot at 'em, their hearts must be pretty well riddled into holes by this time. No, mine's rather higher game than that. My mother's brother-in-law's aunt's sister's cousin's cousin once removed was Viscount Twaddle, and I don't go anything lower than the Peerage."

"What, is it somebody you've met at his Excellency's?"

"Wrong again, beloved Simon. It's nobody I've met at old Stars and Garters', though his lady-wife could no more do without me than without her sal-volatile and flirtations. No, *she* don't go there; she's too high for that sort of thing—sick of it. After all the European Courts, Malta must be rather small and slow. I was introduced to her yesterday, and," continued Little Grand, more solemnly than was his wont, "I do assure you she's superb, divine; and I'm not very easy to please."

"What's her name?" I asked, rather impressed with this view of a lady too high for old Stars and Garters, as we irreverently termed her Majesty's representative in her island of Malta."

Little Grand took his pipe out of his lips to correct me with more dignity.

"Her *title*, my dear Simon, is the Marchioness St. Julian."

"Is that an English peerage, Grand?"

"Hum! What! Oh yes, of course! What else should it be, you owl?"

Not being in a condition to decide this point, I was silent, and he went on, growing more impressive at each phrase:

"She is splendid, really! And I'm a very *difficile* fellow, you know; but such hair, such eyes, one doesn't see every day in those sun-dried Mitchells, or those little pink Bovilliers. Well, yesterday, after that confounded luncheon (how I hate all those complimentary affairs!—one can't enjoy the truffles for talking to the ladies, nor enjoy the ladies for discussing the truffles), I went for a ride with Conran out to Villa Neponte. I left him there, and went down to see the overland steamers come in. While I was waiting, I got into talk, somehow or other, with a very agreeable, gentleman-like fellow, who asked me if I'd only just come to Malta, and all that sort of thing—you know the introductory style of action—till we got quite good friends, and he told me he was living outside this wretched little hole at the Casa di Fiori, and said—wasn't it civil of him?—said he should be very happy to see me if I'd call any time. He gave me his card—Lord Adolphus Fitzhervey—and a man with him called him 'Dolph.' As good luck had it, my weed went out just while we were talking, and Fitzhervey was monstrously pleasant, searched all over him for a fusee, couldn't find one, and asked me to go up with him to the Casa di Fiori and get a light. Of course I did, and he and I and Guatamara had some sherbet and a smoke together, and then he introduced me to the Marchioness St. Julian, his sister—by Jove! such a magnificent woman, Simon, *you* never saw one like her, I'll wager. She was uncommonly agreeable, too, and *such* a smile, my boy! She seemed to like me wonderfully—not rare that, though, you'll say—and asked me to go and take coffee there to-night, after mess, and bring one of my chums with me; and as I like to show you life, young one, and your taste wants improving after Aunt Minerva, you may come, if you like. Hallo! there's Conran. I say, don't tell *him.* I don't want any poaching on my manor."

Conran came in at that minute; he was then a Brevet-Major and Captain in Ours, and one of the older men who spoilt Little Grand in one way, as much as the women did in another. He was a fine, powerful fellow, with eyes like an eagle's, and pluck like a lion's; he had a grave look, and had been of late more silent and self-reticent than the other roystering, débonnair, light-hearted "Dare Devils;" but though, perhaps, tired of the wild escapades which reputation had once attributed to him, was always the most lenient to the boy's monkey tricks, and always the one to whom he went if his larks had cost him too dear, or if he was in a scrape from which he saw no exit. Conran had recently come in for a good deal of money, and there were few bright eyes in Malta that would not have smiled kindly on him; but he did not care much for any of them. There was some talk of a love-affair before he went to India, that was the cause of his hard-heartedness, though I must say he did not look much like a victim to the *grande passion*, in my ideas, which were drawn from valentines and odes in the "Woman, thou fond and fair deceiver" style; in love that turned its collars down and let its hair go uncut and refused to eat, and recovered with a rapidity proportionate to its ostentation; and I did not know that, if a man has lost his treasure, he *may* mourn it so deeply that he may refuse to run about like Harpagon, crying for his *cassette* to an audience that only laughs at his miseries.

"Well, young ones," said Conran, as he came in and threw down his cap and whip, "here you are, spending your hours in pipes and bad wine. What a blessing it is to have a palate that isn't *blasé*, and that will swallow all wine just because it *is* wine! That South African goes down with better relish, Little Grand, than you'll find in Château Margaux ten years hence. As soon as one begins to want touching up with olives, one's real gusto is gone."

"Hang olives, sir! they're beastly," said Little Grand; "and I don't care who pretends they're not. Olives are like sermons and wives, everybody makes a wry face, and would rather be excused 'em, Major; but it's the custom to call 'em good things, and so men bolt 'em in complaisance, and while they hate the salt-water flavour, descant on the delicious rose taste!"

"Quite true, Little Grand! but one takes olives to enhance the wine; and so, perhaps other men's sermons make one enjoy one's racier novel, and other men's wives make one appreciate one's liberty still better. Don't abuse olives; you'll want them figuratively and literally before you've done either drinking or living!"

"Oh! confound it, Major," cried Little Grand, "I do hope and trust a spent ball may have the kindness to double me up and finish me off before then!"

"You're not philosophic, my boy."

"Thank Heaven, no!" ejaculated Little Grand, piously. "I've an uncle, a very great philosopher, beats all the sages hollow, from Bion to Buckle, and writes in the Metaphysical Quarterly, but I'll be shot if he don't spend so much time in trying to puzzle out what life is, that all his has slipped away without his having *lived* one bit. When I was staying with him one Christmas, he began boring me with a frightful theory on the non-existence of matter. I couldn't stand that, so I cut him short, and set him down to the luncheon-table; and while he was full swing with a Strasbourg pâté and Comet hock, I stopped him and asked him if, with them in his mouth, he believed in matter or not? He was shut up, of course; bless your soul, those theorists always are, if you're down upon 'em with a little fact!"

"Such as a Strasbourg pâté?—that *is* an unanswerable argument with most men, I believe," said Conran, who liked to hear the boy chatter. "What are you going to do with yourself to-night, Grand?"

"I am going to—ar—hum—to a friend of mine," said Little Grand, less glibly than usual.

"Very well; I only asked, because I would have taken you to Mrs. Fortescue's with me; they're having some acting proverbs (horrible exertion in this oven of a place, with the thermometer at a hundred and twenty degrees); but if you've better sport it's no matter. Take care what friends you make, though, Grand; you'll find some Maltese acquaintances very costly."

"Thank you. I should say I can take care of myself," replied Little Grand, with immeasurable scorn and dignity.

Conran laughed, struck him across the shoulders with his whip, stroked his own moustaches, and went out again, whistling one of Verdi's airs.

"I don't want him bothering, you know," explained Little Grand; "she's such a deuced magnificent woman!"

She was a magnificent woman, this Eudoxia Adelaida, Marchioness St. Julian; and proud enough Little Grand and I felt when we had that soft, jewelled hand held out to us, and that bewitching smile beamed upon us, and that joyous presence dazzling in our eyes, as we sat in the drawing-room of that Casa di Fiori. She was about thirty-five, I should say (boys always worship those who might have been schoolfellows of their mothers), tall and stately, and imposing, with the most beautiful pink and white skin, with a fine set of teeth, raven hair, and eyes tinted most exquisitely.

Oh! she was magnificent, our Marchioness St. Julian! Into what unutterable insignificance, what miserable washed-out shadows sank Stars and Garters' lady, and the Mitchell girls, and all the belles of La Valetta, whom we hadn't thought so very bad-looking before.

There was a young creature sitting a little out of the radiance of light, reading; but we had no eyes for anybody except the Marchioness St. Julian. We were in such high society, too; there was her brother, Lord Adolphus, and his bosom Pylades, the Baron Guatamara; and there was a big fellow, with hooked nose and very curly hair, who was introduced to us as the Prince of Orangia Magnolia; and a little wiry fellow, with bits of red and blue ribbon, and a star or two in his button-hole, who was M. le Duc de Saint-Jeu. We were quite dazzled with the coruscations of so much aristocracy, especially when they talked across to each other—so familiarly, too—of Johnnie (that was Lord Russell), and Pam, and "old Buck" (my godfather Buckingham, Lord Adolphus explained to us), and Montpensier and old Joinville; and chatted of when they dined at the Tuileries, and stayed at Compiègne, and hunted at Belvoir, and spent Christmas at Holcombe or Longleat. We were in such high society! How contemptible appeared Mrs. Maberly's and the Fortescue's soirées; how infinitesimally small grew Charlie Ruthven, and Harry Villiers, and Gray and Albany, and all the other young fellows who thought it such great guns to be *au mieux* with little Graziella, or invited to Sir George Dashaway's. *We* were a cut above those things now—rather!

That splendid Marchioness! There was a head for a coronet, if you like! And how benign she was!

Grand sat on the couch beside her, and I on an ottoman on her left, and she leaned back in her magnificent toilette, flirting her fan like a Castilian, and flashing upon us her superb eyes from behind it; not speaking very much, but showing her white teeth in scores of heavenly smiles, till Little Grand, the *blasé* man of seventeen, and I the raw Moses of private tutelage, both felt that we had never come across anything like this; never, in fact, seen a woman worth a glance before.

She listened to us—or rather to him, I was too awestruck to advance much beyond monosyllables—and laughed at him, and smiled encouragingly on my *gaucherie* (and when a boy is *gauche*, how ready he is to worship such a helping hand!), and beamed upon us both with an effulgence compared with which the radiance of Helen, Galatea, Œnone, Messalina, Laïs, and all the legendary beauties one reads about, must have been what the railway night-lamps that *never* burn are to the prismatic luminaries of Cremorne. They were all uncommonly pleasant, all except the girl who was reading, whom they introduced as the Signorina da' Guari, a Tuscan, and daughter to Orangia Magnolia, with one of those marvellously beautiful faces that one sees in the most splendid painters' models of the Campagna, who never lifted her head scarcely, though Guatamara and Saint-Jeu did their best to make her. But all the others were wonderfully agreeable, and quite *fête'd* Little Grand and me, at which, they being more than double our age, and seemingly at home alike with Belgravia and Newmarket, the Faubourg and the Pytchley, we felt to grow at least a foot each in the aroma of this Casa di Fiori.

"This is rather stupid, Doxie," began Lord Adolphus, addressing his sister; "not much entertainment for our guests. What do you say to a game of vingt-et-un, eh, Mr. Grandison?"

Little Grand fixed his blue eyes on the Marchioness, and said he should be very happy, but, as for entertainment—*he* wanted no other.

"No compliments, *petit ami*," laughed the Marchioness, with a dainty blow of her fan. "Yes, Dolph, have vingt-et-un, or music, or anything you like. Sing us something, Lucrezia."

The Italian girl thus addressed looked up with a passionate, haughty flush, and answered, with wonderfully little courtesy I considered, "I shall not sing tonight."

"Are you unwell, fairest friend?" asked the Duc de Saint-Jeu, bending his little wiry figure over her.

She shrank away from him, and drew back, a hot colour in her cheeks.

"Signore, I did not address *you*."

The Marchioness looked angry, if those divine eyes could look anything so mortal. However, she shrugged her shoulders.

"Well, my dear Lucrezia, we can't make you sing, of course, if you won't. I, for my part, always do any little thing I can to amuse anybody; if I fail, I fail; I have done my best, and my friends will appreciate the effort, if not the result. No, my dear Prince, do not teaze her," said the Marchioness to Orangia Magnolia, who was arguing, I thought, somewhat imperatively for such a well-bred and courtly man, with Lucrezia; "we will have vingt-et-un, and Lucrezia will give us the delight of her voice some other evening, I dare say."

We had vingt-et-un; the Marchioness would not play, but she sat in her rose velvet arm-chair, just behind Little Grand, putting in pretty little speeches, and questions and bagatelles, and calling attention to the gambols of her darling greyhound Cupidon, and tapping Little Grand with her fan, till, I believe, he neither knew how the game went, nor what money he lost; and I, gazing at her, and cursing him for his facile tongue, never noticed my naturels, couldn't have said what the maximum was if you had paid me for it, and might, for anything I knew to the contrary, have been seeing my life slip away with each card as Balzac's hero with the Peau de Chagrin. Then we had sherbet, and wine, and cognac for those who preferred it; and the Marchioness gave us permission to smoke, and took a dainty hookah with an amber mouthpiece for her own use (divine she did look, too, with that hookah between her ruby lips!); and the smoke, and the cognac, and the smiles, unloosed our tongues, and we spake like very great donkeys, I dare say, but I'm sure with not a tenth part the wisdom that Balaam's ass developed in his brief and pithy conversation.

However great the bosh we talked, though, we found very lenient auditors. Fitzhervey and Guatamara laughed at all our witticisms; the Prince of Orangia Magnolia joined in with a "Per Baccho!" and a "Bravo!" and little Saint-Jeu wheezed, and gave a faint echo of "Mon Dieu!" and "Très bien, très bien, vraiment!" and the Marchioness St. Julian laughed too, and joined in our nonsense, and, what was much more, bent a willing ear to our compliments, no matter how florid; and Saint-Jeu told us a story or two, more amusing than *comme il faut*, at which the Marchioness tried to look grave, and *did* look shocked, but laughed for all that behind her fan; and Lucrezia da' Guari sat in shadow, as still and as silent as the Parian Euphrosyne on the console, though her passionate eyes and expressive face looked the very antipodes of silence and statuetteism, as she flashed half-shy, half-scornful, looks upon us.

If the first part of the evening had been delightful, this was something like Paradise! It was such high society! and with just dash enough of Mabille and coulisses laisser-aller to give it piquancy. How different was the pleasantry and freedom of these *real* aristos, after the humdrum dinners and horrid bores of dances that those snobs of Maberlys, and Fortescues, and Mitchells, made believe to call Society!

What with the wine, and the smoke, and the smiles, I wasn't quite clear as to whether I saw twenty horses' heads or one when I was fairly into saddle, and riding back to the town, just as the first dawn was rising, Aphrodite-like, from the far blue waves of the Mediterranean. Little Grand was better seasoned, but even he was dizzy with the parting words of the Marchioness, which had softly breathed the delicious passport, "Come to-morrow."

"By Jupiter!" swore Little Grand, obliged to give relief to his feelings—"by Jupiter, Simon! did you ever see such a glorious, enchanting, divine, delicious, adorable creature? Faugh! who could look at those Mitchell girls after her? Such eyes! such a smile! such a figure! Talk of a coronet! no imperial crown would be half good enough for her! And how pleasant those fellows are! I like that little chaffy chap, the Duke; what a slap-up story that was about the bal de l'Opéra. And Fitzhervey, too; there's something uncommonly thorough-bred about him, ain't there? And Guatamara's an immensely jolly fellow. Ah, my boy! that's something like society; all the ease and freedom of real rank; no nonsense about them, as there is about snobs. I say, what wouldn't the other fellows give to be in our luck? I think even Conran would warm up about her. But, Simon, she's deucedly taken with me—she is, upon my word; and she knows how to show it you, too! By George! one could die for a woman like that—eh?"

"Die!" I echoed, while my horse stumbled along up the hilly road, and I swayed forward, pretty nearly over his head, while poetry rushed to my lips, and electric sparks danced before my eyes:

> "To die for those we love! oh, there is power
> In the true heart, and pride, and joy, for this.
> It is to live without the vanished light
> That strength is needed!"

"But I'll be shot if it shall be vanished light," returned Little Grand; "it don't look much like it yet. The light's only just lit, 'tisn't likely it's going out again directly; but she's a stunner! and——"

"A stunner!" I shouted; "she's much more than that—she's an angel, and I'll be much obliged to you to call her by her right name, sir. She's a beautiful, noble, loving woman; the most perfect of all Nature's masterworks. She is divine, sir, and you and I are not worthy merely to kiss the hem of her garment."

"Ain't we, though? I don't care much about

kissing her dress; it's silk, and I don't know that I should derive much pleasure from pressing my lips on its texture; but her cheek——

> 'Her cheek is like the Catherine pear,
> The side that's next the sun!'"

I shouted, as my horse went down in a rut. "She's like Venus rising from the sea-shell; she's like Aurora, when she came down on the first ray of the dawn to Tithonus; she's like Briseis———"

"Bother classics! she's like herself, and beats 'em all hollow. She's the finest creature ever seen on earth, and I should like to see the man who'd dare to say she wasn't. And—I say, Simon—*how much did you lose to-night?*"

From sublimest heights I tumbled straight to bathos. The cold water of Grand's query quenched my poetry, extinguished my electric lights, and sobered me like a douche bath.

"I don't know," I answered with a sense of awe and horror stealing over me; "but I had a pony in my waistcoat-pocket that the governor had just sent me; Guatamara changed it for me, and—*I've only sixpence left!*"

"Old boy," said Little Grand to me, the next morning, after early parade, "come in my room, and let's make up some despatches to the governors. You see," he continued, five minutes after—"you see, we're both of us pretty well cleared out; I've only got half a pony, and you haven't a couple of fivers left. Now you know they evidently play rather high at the Casa di Fiori; do everything *en prince*, like nobs who've Barclay's at their back; and one mustn't hang fire; horrid shabby that would look. Besides, fancy seeming mean before *her!* So I've been thinking that, though governors are a screwy lot generally, if we put it to 'em clearly the sort of set we've got into, and show 'em that we can't help, now that we are at Rome, doing as the Romans do, I should say they could hardly help bleeding a little—eh? Now, listen how I've put it. My old boy has a weakness for titles; he married my mother on the relationship to Viscount Twaddles (who doesn't know of her existence, but who does to talk about as 'our cousin'), and he'd eat up miles of dirt for a chance of coming to a strawberry-leaf; so I think this will touch him up beautifully. Listen! ain't I sublimely respectful? 'I'm sure, my dear father, you will be delighted to learn that by wonderful luck, or rather I ought to say Providence, I have fallen on my feet in Malta, and got introduced to the very highest' (wait! let me stick a dash under very)—'the *very* highest society here. They are quite tip-top. To show you what style, I need only mention Lord A. Fitzhervey, the Baron Guatamara, and the Marchioness St. Julian, as among my kindest friends. They have been yachting in the Levant, and are now staying in Malta: they are all most kind to me; and I know you will appreciate the intellectual advantages that such contact must afford me; at the same time you will understand that I can hardly enter such circles as a snob, and you will wish your son to comport himself as a gentleman; but gentlemanising comes uncommon dear, I can tell you, with all the care in the world: and if you *could* let me have another couple of hundred, I should vote you'—a what, Simon?—'an out-and-out brick' is the sensible style, but I suppose 'the best and kindest of parents' is the filial dodge, eh? There! 'With fond love to mamma and Florie, ever your affectionate son, COSMO GRANDISON.' Bravo! that's prime; that'll bring the yellows down, I take it. Here, old fellow, copy it to your governor; you couldn't have a more stunning effusion—short and to the purpose, as cabinet councils ought to be, and ain't. Fire away, my juvenile."

I did fire away! only I, of a more impressionable and poetic nature than Little Grand, gave a certain vent to my feelings in expatiating on the beauty, grace, condescension, &c., &c., of the Marchioness to my mother; I did *not* mention the grivois stories, the brandy, and the hookah: I was quite sure they were the sign of that delicious ease and disregard of snobbish etiquette and convenances peculiar to the "Upper Ten," but I thought the poor people at home, in vicarage seclusion, would be too out of the world to fully appreciate such revelations of our *crême de la crême;* besides, my governor had James's own detestation of the divine weed, and considered that men who "made chimneys of their mouths" might just as well have the mark of the Beast at once.

Little Grand and I were hard-up for cash, and *en attendant* the governors' replies and remittances, we had recourse to the tender mercies and leather bags of napoleons, ducats, florins, and doubloons of a certain Spanish Jew, one Balthazar Miraflores, a shrivelled-skinned, wheezing old cove, who was "most happy to lent anytink to his tear young shentlesmen, but, by Got! he was as poor as Job, he was indeed!" Whether Job ever lent money out on interest or not, I can't say; perhaps he did, as in the finish he ended with having quadrupled his cattle and lands, and all his goods—a knack usurers preserve in full force to this day; but all I can say is, that if he was not poorer than Mr. Miraflores, he was not much to be pitied, for he, miserly old shark, lived in his dark, dirty hole, like a crocodile embedded in Nile mud, and crushed the bones of all unwary adventurers who came within range of his great bristling jaws.

Money, however, Little Grand and I got out of him in plenty, only for a little bit of paper in exchange: and at that time we didn't know that though the paper tax would be repealed at last, there would remain, as long as youths are green and old birds cunning, a heavy and bitter tax on certain bits of paper to which one's hand is put, which Mr. Gladstone, though he achieve the herculean task of making draymen take kindly to vin ordinaire, and the popping of champagne corks a familiar sound by cottage-hearths, will never be able to include, in his budgets to come, among the Taxes that are Repealed!

Well, we had our money from old Balthazar that morning, and we played with it again that night up at the Casa di Fiori. Loo this time, by way of change. Saint-Jeu said he always thought it well to change your game as you change your loves: constancy, whether to cards or women, was most fatiguing. We liked Saint-Jeu very much: we thought him such a funny fellow. They said they did not care to play much—of course they didn't, when Guatamara had had écarté with the Grand-Duke of Chaffsandlarkstein at half a million a side, and Lord Dolph had broken the bank at Homburg "just for fun—no fun to old Blanc, who farms it, though, you know." But the Marchioness, who was doubly gracious that night, told them they must play, because it amused her *chers petits amis*. Besides, she said, in her pretty, imperious way, she liked to see it—it amused her. After that, of course, there was no more hesitation: down we sat, and young Heavystone with us.

The evening before we had happened to mention him, said he was a fellow of no end of tin, though as stupid an owl as ever spelt his own name wrong when he passed a military examination, and the Marchioness, recalling the name, said she remembered his father, and asked us to bring him to see her; which we did, fearing no rival in "old Heavy."

So down we three sat, and had the evening before over again, with the cards, and the smiles, and wiles of our divinity, and Saint-Jeu's stories and Fitzhervey's cognac and cigars; with this difference, that we found loo more exciting than vingt-et-un. They played it so fast, too, it was like a breathless heat for the Goodwood Cup, and the Marchioness watched it, leaning alternately over Grand's, and Heavy's, and my chair, and saying, with such naïve delight, "Oh, do take miss, Cosmo; I would risk it if I were you, Mr. Heavystone; *pray* don't let my naughty brother win everything," that I'd have defied the stiffest of the Stagyrites or the chilliest of Calvinists to have kept their head cool with that syren voice in their ear.

And La Lucrezia sat, as she had sat the night before, by the open window, still and silent, the Cape jasmines and Southern creepers framing her in a soft moonlight picture, contrast enough to the brilliantly lighted room, echoing with laughter at Saint-Jeu's stories, perfumed with Cubas and narghilés, and shrining the magnificent, full-bloom, jewelled beauty of our

Marchioness St. Julian, with which we were as rapidly, as madly, as unreasoningly, and as sentimentally in love as any boys of seventeen or eighteen ever could be. What greater latitude, you will exclaim, recalling certain buried-away episodes of *your* hobbedehoyism, when you addressed Latin distiches to that hazel-eyed Hebe who presided over oyster patties and water ices at the pastrycook's in Eton; or ruined your governor's young plantations cutting the name of Adeliza Mary, your cousin, at this day a portly person in velvet and point, whom you can now call, with a thanksgiving in the stead of the olden tremor, Mrs. Hector M'Cutchin? Yes, we were in love in a couple of evenings, Little Grand vehemently and unpoetically, I shyly and sentimentally, according to our temperaments, and as the fair Emily stirred feud between the two Noble Kinsmen, so the Marchioness St. Julian began to sow seeds of jealousy and detestation between us, sworn allies as we were. But "*le véritable amant ne connait point d'amis*," and as soon as we began to grow jealous of each other, Little Grand could have kicked me to the devil, and I could have kicked *him*, with the greatest pleasure in life.

But I was shy, Little Grand was blessed with all the audacity imaginable; the consequence was, that when our horses came round, and the Maltese who acted as cherub was going to close the gates of Paradise upon us, he managed to slip into the Marchioness's boudoir to get a tête-à-tête farewell, while I strode up and down the verandah, not heeding Saint-Jeu, who was telling me a tale, to which, in any other saner moments, I should have listened greedily, but longing to execute on Little Grand some fierce and terrible vengeance, to which the vendetta should be baby's play. Saint-Jeu left me to put his arm over Heavy's shoulder, and tell him if ever he came to Paris he should be transported to receive him at the Hôtel de Millefleurs, and present him at the Tuileries; and I stood swearing to myself, and breaking off sprays of the verandah creepers, when I heard somebody say, very softly and low,

"Signore, come here a moment."

It was that sweetly pretty mute whom we had barely noticed, absorbed as we were in the worship of our maturer idol, leaning out of the window, her cheeks flushed, her lips parted, her eyes sad and anxious. Of course I went to her, surprised at her waking up so suddenly to any interest in me. She put her hand on my coat-sleeve, and drew me down towards her.

"Listen to me a moment. I hardly know how to warn you, and yet I must. I cannot sit quietly by and see you and your young friends being deceived as so many have been before you. Do not come here again —do not——"

"Figlia mia! are you not afraid of the night air?" said the Prince of Orangia Magnolia, just behind us.

His words were kind, but there was a nasty glitter in his eyes. Lucrezia answered him in passionate Italian—of which I had no knowledge—with such fire in her eyes, such haughty gesticulation, and such a torrent of words, that I really began to think, pretty soft little dear as she looked, that she must positively be a trifle out of her mind, her silence before, and her queer speech to me, seemed such odd behaviour for a young lady in such high society. She was turning to me again when Little Grand came out into the verandah, looking flushed, proud, and self complaisant, as such a winner and slayer of women would do. My hand clenched on the jasmine, I thirsted to spring on him as he stood there with his provoking, self-contented smile, and his confounded coxcombical air, and his cursed fair curls—*my* hair was dust-coloured and as rebellious as porcupine-quills—and wash out in his blood or mine——A touch of a soft hand thrilled through my every nerve and fibre; the Marchioness was there, and signed me to her. Lucrezia, Little Grand, and all the rest of the universe vanished from my mind at the lightning of that angel smile and the rustle of that moire-antique dress. She beckoned me to her into the empty drawing-room.

"Augustus" (I never thought my name could sound so sweet before), "tell me, what was my niece Lucrezia saying to you just now?"

Now I had a sad habit of telling the truth; it was an out-of-the-world custom taught me, among other old-fashioned things, at home, though I soon found how inconvenient a *bêtise* modern society considers it; and I blurted the truth out here, not distinctly or gracefully, though, as Little Grand would have done, for I was in that state of exaltation ordinarily expressed as not knowing whether one is standing in one's Wellingtons or not.

The Marchioness sighed.

"Ah, did she say that? Poor dear girl! She dislikes me so much, it is quite an hallucination, and yet, O Augustus, I have been to her like an elder sister, like a mother. Imagine how it grieves me," and the

Marchioness shed some tears—pearls of price, thought I, worthy to drop from angel eyes—"it is a bitter sorrow to me, but, poor darling! she is not responsible."

She touched her veiny temple significantly as she spoke, and I understood, and felt tremendously shocked at it, that the young, fair Italian girl was a fierce and cruel maniac, who had the heart (oh! most extraordinary madness did it seem to me; if *I* had lost my senses I could never have harmed *her!*) to hate, absolutely hate, the noblest, tenderest, most beautiful of women!

"I never alluded to it to any one," continued the Marchioness. "Guatamara and Saint-Jeu, though such intimate friends, are ignorant of it. I would rather have any one think ever so badly of me, than reveal to them the cruel misfortune of my sweet Lucrezia——"

How noble she looked as she spoke!

"But you, Augustus, you," and she smiled upon me till I grew as dizzy as after my first taste of milk-punch, "I have not the courage to let *you* go off with any bad impression of me. I have known you a very little while, it is true—but a few hours, indeed—yet there are affinities of heart and soul which overstep the bounds of time, and, laughing at the chill ties of ordinary custom, make strangers dearer than old friends——"

The room revolved round me, the lights danced up and down, my heart beat like Thor's hammer, and my pulse went as fast as a favourite saving the distance. *She* speaking so to me! My senses whirled round and round like fifty thousand witches on a Walpurgis Night, and down I went on my knees before my magnificent idol, raving away I couldn't tell you what now—the essence of everything I'd ever read, from Ovid to Alexander Smith. It must have been something frightful to hear, though Heaven knows I meant it earnestly enough. Suddenly I was pulled up with a jerk, as one throws an unbroken colt back on his haunches in the middle of his first start. *I thought I heard a laugh.*

She started up too. "Hush! another time! We may be overheard." And drawing her dress from my hands, which grasped it as agonisingly as a cockney grasps his saddle-bow, holding on for dear life over the Burton or Tedworth country, she stooped kindly over me, and floated away before *I* was recovered from the exquisite delirium of my ecstatic trance.

She loved me! The superb creature loved me! There was not a doubt of it; and how I got back to the barracks that night in my heavenly state of mind I could never have told. All I know is, that Grand and I never spoke a word, by tacit consent, all the way back; that I felt a fiendish delight when I saw his proud triumphant air, and thought how little he guessed, poor fellow!——And that Dream of One Fair Woman was as superior in rapture to the "Dream of Fair Women" as Tokay to the "Fine Fruity Port" that results from damsons and a decoction of sloes!

The next day there was a grand affair in Malta to receive some foreign Prince, whose name I do not remember now, who called on us *en route* to England. Of course all the troops turned out, and there was an inspection of us, and a grand luncheon and dinner, and ball, and all that sort of thing, which a month before I should have considered prime fun, but which now, as it kept me out of my paradise, I thought the most miserable bore that could possibly have chanced.

"I say," said Heavy to me, as I was getting into harness—"I say, don't you wonder Fitzhervey and the Marchioness ain't coming to the palace to-day? One would have thought old Stars and Garters would have been sure to ask them."

"Ask them? I should say so," I returned with immeasurable disdain. "Of course he asked them; but she told me she shouldn't come, last night. She is so tired of such things. She came yachting with Fitzhervey solely to try and have a little quiet. She says people never give her a moment's rest when she is in Paris or London. She was sorry to disappoint Stars and Garters, but I don't think she likes his wife much: she don't consider her good ton."

On which information Heavy lapsed into a state of profoundest awe and wonderment, it having been one of his articles of faith, for the month that we had been in Malta, that the palace people were exalted demigods, whom it was only permissible to worship from a distance, and a very respectful distance too. Heavy had lost some twenty odd pounds the night before— of course we lost, young hands as we were, unaccustomed to the society of that entertaining gentleman Pam—and had grumbled not a little at the loss of his gold bobs. But now I could see that such a contemptibly pecuniary matter was clean gone from his memory, and that he would have thought the world well lost for the honour of playing cards with people who could afford to disappoint old Stars and Garters.

The inspection was over at last; and if any other than Conran had been my senior officer, I should have come off badly, in all probability, for the abominable manner in which I went through my evolutions. The day came to an end somehow or other, though I began to think it never would, the luncheon was ended, the bigwigs were taking their sieste, or otherwise occupied, and I, trusting to my absence not being noticed, tore off as hard as a man can who has Cupid for his Pegasus. With a bouquet as large as a drum-head, clasped round with a bracelet, about which I had many doubts as to the propriety of offering to the possessor of such jewellery as the Marchioness must have, yet on which I thought I might venture after the scene of last night, I was soon on the verandah of the Casa di Fiori, and my natural shyness being stimulated into a distant resemblance of Little Grand's enviable brass, seeing the windows of the drawing-room open, I pushed aside the green venetians and entered noiselessly. The room did not look a quarter so inviting as the night before, though it was left in precisely a similar state. I do not know how it was, but those cards lying about on the floor, those sconces with the wax run down and dripping over them, those emptied caraffes that had diffused an odour not yet dissipated, those tables and velvet couches all *à tort et à travers*, did not look so very inviting after all, and, even to my unsophisticated senses, scarcely seemed fit for a Peeress.

There was nobody in the room, and I walked through it towards the boudoir; from the open door I saw Fitzhervey, Guatamara, and my Marchioness—but oh! what horror unutterable! doing—*que pensez-vous?* Drinking bottled porter!—and drinking bottled porter in a *peignoir* not of the cleanliest, and with raven tresses not of the neatest!

Only fancy! she, that divine *spirituelle* creature, who had talked but a few hours before of the affinity of souls, to have come down, like any ordinary woman, to Guinness's stout, and a checked dressing-gown and unbrushed locks! To find your prophet without his silver veil, or your Leila dead drowned in a sack, or your Guinevere flown over with Sir Lancelot to Boulogne, or your long-esteemed Griselda gone off with your cockaded Jeames, is nothing to the torture, the unutterable anguish, of seeing your angel, your divinity, your bright particular star, your hallowed Arabian rose, come down to—Bottled Porter! Do not talk to me of Doré, sir, or Mr. Martin's pictures; their horrors dwindle into insignificance compared with the horror of finding an intimate liaison between one's first love and Bottled Porter!

In my first dim, unutterable anguish, I should have turned and fled; but my syren's voice had not lost all its power, despite the stout and dirty dressing-gown, for she *was* a very handsome woman, and could stand such things as well as anybody. She came towards me, with her softest smile, glancing at the bracelet on the bouquet, apologising slightly for her négligé:—"I am so indolent. I only dress for those I care to please —and I never hoped to see *you* to-day." In short, magnetising me over again, and smoothing down my outraged sensibilities, till I ended by becoming almost blind (*quite* I could not manage) to the checked *robe de chambre* and the unbrushed bandeaux, by offering her my braceleted bouquet, which was very graciously accepted, and even by sharing the atrocious London porter, "that horrid stuff," she called it, "how I hate it! but it is the only thing Sir Benjamin Brodie allows me, I am so very delicate, you know, my sensibilities so frightfully acute!"

I had not twenty minutes to stay, having to be back at the barracks, or risk a reprimand, which, happily, the checked *peignoir* had cooled me sufficiently to enable me to recollect. So I took my farewell—one not unlike Medora's and Conrad's, Fitzhervey and Guatamara having kindly withdrawn as soon as the bottled porter was finished—and I went out of the house in a very blissful state, despite Guinness and the unwelcome demi-toilette, which did not accord with Eugène Sue's and the Parlour Library's description of the general getting-up and stunning appearance of heroines and peeresses "reclining, in robes of cloud-like tissue and folds of the richest lace, on a cabriole couch of amber velvet, while the air was filled with the voluptuous perfume of the flower-children of the South, and music from unseen choristers lulled the senses with its divinest harmony," &c. &c. &c.

Bottled porter and a checked dressing-gown! Say what you like, sirs, it takes a very strong passion to overcome *those*. I have heard men ascribe the waning of their affections after the honeymoon to the constant sight of their wives—whom before they had only seen making papa's coffee with an angelic air and a toilette *tirée à quatre épingles*—everlastingly coming down too late for breakfast in a dressing-gown; and, upon my soul, if ever I marry, which Heaven in pitiful mercy forfend! and my wife make her appearance in one of those confounded *peignoirs*, I will give that much-run-after and deeply-to-be-pitied public character, the

Divorce Judge, some more work to do—I will upon my honour.

However, the *peignoir* had not iced me enough that time to prevent my tumbling out of the house in as delicious an ecstasy as if I had been eating some of Monte Cristo's "hatchis." As I went out, not looking before me, I came bang against the chest of somebody else, who, not admiring the rencontre, hit my cap over my eyes, and exclaimed, in not the most courtly manner you will acknowledge, "You cursed owl, take that, then! What are you doing here, I should like to know?"

"Confound your impudence!" I retorted, as soon as my ocular powers were restored, and I saw the blue eyes, fair curls, and smart figure of my ancient Iolaüs, now my bitterest foe—"confound your impertinence! what are *you* doing here? you mean."

"Take care, and don't ask questions about what doesn't concern you," returned Little Grand, with a laugh—a most irritating laugh. There are times when such cachinnations sting one's ears more than a volley of oaths. "Go home and mind your own business, my chicken. You are a green bird, and nobody minds you; but still you'll find it as well not to come poaching on other men's manors."

"Other men's manors! Mine, if you please," I shouted, so mad with him I could have floored him where he stood.

"Phew!" laughed Little Grand, screwing up his lips into a contemptuous whistle, "you've been drinking too much Bass, my daisy; 'tisn't good for young heads—can't stand it. Go home, innocent."

The insult, the disdainful tone, froze my blood.

My heart swelled with a sense of outraged dignity and injured manhood. With a conviction of my immeasurable superiority of position, as the beloved of that divine creature, I emancipated myself from the certain sort of slavery I was generally in to Little Grand, and spoke as I conceived it to be the habit of gentlemen whose honour had been wounded to speak.

"Mr. Grandison, you will pay for this insult. I shall expect satisfaction."

Little Grand laughed again—absolutely grinned, the audacious young imp—and he twelve months younger than I, too!

"Certainly, sir. If you wish to be made a target of, I shall be delighted to oblige you. I can't keep ladies waiting. It is always Place aux dames! with me; so, for the present, good morning!"

And off went the young coxcomb into the Casa di Fiori, and I, only consoled by the reflection of the different reception he would receive to what mine had been (*he* had a braceleted bouquet, too, the young pretentious puppy!), started off again, assuaging my lacerated feelings with the delicious word of Satisfaction. I felt myself immeasurably raised above the heads of every other man in Malta—a perfect hero of romance; in fact, fit to figure in my beloved Alexandre's most highly-wrought yellow-papered *roman*, with a duel on my hands, and the love of a magnificent creature like my Eudoxia Adelaida. She had become Eudoxia Adelaida to me now, and I had forgiven, if not forgotten, the dirty dressing-gown: the bottled porter lay, of course, at Brodie's' door. If he would condemn spiritual forms of life and light to the common realistic aliments of horrible barmaids and draymen, she could not help

5*

it, nor I either. If angels come down to earth, and are separated from their natural nourishment of manna and nectar, they must take what they can get, even though it be so coarse and sublunary a thing as Guinness's XXX, must they not, sir? Yes, I felt very *exalté* with my affair of honour and my affair of the heart, Little Grand for my foe, and my Marchioness for a love. I never stopped to remember that I might be smashing with frightful recklessness the Sixth and the Seventh Commandments. If Little Grand got shot, he must thank himself; he should not have insulted me; and if there was a Marquis St. Julian, why—I pitied him, poor fellow! that was all.

Full of these sublime sensations—grown at least three feet in my varnished boots—I lounged into the ball-room, feeling supreme pity for ensigns who were chattering round the door, admiring those poor, pale garrison girls. *They* had not a duel and a Marchioness; *they* did not know what beauty meant—what life was!

I did not dance—I was above that sort of thing now—there was not a woman worth the trouble in the room; and about the second waltz I saw my would-be rival talking to Ruthven, a fellow in Ours. Little Grand did not look glum or dispirited, as he ought to have done after the interview he must have had; but probably that was the boy's brass. He would never look beaten if you had hit him till he was black and blue. Presently Ruthven came up to me. He was not overused to his business, for he began the opening chapter in rather schoolboy fashion.

"Hallo, Gus! so you and Little Grand have been falling out. Why don't you settle it with a little mill?

A vast deal better than pistols. Duels always seem to me no fun. Two men stand up like fools, and——"

"Mr. Ruthven," said I, very haughtily, "if your principal desires to apologise——"

"Apologise! Bless your soul, no! But——"

"Then," said I, cutting him uncommonly short, indeed, "you can have no necessity to address yourself to me, and I beg to refer you to my friend and second, Mr. Heavystone."

Wherewith I bowed, turned on my heel, and left him.

I did not sleep that night, though I tried hard, because I thought it the correct thing for heroes to sleep sweetly till the clock strikes the hour of their duel, execution, &c., or whatever it may hap. Egmont slept, Argyle slept, Philippe Egalité, scores of them, but I could not. Not that I funked it, thank Heaven—I never had a touch of that—but because I was in such a delicious state of excitement, self-admiration, and heroism, which had not cooled when I found myself walking down to the appointed place by the beach with poor old Heavy, who was intensely impressed by being charged with about five quires of the best cream-laid, to be given to the Marchioness in case I fell. Little Grand and Ruthven came on the ground at almost the same moment, Little Grand eminently jaunty and most *confoundedly* handsome. We took off our caps with distant ceremony; the Castilian hidalgos were never more stately; but, then, what Knights of the Round Table ever splintered spears for such a woman?

The paces were measured, the pistols taken out of their case. We were just placed, and Ruthven, with a handkerchief in his hand, had just enumerated, in awful accents, "One! two!"—the "three!" yet hovered on his lips, when we heard a laugh—the third laugh that had chilled my blood in twenty-four hours. Somebody's hand was laid on Little Grand's shoulder, and Conran's voice interrupted the whole thing.

"Hallo, young ones! what farce is this?"

"Farce, sir!" retorted Little Grand, hotly—"farce? It is no farce. It is an affair of honour, and——"

"Don't make me laugh, my dear boy," smiled Conran; "it is much too warm for such an exertion. Pray, why are you and your once sworn friend making popinjays of each other?"

"Mr. Grandison has grossly insulted me," I began, "and I demand satisfaction. I will not stir from the ground without it, and——"

"You *shan't*," shouted Little Grand. "Do you dare to pretend I want to funk, you little contemptible——"

Though it was too warm, Conran went off into a fit of laughter.

I dare say our sublimity had a comic touch in it of which we never dreamt. "My dear boys, pray don't, it is too fatiguing. Come, Grand, what is it all about?"

"I deny your right to question me, Major," retorted Little Grand in a fury. "What have you to do with it? I mean to punish that young owl yonder—who didn't know how to drink anything but milk-and-water, didn't know how to say bo! to a goose, till I taught him—for very abominable impertinence, and I'll——"

"My impertinence! I like that!" I shouted. "It is

your unwarrantable, overbearing self-conceit, that makes you the laughing-stock of all the mess, which——"

"Silence!" said Conran's still stern voice, which subdued us into involuntary respect. "No more of this nonsense! Put up those pistols, Ruthven. You are two hot-headed, silly boys, who don't know for what you are quarrelling. Live a few years longer, and you won't be so eager to get into hot water, and put cartridges into your best friends. No, I shall not hear any more about it. If you do not instantly give me your words of honour not to attempt to repeat this folly, as your senior officer I shall put you under arrest for six weeks."

O Alexander Dumas!—O Monte Cristo!—O heroes of yellow paper and pluck invincible! I ask pardon of your shades; I must record the fact, lowering and melancholy as it is, that before our senior officer our heroism melted like Vanilla ice in the sun, our glories tumbled to the ground like twelfth-cake ornaments under children's fingers, and before the threat of arrest the lions lay down like lambs.

Conran sent us back, humbled, sulky, and crestfallen, and resumed his solitary patrol upon the beach, where, before the sun was fairly up, he was having a shot at curlews. But if he was a little stern, he was no less kind-hearted; and in the afternoon of that day, while he lay, after his siesta, smoking on his little bed, I unburdened myself to him. He did not laugh at me, though I saw a quizzical smile under his black moustaches.

"What is your divinity's name?" he asked, when I had finished.

"Eudoxia Adelaida, Marchioness St. Julian."

"The Marchioness St. Julian! Oh!"

"Do you know her?" I inquired, somewhat perplexed by his tone.

He smiled straight out this time.

"I don't know *her*, but there are a good many Peeresses in Malta and Gibraltar, and along the line of the Pacific, as my brother Ned, in the *Belisarius*, will tell you. I could count two score such of my acquaintance off at this minute."

I wondered what he meant. I dare say he knew all the Peerage; but that had nothing to do with me, and I thought it strange that all the Duchesses, and Countesses, and Baronesses should quit their country-seats and town-houses to locate themselves along the line of the Pacific.

"She's a fine woman, St. John?" he went on.

"Fine!" I reiterated, bursting into a panegyric, with which I won't bore you as I bored him.

"Well, you're going there to-night, you say; take me with you, and we'll see what I think of your Marchioness."

I looked at his fine figure and features, recalled certain tales of his conquests, remembered that he knew French, Italian, German, and Spanish; but, not being very able to refuse, acquiesced with a reluctance I could not entirely conceal. Conran, however, did not perceive it, and after mess took his cap, and went with me to the Casa di Fiori.

The rooms were all right again, my Marchioness was *en grande tenue*, amber silk, black lace, diamonds, and all that sort of style. Fitzhervey and the other men were in evening dress, drinking coffee; there was not a trace of bottled porter anywhere, and it was all very brilliant and presentable. The Marchioness St. Julian rose with the warmest effusion, her dazzling white teeth showing in the sunniest of smiles, and both hands outstretched.

"Augustus, *bien aimé*, you are rather——"

"Late," I suppose she was going to say, but she stopped dead short, her teeth remained parted in a stereotyped smile, a blankness of dismay came over her luminous eyes. She caught sight of Conran, and I imagined I heard a very low-breathed "Curse the fellow!" from courteous Lord Dolph. Conran came forward, however, as if he did not notice it; there was only that queer smile lurking under his moustaches. I introduced him to them, and the Marchioness smiled again, and Fitzhervey almost resumed his wonted extreme urbanity. But they were somehow or other wonderfully ill at ease—wonderfully, for people in such high society; and I was ill at ease too, from being only able to attribute Eudoxia Adelaida's evident consternation at the sight of Conran to his having been some time or other an old love of hers. "Ah!" thought I, grinding my teeth, "that comes of loving a woman older than oneself."

The Major, however, seemed the only one who enjoyed himself. The Marchioness was beaming on him graciously, though her ruffled feathers were not quite smoothed down, and he was sitting by her with an intense amusement in his eyes, alternately talking to her about Stars and Garters, whom, by her answers, she did not seem to know so very intimately after all, and chatting with Fitzhervey about hunting, who, for a man that had hunted over every country, according to his own account, seemed to confuse Tom Edge with Tom Smith, the Burton with the Tedworth, a bullfinch with an ox-rail, in queer style, under Conran's cross-questioning. We had been in the room about ten minutes, when a voice, rich, low, sweet, rang out from some inner room, singing the glorious "Inflammatus." How strange it sounded in the Casa di Fiori!

Conran started, the dark blood rose over the clear bronze of his cheek. He turned sharply on to the Marchioness. "Good Heaven! whose voice is that?"

"My niece's," she answered, staring at him, and touching a hand-bell. "I will ask her to come and sing to us nearer. She has really a lovely voice."

Conran grew pale again, and sat watching the door with the most extraordinary anxiety. Some minutes went by; then Lucrezia entered, with the same haughty reserve which her soft young face always wore when with her aunt. It changed, though, when her glance fell on Conran, into the wildest rapture I ever saw on any countenance. He fixed his eyes on her with the look Little Grand says he's seen him wear in a battle —a contemptuous smile quivering on his face.

"Sing us something, Lucrezia dear," began the Marchioness. "You shouldn't be like the nightingales, and give your music only to night and solitude."

Lucrezia seemed not to hear her. She had never taken her eyes off Conran, and she went, as dreamily as that dear little *Amina* in the "Sonnambula," to her seat under the jasmines in the window. For a few minutes Conran, who didn't seem to care two straws what the society in general thought of him, took his leave, to the relief, apparently, of Fitzhervey and Guatamara.

As he went across the verandah—that memorable verandah!—I sitting in dudgeon near the other window, while Fitzhervey was proposing écarté to Heavy, whom we had found there on our entrance, and the Marchioness had vanished into her boudoir for a moment, I saw the Roman girl spring out after him, and catch hold of his arm:

"Victor! Victor! for pity's sake!—I never thought we should meet like this!"

"Nor did I."

"Hush! hush! you will kill me. In mercy, say some kinder words!"

"I can say nothing that it would be courteous to you to say."

I couldn't have been as inflexible, whatever her sins might have been, with her hands clasped on me, and her face raised so close to mine. Lucrezia's voice changed to a piteous wail:

"You love me no longer, then?"

"Love!" said Conran, fiercely—"love! How dare you speak to me of love? I held you to be fond, innocent, true as Heaven: as such, you were dearer to me than life, as dear as honour. I loved you with as deep a passion as ever a man knew—Heaven help me! I love you now! How am I rewarded? By finding you the companion of blackguards, the associate of swindlers, one of the arch-intriguantes who lead on youths to ruin with base smiles and devilish arts. Then you dare talk to me of love!"

With those passionate words he threw her off him. She fell at his feet with a low moan. He either did not hear, or did not heed it; and I, bewildered by what I heard, mechanically went and lifted her from the ground. Lucrezia had not fainted, but she looked so wild, that I believed the Marchioness, and set her down as mad; but then Conran must be mad as well, which seemed too incredible a thing for me to swallow—our cool Major mad!

"Where does he live?" asked Lucrezia of me, in a breathless whisper.

"He? Who?"

"Victor—your officer—Signor Conran."

"Why, he lives in Valetta, of course."

"Can I find him there?"

"I dare say, if you want him."

"Want him! Oh, Santa Maria! is not his absence death? Can I find him?"

"Oh yes, I dare say. Anybody will show you Conran's rooms."

"Thank you."

With that, this mysterious young lady left me, and I turned in through the window again. Heavy and the men were playing at lansquenet, that most perilous, rapid, and bewitching of all the resistless Card Circes. There was no Marchioness, and having done it once with impunity, I thought I might do it again, and lifted the amber curtain that divided the boudoir from the drawing-room. What did I behold? Oh! torture unexampled! Oh! fiendish agony! There was Little Grand—self-conceited, insulting, impertinent, abominable, unendurable Little Grand—on the amber satin couch, with the Marchioness leaning her head on his shoulder, and looking up in his thrice-confounded face with her most adorable smile, *my* smile, that had beamed, and, as I thought, beamed only upon me!

If Mephistopheles had been by to tempt me, I would have sold my soul to have wreaked vengeance on them both. Neither saw me, thank Heaven! and I had self-possession enough not to give them the cruel triumph of witnessing my anguish. I withdrew in silence, dropped the curtain, and rushed to bury my wrongs and sorrows in the friendly bosom of the gentle night. It was my first love, and I had made a fool of myself. The two are synonymous.

How I reached the barracks I never knew. All the night long I sat watching the stars out, raving to them of Eudoxia Adelaida, and cursing in plentiful anathemas my late Orestes. How should I bear his impudent grin every mortal night of my life across the mess-table? I tore up into shreds about a ream of paper, inscribed with tender sonnets to my faithless idol. I trampled into fifty thousand shreds a rosette off her dress, for which, fool-like, I had begged the day before. I smashed the looking-glass, which could only show me the image of a pitiful donkey. I called on Heaven to redress my wrongs. Oh! curse it! never was a fellow at once so utterly done for and so utterly done brown!

And in the vicarage, as I learnt afterwards, when my letter was received at home, there was great glorification and pleasure. My mother and the girls were enraptured at the high society darling Gussy was moving in; "but then, you know, mamma, dear Gussy's manners are so gentle, so gentlemanlike, they are sure to please wherever he goes!" Wherewith my mother cried, and dried her eyes, and cried again, over that abominable letter copied from Little Grand's, and smelling of vilest tobacco.

Then entered a rectoress of a neighbouring parish, to whom my mother and the girls related with innocent exultation of my grand friends at Malta; how Lord A. Fitzhervey was my sworn ally, and the Marchioness St. Julian had quite taken me under her wing. And the rectoress, having a son of her own, who was not doing anything so grand at Cambridge, but principally sotting beer at a Cherryhinton public, smiled and was wrathful, and said to her lord at dinner:

"My dear, did you ever hear of a Marchioness St. Julian?"

"No, my love, I believe not—never."

"Is there one in the Peerage?"

"Can't say, my dear. Look in Burke."

So the rectoress got Burke, and closed it, after deliberate inspection, with malignant satisfaction.

"I thought not. How ridiculous those St. Johns are about that ugly boy Augustus. As if Tom were not worth a hundred of him!"

I was too occupied with my own miseries then to think about Conran and Lucrezia, though some time after I heard all about it. It seems that, a year before, Conran was on leave in Rome, and at Rome, loitering about the Campagna one day, he made a chance acquaintance with an Italian girl, by getting some flowers for her she had tried to reach and could not. She was young, enthusiastic, intensely interesting, and had only an old Roman nurse, deaf as a post and purblind with her. The girl was Lucrezia da' Guari, and Lucrezia was lovely as one of her own myrtle or orange flowers. Somehow or other Conran went there the next day, and the next, and the next, and so on for a good many days, and always found Lucrezia. Now, Conran had at bottom a touch of unstirred romance, and, moreover, his own idea of what sort of woman he could love. Something in this untrained yet winning Campagna flower answered to both. He was old enough to trust his own discernment, and, after a month or two's walks and talks, Conran, one of the proudest men going, offered himself and his name to a Roman girl of whom he knew nothing, except that she seemed to care for him as he had had a fancy to be cared for all his life. It was a deucedly romantic thing—however, he did it! Lucrezia had told him her father was a military officer, but somehow or other this father never came to light, and when he called at their house—or rather rooms—Conran always found him out, which he thought queer, but, on the whole, rather providential, and he set the accident down to a foreigner's roaming habits.

The day Conran had really gone the length of offering to make an unknown Italian his wife, he went for the first time in the evening, to Da Guari's house. The servant showed him in unannounced to a brightly-lighted chamber, reeking with wine and smoke, where a dozen men were playing trente et quarante at an amateur bank, and two or three others were gathered round what he had believed his own fair and pure Campagna flower. He understood it all; he turned away with a curse upon him. He wanted love and innocence; adventuresses he could have by the score, and he was sick to death of them. From that hour he never saw her again till he met her at the Casa di Fiori.

The next day I went to Conran while he was breakfasting, and unburdened my mind to him. He looked ill and haggard, but he listened to me very kindly, though he spoke of the people at the Casa di Fiori in a hard, brief, curious manner.

"Plenty have been taken in like you, Gus," he said. "I was, years ago in my youth, when I joined the army. There are scores of such women, as I told you, down the line of the Pacific, and about here; anywhere, in fact, where the army and navy give them fresh pigeons to be gulled. They take titles that sound grand in boys' ears, and fascinate them till they've won all their money, and then——send them to the dogs. Your Marchioness St. Julian's name is Sarah Briggs."

I gave an involuntary shriek. Sarah Briggs finished me. It was the death-stroke, that could never be got over.

"She was a ballet-girl in London," continued Conran; "then, when she was sixteen, married that Fitzhervey, *alias* Briggs, *alias* Smith, *alias* what you please, and set up in her present more lucrative employment with her three or four confederates. Saint-Jeu was expelled from Paris for keeping a hell in the Chaussée d'Antin, Fitzhervey was a leg at Newmarket, Orangia Magnolia a lawyer's clerk, who was had up for forgery, Guatamara is—by another name—a scoundrel of Rome. There is the history of your Maltese Peerage, Gussy. Well, you'll be wider awake next time. Wait, there is somebody at my door. Stay here a moment, I'll come back to you."

Accordingly, I stayed in his bedroom, where I had found him writing, and he went into his sitting-room, of which, from the diminutiveness of his domicile, I commanded a full view, sit where I would. What was my astonishment to see Lucrezia! I went to his bedroom door; it was locked from the outside, so I perforce remained where I was, to, *nolens volens*, witness the finish of last night's interview.

Stern to the last extent and deadly pale, Conran stood, too surprised to speak, and most probably at a loss for words.

Lucrezia came up to him nevertheless with the abandonment of youth and southern blood.

"Victor! Victor! let me speak to you. You shall listen; you shall not judge me unheard."

"Signorina, I have judged you by only too ample evidence."

He had recovered himself now, and was as cool as needs be.

"I deny it. But you love me still?"

"Love you? More shame on me! A laugh, a compliment, a caress, a cashmere, is as much as such women as you are worth. Love becomes ridiculous named in the same breath with you."

She caught hold of his hand and crushed it in both her own.

"Kill me if you will. Death would have no sting from your hand, but never speak such words to *me.*"

His voice trembled.

"How can I choose but speak them? You know what I believed you in Italy, and how on that belief I offered you my name—a name never yet stained, never yet held unworthy. I lost you, to find you in society which stamped you for ever. A lovely fiend, holding raw boys enchained, that your associates might rifle their purses with marked cards and cogged dice. I hoped to have found a diamond, without spot or flaw. I discovered my error too late; it was only glass, which all men were free to pick up and trample on at their pleasure."

He tried to wrench his hand away, but she would not let it go.

"Hush! hush! listen to me first. If you once thought me worthy of your love, you may, surely, now accord me pity. I shall not trouble you long. After this, you need see me no more. I am going back to my old convent. You and the world will soon forget me, but I shall remember you, and pray for you, as dearer than my own soul."

Conran's head was bent down now, and his voice was thick, as he answered briefly,

"Go on."

This scene half consoled me for Eudoxia Adelaida —(I mean, O Heavens, Sarah Briggs!)—it was so exquisitely romantic, and Conran and Lucrezia wouldn't have done at all badly for Monte Cristo and that dear little Haidee. I was fearfully poetic in those days.

"When I met you in Rome," Lucrezia went on, in obedience to his injunction, "two years ago, you remember I had only left my convent and lived with my father but a month or two. I told you he was an officer. I only said what I had been told, and I knew no more than you that he was the keeper of a gambling-house."

She shuddered as she paused, and leaned her forehead on Conran's hand. He did not repulse her, and she continued, in her broken, simple English:

"The evening you promised me what I should have needed to have been an angel to be worthy of—your love and your name—that very evening, when I reached home, my father bade me dress for a soirée he was going to give. I obeyed him, of course. I knew nothing but what he told me, and I went down, to find a dozen young nobles and a few Englishmen drinking and playing on a table covered with green cloth. Some few of them came up to me, but I felt frightened; their looks, their tones, their florid compliments, were so different to yours. But my father kept his eye upon me, and would not let me leave. While they were leaning over my chair, and whispering in my ear, *you* came to the door of the salon, and I went towards you, and you looked cold and harsh, as I had never seen you before, and put me aside, and turned away without a word. Oh, Victor! Why did you not kill me then? Death would have been kindness. Your Othello was kinder to Desdemona; he slew her—he did not *leave* her. From that hour I never saw you, and from that hour my father persecuted me because I would never join in his schemes, nor enter his vile gaming-rooms. Yet I have lived with him because I could not get away. I have been too carefully watched. We Italians are not free, like your happy English girls. A few weeks ago we were compelled to leave Rome, the young Contino di Firenze had been stilettoed leaving my father's rooms, and he could stay in Italy no longer. We came here, and joined that hateful woman, who calls herself Marchioness St. Julian; and, because she could not bend me to her will, gives out that I am her niece, and mad! I wonder I am *not* mad, Victor. I wish hearts would break, as the romancers make them; but how long one suffers, and lives on! Oh, my love, my soul, my life, only say that you believe me, and look kindly at me once again, then I will never trouble you again, I will only pray for you. But believe me, Victor. The Mother Superior of my convent will tell you it is the truth that I speak. O, for the love of Heaven, believe me! Believe me, or I shall die!"

It was not in the nature of man to resist her; there was truth in the girl's voice and face, if ever truth walked abroad on earth. And Conran did believe her, and told her so in a few unconnected words, lifting her up in his arms, and vowing, with most unrighteous oaths, that her father should never have power to persecute her again as long as he himself lived to shelter and take care of her.

I was so interested in my Monte Cristo and Haidee (it was so like a chapter out of a book), that I entirely forgot my durance vile, and my novel and excessively disgraceful, though enforced, occupation of spy; and there I stayed, alternating between my interest in them and my agonies at the revelations concerning my Eudoxia Adelaida—oh, hang it! I mean Sarah Briggs—till, after a most confounded long time, Conran saw fit to take Lucrezia off, to get asylum for her with the Colonel's wife for a day or two, that "those fools might not misconstrue her." By which comprehensive epithet he, I suppose, politely designated "Ours."

Then I went my ways to my own room, and there I found a scented, mauve-hued, creamy billet-doux, in uncommon bad handwriting, though, from my miserable Eudoxia Adelaida to the "friend and lover of her soul." Confound the woman!—how I swore at that daintily-perfumed and most vilely-scrawled letter. To think that where that beautiful signature stretched from one side to the other—"Eudoxia Adelaida St. Julian" —there *ought* to have been that short, vile, low-bred, hideous, Billingsgate cognomen of "Sarah Briggs!"

In the note she reproached me—the wretched hypocrite!—for my departure the previous night, "without one farewell to your Eudoxia, O cruel Augustus!" and asked me to give her a rendezvous at some vineyards lying a little way off the Casa di Fiori, on the road to Melita. Now, being a foolish boy, and regarding myself as having been loved and wronged, whereas I had only been playing the very common *rôle* of pigeon, I could not resist the temptation of going, just to take one last look of that fair, cruel face, and upbraid her with being the first to sow the fatal seeds of lifelong mistrust and misery in my only too fond and faithful, &c. &c. &c.

So, at the appointed hour, just when the sun was setting over the far-away Spanish shore, and the hush of night was sinking over the little, rocky, peppery, military-thick, Mediterranean isle, I found myself *en route* to the vineyards; which, till I came to Malta, had been one of my delusions, Idea picturing them in wreaths and avenues, Reality proving them hop-sticks and parched earth. I drew near; it was quite dark now, the sun had gone to sleep under the blue waves, and the moon was not yet up. Though I knew she was Sarah Briggs, and an adventuress who had made game of me, two facts that one would fancy might chill the passion out of anybody, so mad was I about that woman, that if I had met her then and there, I should have let her wheedle me over, and gone back to the Casa di Fiori with her and been fleeced again: I am sure I should, sir, and so would you, if, at eighteen, new to life, you had fallen in with Eudox——pshaw! —with Sarah Briggs, my Marchioness St. Julian.

I drew near the vineyards: my heart beat thick. I could not see, but I was certain I heard the rustle of her dress, caught the perfume of her hair. All her sins vanished: how could I upbraid her, though she were three times over Sarah Briggs? Yes, she was coming; I *felt* her near; an electric thrill rushed through me as soul met soul. I heard a murmured "Dearest, sweetest?" I felt a warm clasp of two arms, but—— a cold row of undress waistcoat-buttons came against my face, and a voice I knew too well cried out, as I rebounded from him, impelled thereto by a not gentle kick,

"The devil! get out! Who the deuce are you?"

We both stopped for breath. At that minute up rose the silver moon, and in its tell-tale rays we glared on one another, I and Little Grand.

That silence was sublime: the pause between Beethoven's andante and allegro—the second before the Spanish bull rushes upon the torreador.

"You little miserable wretch!" burst out Grand, slowly and terribly; "you little, mean, sneaking, spying, contemptible milksop! I should like to know what you mean by bringing out your ugly phiz at this hour, when you used to be afraid of stirring out for fear of nurse's bogies? And to dare to come lurking after me!"

"After you, Mr. Grandison!" I repeated, with grandiloquence. Really you put too much importance on your own movements. I came by appointment to meet the Marchioness St. Julian, whom, I presume, as you are well acquainted with her, you know in her real name of Sarah Briggs, and to——"

"Sarah Briggs!—*you* come by appointment?" stammered Little Grand.

"Yes, sir; if you disbelieve my word of honour, I will condescend to show you my invitation."

"You little ape!" swore Grand, coming back to his previous wrath; "it is a lie, a most abominable, unwarrantable lie! *I* came by appointment, sir; you did no such thing. Look there!"

And he flaunted before my eyes in the moonlight the facsimile of my letter, verbatim copy, save that in his Cosmo was put in the stead of Augustus.

"Look there!" said I, giving him mine.

Little Grand snatched it, read it over once, twice, thrice, then drooped his head, with a burning colour in his face, and was silent.

The "knowing hand" was done!

We were both of us uncommonly quiet for ten minutes; neither of us liked to be the first to give in.

At last Little Grand looked up and held out his hand, no more nonsense about him now.

"Simon, you and I have been two great fools; we can't chaff one another. She's a cursed actress, and —let's make it up, old boy."

We made it up accordingly—when Little Grand was not conceited he was a very jolly fellow—and then I gave him my whole key to the mysteries, intricacies, and charms of our Casa di Fiori. We could not chaff one another, but poor Little Grand was pitiably sore then, and for long afterwards. He, the "old bird," the cool hand, the sharp one of Ours, to have been done brown, to be the joke of the mess, the laugh of all the men, down to the weest drummer-boy! Poor Little Grand! He was too done up to swagger, too thoroughly angry with himself to swear at anybody else. He only whispered to me, "Why the dickens could she want you and me to meet ourselves?"

"To give us a finishing hoax, I suppose," I suggested.

Little Grand drew his cap over his eyes, and hung his head down in abject humiliation.

"I suppose so. What fools we have been, Simon! And, I say, I've borrowed three hundred of old Miraflores, and it's all gone up at that devilish Casa; and how I shall get it from the governor, Heaven knows, for *I* don't."

"I'm in the same pickle, Grand," I groaned. "I've given that old rascal notes of hand for two hundred pounds, and, if it don't drop from the clouds, I shall never pay it. Oh, I say, Grand, love comes deucedly expensive."

"Ah!" said he, with a sympathetic shiver, "think what a pair of hunters we might have had for the money!" With which dismal and remorseful remembrance the old bird, who had been trapped like a young pigeon, swore mightily, and withdrew into humbled and disgusted silence.

Next morning we heard, to our comfort—what lots of people there always are to tell us how to lock our stable door when our solitary mare has been stolen—that, with a gentle hint from the police, the Marchioness St. Julian, with her *confrères*, had taken wing to the Ionian Isles, where, at Corfu or Cephalonia, they will re-erect the Casa di Fiori, and glide gently on again from vingt-et-un to loo, and from loo to lansquenet, under eyes as young and blinded as our own. They went without Lucrezia. Conran took her into his own hands. Any other man in the regiment would have been pretty well ridiculed at taking a bride out of the Casa di Fiori; but the statements made by the high-born Abbess of her Roman convent were so clear, and so to the girl's honour, and he had such a way of holding his own, of keeping off liberties from himself and anything belonging to him, and was, moreover, known to be of such fastidious honour, that his young wife was received as if she had been a Princess in her own right. With her respected parent Conran had a brief interview previous to his flight from Malta, in which, with a few gentle hints, he showed that worthy it would be wiser to leave his daughter unmolested for the future, and I doubt if Mr. Orangia Magnolia, *alias* Pepe Guari, would know his own child in the joyous, graceful, daintily-dressed mistress of Conran's handsome Parisian establishment.

Little Grand and I suffered cruelly. We were the butts of the mess for many a long month afterwards, when every idiot's tongue asked us on every side after the health of the Marchioness St. Julian? when we were going to teach them lansquenet? how often we heard from the aristocratic members of the Maltese Peerage? with like delightful pleasantries, which the questioners deemed high wit. We paid for it, too, to that arch old screw Balthazar; but I doubt very much if the money were not well lost, and the experience well gained. It cured me of my rawness and Little Grand of his self-conceit, the only thing that had before spoilt that good-hearted, quick-tempered, and clever-brained little fellow. Oh, Pater and Materfamilias, disturb not yourselves so unnecessarily about the crop of wild oats which your young ones are sowing broadcast. Those wild oats often spring from a good field of high spirit, hot courage, and thoughtless generosity, that are the sign and basis of nobler virtues to come, and from them very often rise two goodly plants—Experience and Discernment.

LADY MARABOUT'S TROUBLES;

OR,

THE WORRIES OF A CHAPERONE.

IN THREE SEASONS.

SEASON THE FIRST.—THE ELIGIBLE.

ONE of the kindest-natured persons that I ever knew on this earth, where kind people are as rare as black eagles or red deer, is Helena, Countess of Marabout, *née* De Boncœur. She has foibles, she has weaknesses—who amongst us has not?—she will wear her dresses *décollettes*, though she's sixty, if Burke tells us truth; she will rouge and practise a thousand other little toilette tricks; but they are surely innocent, since they deceive nobody; and if you wait for a woman who has no artifices, I am afraid you shall have to forswear the sex *in toto*, my friends, and come growling back to your Diogenes' tub in the Albany, with your lantern still lit every day of your lives.

Lady Marabout is a very charming person. As for her weaknesses, she is all the nicer for them, to my taste. I like people with weaknesses myself; those without them do look so dreadfully scornfully and unsympathisingly upon one from the altitude of their superiority, *de toute la hauteur de sa bêtise*, as a witty

Frenchman says. Humanity was born with weaknesses. If I were a beggar I might hope for a coin from a man with some; a man without any, I know, would shut up his porte-monnaie, with an intensified click, to make me feel trebly envious, and consign me to D 15 and his truncheon, on the score of vagrancy.

Lady Marabout is a very charming person, despite her little foibles, and she gives very pleasant little dinners, both at her house in Lowndes-square and in her jointure-villa at Twickenham, where the bad odours of the Thames are drowned in the fragrance of the geraniums, piled in great heaps of red, white, and variegated blossom in the flower-beds on the lawn. She has been married twice, but has only one son, by her first union—Carruthers, of the Guards—a very good fellow, whom his mother thinks perfection, though if she *did* know certain scenes in her adored Philip's life, the good lady might hesitate before she endowed her son with all the cardinal virtues as she does at the present moment. She has no daughters, therefore you will wonder to hear that the prime misery, burden, discomfort, and worry of her life is chaperonage. But so it is.

Lady Marabout is the essence of good nature; she can't say No: that unpleasant negative monosyllable was never heard to issue from her full, smiling, kind-looking lips: she *is* in a high position, she has an extensive circle, thanks to her own family and those of the baronet and peer she successively espoused; and some sister, or cousin, or friend, is incessantly hunting her up to bring out their girls, and sell them well off out of hand; young ladies being goods extremely likely to hang *on* hand now-a-days.

"Of all troubles, the troubles of a chaperone are the greatest," said Lady Marabout to me at the wedding déjeûner of one of her protégées. "In the first place, one looks on at others' campaigns instead of conducting them oneself; secondly, it brings back one's own bright days to see the young things' smiles and blushes, like that girl's just now (I do hope she'll be happy!); and thirdly, one has all the responsibility, and gets all the blame if anything goes wrong. I'll never chaperone anybody again now I have got rid of Leila."

So does Lady Marabout say twenty times; yet has she invariably some young lady under her wing, whose relatives are defunct, or invalided, or in India, or out of society somehow; and we all of us call her house The Yard, and her (among ourselves) not Lady Marabout but Lady Tattersall. The worries she has in her chaperone's office would fill a folio, specially as her heart inclines to the encouragement of romance, but her reason to the banishment thereof; and while her tenderness suffers if she thwarts her protégées' leanings, her conscience gives her neuralgic twinges if she abets them to unwise matches while under her dragonnage.

"What's the matter, mother?" asked Carruthers, one morning. He's very fond of his mother, and will never let any one laugh at her in his hearing.

"Matter? Everything!" replied Lady Marabout, concisely and comprehensively, as she sat on the sofa in her boudoir, with her white ringed hands and her *bien conservé* look, and her kindly pleasant eyes and her rich dress; one could see what a pretty woman she had been, and that Carruthers may thank her for his good looks. "To begin with, Félicie has been so stupid as to marry; married the greengrocer (whom she will ruin in a week!), and has left me to the mercies of a stupid woman who puts pink with cerise, mauve with magenta, and sky-blue with azureline, and has no recommendation except that she is as ugly as the Medusa, and so will not tempt you to——"

"Make love to her, as I did to Marie," laughed Carruthers. "Marie was a pretty little dear; it was very severe in you to send her away."

Lady Marabout tried hard to look severe and condemnatory, but failed signally: nature had formed the smooth brow and the kindly eyes in far too soft a mould.

"Don't jest about it, Philip; you know it was a great pain, annoyance, and scandal to me. Well! Félicie is gone, and Oakes was seen pawning some of my Mechlin the other day, so I have been obliged to discharge *her;* and they both of them suited me so well! Then Bijou is ill, poor little pet——"

"With repletion of chicken panada?"

"No; Bijou isn't such a gourmet. You judge him by yourself, I suppose; men always do! Then Lady Hautton told me last night that you were the wildest man on town, and at forty——"

"You think I ought to *ranger?* So I will, my dear mother, some day; but at present I am—so very comfortable; it would be a pity to alter! What pains one's friends are always at to tell unpalatable things; if they would but be only half so eager to tell us the pleasant ones! I shall expect you to cut Lady Hautton if she speak badly of me. I can't afford to lose your worship, mother!"

"My worship? How conceited you are, Philip! As

for Lady Hautton, I believe she does dislike you, because you did not engage yourself to Adelina, and were selected aide-de-camp to her Majesty, instead of Hautton; still, I am afraid she spoke too nearly the truth."

"Perhaps Marie has entered her service and told tales."

But Lady Marabout wouldn't laugh, she always looks very grave about Marie.

"My worst trouble," she began, hastily, "is that your Aunt Honiton is too ill to come to town; no chance of her being well enough to come at all this season; and of course the charge of Valencia has devolved on me. You know how I hate chaperoning, and I did *so* hope I should be free this year; besides, Valencia is a great responsibility, very great; a girl of so much beauty always is; there will be sure to be so many men about her at once, and your aunt will expect me to marry her so very well. It is excessively annoying."

"My poor dear mother!" cried Carruthers. "I grant you *are* an object of pity. You are everlastingly having young fillies sent you to break in, and they want such a tight hand on the ribbons."

"And a tight hand, as you call it, I never had, and never shall have," sighed Lady Marabout. "Valencia will be no trouble to me on that score, however; she has been admirably educated, knows all that is due to her position, and will never give me a moment's anxiety by any imprudence or inadvertence. But she is excessively handsome, and a beauty is a great responsibility when she first comes out."

"Val was always a handsome child, if I remember. I dare say she is a beauty now. When is she coming up? because I'll tell the men to mark the house and keep clear of it," laughed Carruthers. "You're a dreadfully dangerous person, mother; you have always the best-looking girl in town with you. Fulke Nugent says if he should ever want such a thing as a wife when he comes into the title, he shall take a look at the Marabout Yearlings' Sale."

"Abominably rude of you and your friends to talk me over in your turf slang! I wish *you* would come and bid at the sale, Philip; I should like to see you married—well married, of course."

"My beloved mother!" cried Carruthers. "Leave me in peace, if you please, and catch the others if you can. There's Goodey, now; every chaperone and débutante in London has set traps for him for the last I don't know how many years; wouldn't he do for Valencia?"

"Goodwood? Of course he would; he would do for any one; the Dukedom's the oldest in the peerage. Goodwood is highly eligible. Thank you for reminding me, Philip. Since Valencia is coming, I must do my best for her." Which phrase meant with Lady Marabout that she must be very lynx-eyed as to settlements, and a perfect dragon to all detrimental connexions, must frown with Medusa severity on all horrors of younger sons, and advocate with all the weight of personal experience the advantage and agrémens of a good position, in all of which practicalities she generally broke down, with humiliation unspeakable, immediately her heart was enlisted and her sympathies appealed to on the enemy's side. She sighed, played with her bracelets thoughtfully, and then, heroically resigning herself to her impending fate, brightened up a little, and asked her son to go and choose a new pair of carriage-horses for her.

To look at Lady Marabout as she sat in her amber satin couch that morning, pleasant, smiling, well dressed, well looking, with the grace of good birth and the sunniness of good nature plainly written on her smooth brow and her kindly eyes, and wealth—delicious little god!—stamping itself all about her, from the diamond rings on her soft white fingers to the broidered shoe on the feet, of whose smallness she was still proud, one might have ignorantly imagined her to be the most happy, enviable, well-conditioned, easy-going dowager in the United Kingdom. But appearances are deceptive, and if we believe what she constantly asserted, Lady Marabout was very nearly worn into her grave by a thousand troubles; her almshouses, whose roofs would eternally blow off with each high wind; her dogs, whom she would overfeed; her ladies' maids, who were hired only to steal, tease, or scandalise her; the begging-letter writers, who distilled tears from her eyes and sovereigns from her purse, let Carruthers disclose their hypocrisies as he might; the bolder begging-letters, written by hon. secs., and headed by names with long handles, belonging to Pillars of the State and Lights of the Church, which compelled her to make a miserable choice between a straitened income or a remorseful conscience—tormented, in fine, with worries small and large, from her ferns, on which she spent a large fortune, and who drooped maliciously in their glass cases, with an ill-natured obstinacy characteristic of desperately-courted individuals, whether of the floral or the human world, to those marriageable young ladies whom she took under her wing to usher into the great world, and who were certain to run counter to her wishes and overthrow her plans, to marry ill, or not marry at all, or do something or other to throw discredit on her chaperoning abilities. She was, she assured us, *pétrie* with worries, small and large, specially as she was so eminently sunny, affable, and radiant a looking person, that all the world took their troubles to her, selected her as their confidante, and made her the repository of their annoyances; but her climax of misery was to be compelled to chaperone, and as a petition for some débutante to be entrusted to her care was invariably made each season, and "No" was a monosyllable into which her lips utterly refused to form themselves, each season did her life become a burden to her. There was never any rest for the soul of Helena, Countess of Marabout, till her house in Lowndes-square was shut up, and her charges off her hand, and she could return in peace to her jointure-villa at Twickenham, or to Carruthers' old Hall of Deepdene, and among her flowers, her birds, and her hobbies, throw off for a while the weary burden of her worries as a chaperone.

"Valencia will give me little trouble, I hope. So admirably brought-up a girl, and so handsome as she is, will be sure to marry soon, and marry well," thought Lady Marabout, self-congratulatorily, as she dressed for dinner the day of her niece's arrival in town, running over mentally the qualifications and attractions of Valencia Valletort, while Félicie's successor, Mademoiselle Despréaux, whose crime was to put pink with cerise, mauve with magenta, and sky-blue with azure-line, gave the finishing touches to her toilette—"Valencia will give me no trouble; she has all the De Boncœur beauty, with the Valletort dignity. Who would do for her? Let me see; eligible men are not abundant, and those that are eligible are shy of being marked, as Philip would say—perhaps from being hunted so much, poor things! There is Fulke Nugent, heir to a barony, and his father is ninety—very rich, too—he would do; and Philip's friend, Caradoc, poor, I know, but their Earldom's the oldest peerage patent. There is Eyre Lee, too; I don't much like the man, supercilious and empty-headed; still he's an unobjectionable alliance. And there is Goodwood. Every one has tried for Goodwood, and failed. I should like Valencia to win him; he is decidedly the most eligible man in town. I will invite him to dinner. If he is not attracted by Valencia's beauty, nothing can attract him——*Despréaux! comme vous êtes bête! Otez ces panaches, de grace!*"

"Valencia will give me no trouble; she will marry at once," thought Lady Marabout again, looking across the dinner-table at her niece.

If any young patrician might be likely to marry at once, it was the Hon. Valencia Valletort; she was, to the most critical, a beauty: her figure was perfect, her features were perfect, and if you complained that her large glorious eyes were a trifle too changeless in expression, that her cheek, exquisitely independent of Maréchale powder, Blanc de Perle, and liquid rouge, though it was, rarely varied with her thoughts and feelings, why, you were very exacting, my good fellow, and should remember that nothing is quite perfect on the face of this earth—not even a racer or a woman— and that whether you bid at the Marabout Yearlings Sale or the Rawcliffe, if you wish to be pleased you'd better leave a hypercritical spirit behind you, and not expect to get *all* points to your liking. The best filly will have something faulty in temper or breeding, symmetry or pace, for your friend Jack Martingale to have the fun of pointing out to you when your money is paid and the filly in your stall; and your wife will have the same, only Martingale will point *her* flaws out behind your back, and only hint them to you with an all-expressive "Not allowed to smoke in the dining-room *now!*" "A little bit of a flirt, madame—ne'st-ce pas, Charlie?" "Reins kept rather tight, eh, old fellow?" or something equally ambiguous, significant, and unpleasant.

"I must consider, Philip, I have brought out the beauty of the season," said Lady Marabout to Carruthers, eyeing her niece as she danced at her first ball at the Dowager-Duchess of Amandine's, and beginning to brighten up a little under the weight of her responsibilities.

"I think you have, mother. Val's indisputably handsome. You must tell her to make play with Goodwood or Nugent."

Lady Marabout unfurled her fan, and indignantly interrupted him:

"My dear Philip! do you suppose I would teach Valencia, or any girl under my charge, to lay herself out for any man, whoever, or whatever he might be? I trust your cousin would not stoop to use such manœuvres, did I even stoop to counsel them. Depend on it, Philip, it is precisely those women who try to 'make play,' as you call it, with your sex that fail most to charm them. It is abominable the way in which you men talk, as if we all hunted you down, and would drive you to St. George's *nolens volens!*"

"So you would, mother," laughed Carruthers. "We 'eligible men' have a harder life of it than rabbits in a warren, with a dozen beagles after them. From the minute we're of age, we're beset with traps for the unwary, and the spring-guns are so dexterously covered with an inviting, innocent-looking turf of courtesies and hospitalities that it's next to a moral impossibility to escape them, let one retire into oneself, keep to monosyllables through all the courses of all the dinners and all the turns of all the valses, and avoid everything 'compromising,' as one may. I've suffered, and can tell you. I suffer still, though I believe and hope they are beginning to look on me as an incurable, given over to the clubs, the coulisses, and the coverside. There's a fellow that's known still more of the *peins fortes et dures* than I. Goodwood's coming to ask for an introduction to Val, I would bet."

He was coming for that purpose, and though Lady Marabout had so scornfully and sincerely repudiated her son's counsel relative to making play with Goodwood, blandly ignorant of her own weaknesses like a good many other people, Lady Marabout was not above a glow of chaperone gratification when she saw the glance of admiration, which the Pet Eligible of the season bestowed on Valencia Valletort. Goodwood was a good-looking fellow—a clever fellow—though possibly he shone best alone at a mess luncheon, in a chat driving to Hornsey Wood, round the fire in a smoking-room, on a yacht deck, or anywhere where ladies of the titled world were not encountered, he having become afraid of them by dint of much persecution, as any October partridge of a setter's nose. He was passably good-looking, ordinarily clever, a very good fellow as I say, and—he was elder son of his Grace of Doncaster, which fact would have made him the desired of every unit of the *beau sexe*, had he been hideous as the Veiled Prophet or brutal Gilles de Rayes. The Beauty often loves the Beast in our day, as in the days of fairy lore. We see that beloved story of our petticoat days not seldom acted out, and when there is no possibility of personal transmogrification and amelioration for the Beast moreover; only—the Beauty has always had whispered in her little ear the title she will win, and the revenues she will gain, and the cloth of gold she will wear, if she caresses Bruin the enamoured, swears his ugly head is god-like, and vows fidelity unswerving!

Goodwood was no uncouth Bruin, and he had strawberry-leaves in his gift; none of your lacquered, or ormolu, or silver-gilt coronets, such as are cast about now-a-days with a liberality that reminds one of flinging a handful of halfpence from a balcony, where the nimblest beggar is first to get the prize; but of the purest and best gold; and Goodwood had been tried for accordingly by every woman he came across for the last dozen years. Women of every style and every order had primed all their rifles, and had their shot at him, and done their best to make a centre and score themselves as winner: belles and bas bleus, bewitching widows and budding débutantes, fast young ladies who tried to capture him in the hunting-field by clearing a bull-finch; saintly young ladies, who illuminated missals, and hinted they would like to take his conversion in hand; brilliant women, who talked at him all through a long rainy day, when Perthshire was flooded, and the black-fowl unattainable; showy women, who *posed* for him whole evenings in their opera-boxes, whole mornings in their boudoir—all styles and orders had set at him, till he had sometimes sworn in his haste that all women were mantraps, and that he wished to Heaven he were a younger son in the Foreign Office, or a poor devil in the Line, or anything, rather than what he was; the Pet Eligible of his day.

"Goodwood is certainly struck with her," thought Lady Marabout, as Despréaux disrobed her that night, running over with a retrogressive glance Valencia Valletort's successes at her first ball. "Very much struck, indeed, I should say. I will issue cards for another 'At Home.' As for 'making play' with him, as Philip terms it, of course that is only a man's nonsense. Valencia will need none of those trickeries, I trust; still, it is any one's duty to make the best alliance possible for such a girl, and—dear Adeliza would be very pleased."

With which amiable remembrance of her sister (whom, conceiving it her duty to love, Lady Marabout persuaded herself that she *did* love, from a common feminine opticism that there's an eleventh commandment which makes it compulsory to be attached to relatives *n'importe* of whatever degree of disagreeability, though Lady Honiton was about the most odious hypochondriac going, in a perpetual state of unremitting battle with the whole outer world in general, and allopathists, homœopathists, and hydropathists in especial), the most amiable lady in all Christendom bade Despréaux bring up a cup of coffee an hour earlier in the morning, she had so much to do! asked if Bijou had had some panada set down by his basket in case he wanted something to take in the night; wished her maid good-night, and laid her head on her pillow as the dawn streamed through the shutters, already settling what bridal presents she should give her niece Valencia, when she became present Marchioness of Goodwood and prospective Duchess of Doncaster before the altar rails of St. George's.

"That's a decidedly handsome girl, that cousin of yours, Phil," said Goodwood, on the pavement before her Grace of Amandine's, in Grosvenor-place, at the same hour that night.

"I think she *is* counted like me!" said Carruthers. "Of course she's handsome; hasn't she De Boncœur blood in her, my good fellow? We're all of us good-looking, always have been, thank God! If you're inclined to sacrifice, Goodwood, now's your time, and my mother 'll be delighted. She's brought out about half a million of débutantes, I should say, in her time, and all of 'em have gone wrong, somehow; wouldn't go off at all, like damp gunpowder, or would go off too quick in the wrong direction, like a volunteer's rifle charge; married ignominiously or married obstinately, or never excited pity in the breast of any man, but had to retire to single-blessedness in the country, console themselves with piety and an harmonium, and spread nets for young clerical victims. Give her a triumph at last, and let her have glory for once, as a chaperone, in catching *you!*"

Goodwood gave a little shiver, and tried to light a Manilla, which utterly refused to take light, for the twelfth time in half a minute.

"Hold your tongue! If the Templars' Order were extant, wouldn't I take the vows and bless them! What an unspeakable comfort and protection that white cross would be to us, Phil, if we could stick it on our coats, and know it would say to every woman that looked at us, 'No go, my pretty little dears—not to be caught!' Marriage! I can't remember any time that that word wasn't my bugbear. When I was but a little chicken, some four years old, I distinctly remember, when I was playing with little Ida Keane on the terrace, hearing her mother simper to mine, 'Perhaps darling Goodwood may marry my little Ida some day, who knows?' I never would play with Ida afterwards; instinct preserved me; she's six or seven-and-thirty now, and weighs ten stone, I'm positive. Why *won't* they let us alone? The way journalists and dowagers, the fellows who want to write a taking article, and the women who want to get rid of a taking daughter, all badger us, in public and private, about marriage just now, is abominable, on my life; the affair's *ours*, I should say, not theirs, and to marry isn't the ultimatum of a man's existence, nor anything like it."

"I hope not! It's more like the extinguisher. Good-night, old fellow." And Carruthers drove away in his hansom, while Goodwood got into his night-brougham, thinking that for the sake of the title, the evil (nuptial) day *must* come, sooner or later, but dashed off to forget the disagreeable obligation over the supper-table of the most sparkling empress of the demi-monde.

Lady Marabout had her wish; she brought out the belle of the season, and when a little time had slipped by, when the Hon. Val had been presented at the first

Drawing-room, and shone there despite the worry, muddle, and squeeze incidental to that royal and fashionable ceremony, and she had gathered second-hand from her son what was said in the clubs relative to this new specimen of the Valletort beauty, she began to be happier under her duties than she had ever been before, and wrote letters to "dearest Adeliza," brimful of superlative adjectives and genuine warmth.

"Valencia will do me credit: I shall see her engaged, before the end of June; she will have only to choose," Lady Marabout would say to herself some twenty times in the pauses of the morning concerts, the morning parties, the bazaar committees, the toilette consultations, the audiences to religious beggars, whose name was Legion and rapacity unmeasured, the mass of unanswered correspondence whose debt lay as heavily on Lady Marabout as his chains on a convict, and were about as little likely to be knocked off, and all the other things innumerable that made her life in the season one teetotum whirl of small worries and sunshiny cares, from the moment she began her day, with her earliest cup of Mocha softened with cream from that pet dairy of hers at Fernditton, where, according to Lady Marabout, the cows were constantly *in articulo mortis*, but the milk invariably richer than anywhere else, an agricultural anomaly which presented no difficulties to *her* reason. Like all women, she loved paradoxes, defied logic recklessly, and would clear at a bound a chasm of solecisms that would have kept Plato in difficulties about crossing it, and in doubt about the strength of his jumping-pole, all his life long.

"She will do me great credit," the semi-consoled chaperone would say to herself with self-congratulatory relief; and if Lady Marabout thought now and then, "I wish she were a trifle—a trifle more—demonstrative," she instantly checked such an ungrateful and hypercritical wish, and remembered that a heart is a highly treacherous and unadvisable possession for any young lady, and a most happy omission in her anatomy, though Lady Marabout had, she would confess to herself on occasions with great self-reproach, an unworthy and lingering weakness for that contraband article, for which she scorned and scolded herself with the very worst success.

Lady Marabut *had* a heart herself; to it she had had to date the greatest worries, troubles, imprudences, and vexations of her life; she had had to thank it for nothing, and to dislike it for much; it had made her grieve most absurdly for other people's griefs; it had given her a hundred unphilosophical pangs at philosophic ingratitude from people who wanted her no longer; it had teased, worried, and plagued her all her life long, had often interfered in the most meddling and inconvenient manner between her and her reason, her comfort and her prudence; and yet she had a weakness for the same detrimental organ in other people— a weakness of which she could no more have cured herself than of her belief in the detection-defying powers of liquid rouge, the potentiality of a Lilliputian night-bolt against an army of burglars, the miraculous properties of sal-volatile, the efficacy of sermons, and such-like articles of faith common to feminine orthodoxy. A weakness of which she never felt more ignominiously convicted and more secretly ashamed than in the presence of Miss Valletort, that young lady having a lofty and magnificent disdain for all such follies, quite unattainable to ordinary mortals, which oppressed Lady Marabout with a humiliating sense of inferiority to her niece of eighteen summers. "So admirably educated! so admirably brought up!" she would say to herself over and over again, and if heretic suggestions that the stiffest trained flowers are not always the best, that the upright and spotless arum-lily isn't so fragrant as the careless, brilliant, tangled clematis; that rose-boughs, tossing free in sunshine and liberty, beat hollow the most carefully-pruned standard that ever won a medal at Regent's Park, with such-like allegories, arising from contemplation of her conservatory or her balcony flowers, *would* present themselves, Lady Marabout repressed them dutifully, and gratefully thought how many pounds' weight lighter became the weary burden of a chaperone's responsibilities when the onerous charge had been educated "on the best system."

"Goodwood's attentions *are* serious, Philip, say what you like," said the Countess to her son, as determinedly as a theologian states his pet points with wool in his ears, that he may not hear any Satan-inspired, rational, and mathematical disproval of them, with which you may rashly seek to soil his tympana and smash his arguments—"Goodwood's intentions *are* serious, Philip, say what you like," said her ladyship, at a morning party at Kew, eating her Neapolitan ice, complacently glancing at the "most eligible alliance of the season," who was throwing the balls at lawn-billiards, and talking between whiles to the Hon. Val with praiseworthy and promising animation.

"Serious indeed, mother, if they tend matrimony,

wards!" smiled Carruthers. "It's a very serious time indeed for unwary sparrows when they lend an ear to the call-bird, and think about hopping on to the lime-twigs. I should think it's from a sense of compunction for the net you've led us into, that you all particularise our attentions, whenever they point near St. George's, by that very suggestive little adjective 'serious!' Yes, I am half afraid poor Goodey *is* a little touched. He threw over our Derby sweepstakes up at Hornsey Wood yesterday to go and stifle himself in Willis's Rooms at your bazaar, and buy a guinea cup of Souchong from Valencia; and, considering he's one of the best shots in England, I don't think you could have a more conclusive, if you could have a more poetic, proof of devoted renunciation. *I*'d fifty times rather get a spear in my side, à la Ivanhoe, for a woman than give up a Pigeon-match, a Cup-day, or a Field-night:"

"You'll never do either!" laughed Lady Marabout, who made it one of her chief troubles that her son would not marry, chiefly, probably, because if he *had* married she would have been miserable, and thought no woman good enough for him, would have been jealous of his wife's share of his heart, and supremely wretched, I have no doubt, at his throwing himself away, as she would have thought it, had his handkerchief lighted on a Princess born, lovely as Galatea, and blessed with Venus's cestus.

"Never, *plaise à Dieu!*" responded her son, piously over his ice; "but if Goodwood's serious, what's Cardonnel? *He's* lost his head, if you like, after the Valletort beauty."

"Major Cardonnel!" said Lady Marabout, hastily. "Oh no, I don't think so. I hope not—I trust not."

"Why so? He's one of the finest fellows in the Service."

"I dare say; but you see, my dear Philip, he's not —not—desirable."

Carruthers stroked his moustaches and laughed:

"Fie, fie, mother! if all other Belgraviennes are Mammon-worshippers, I thought you kept clear of the paganism. I thought your freedom from it was the only touch by which you weren't 'purely feminine,' as the lady novelists say of their pet bits of chill propriety."

"Worship Mammon! Heaven forbid!" ejaculated Lady Marabout. "But there are duties, you see, my dear; your friend is a very delightful man, to be sure; I like him excessively, and if Valencia felt any *great* preference for him——"

"You'd feel it *your* duty to counsel her to throw him over for Goodwood?"

"I never said so, Philip," interrupted Lady Marabout, with as near an approach to asperity as she could achieve, which approach was less like vinegar than most people's best honey."

"But you implied it. What are 'duties' else, and why is poor Cardonnel 'not desirable'?"

Lady Marabout played a little tattoo with her spoon in perplexity:

"My dear Philip, you know as well as I do what I mean. One might think you were a boy of twenty to hear you!"

"My dear mother, like all disputants, when beaten in argument and driven into a corner, you resort to vituperation of your opponent!" laughed Carruthers, as he left her and lounged away to pick up the stick with which pretty Flora Elmers had just knocked the pipe out of Aunt Sally's head on to the velvet lawn of Lady George Frangipane's dower-house, leaving his mother by no means tranquillised by his suggestions.

"Dear me!" thought Lady Marabout, uneasily, as she conversed with the Dowager-Countess of Patchouli on the respective beauties of two new pelargonium seedlings, the Leucadia and the Beatrice, for which her gardener had won prizes the day before at the Regent's Park show—"dear me! why is there invariably this sort of cross-purposes in everything? It will be so grievous to lose Goodwood (and he *is* decidedly struck with her; when he bought that rosebud yesterday of her at the bazaar, and put it in the breast of his waistcoat, I heard what he said, and it was no nonsense, no mere flirting complaisance either)—it would be so grievous to lose him; and yet if Valencia really care for Cardonnel—and sometimes I almost fancy she does—I shouldn't know which way to advise. I thought it would be odd if a season could pass quietly without my having some worry of this sort! With fifty men always about Valencia, as they are, how *can* I be responsible for any mischief that may happen, though, to hear Philip talk, one would really imagine it was *my* fault that they lost their heads, as he calls it! As if a forty-horse steam-power could stop a man when he's once off down the incline into love! The more you try to pull him back the more impetus you give him to go headlong down. I wish Goodwood would propose, and we could settle the affair definitively. It is singular, but she has had no offers hardly with all her beauty. It is very singular, in *my* first season I had almost as many as I had names on my tablets at Almack's. But men don't marry now, they say. Perhaps 'tisn't to be wondered at, though I wouldn't allow it to Philip. Poor things! they lose a very great many pleasant things by it, and get nothing, I'm sure, nine times out of ten, except increased expenses and unwelcome worries. I don't think I would have married if I'd been a man, though I'd never admit it, of course, to one of them. There are plenty of women who know too much of their own sex ever to wonder that a man doesn't marry, though of course we don't say so; 'twouldn't be to our interest. Sculptors might as well preach iconoclasm, or wine-merchants teetotalism, as women misogynism, however little in our hearts we may marvel at it. Oh, my dear Lady Patchouli! you praise the Leucadia too kindly—you do indeed—but if you really think so much of it, let me send you some slips. I shall be most happy, and Fenton will be only too proud; it is his favourite seedling."

Carruthers was quite right. One fellow at least had lost his head after the beauty of the season, and he was Cardonnel, of the—Lancers, as fine a fellow, as Philip said, as any in the Queen's, but a dreadful detrimental in the eyes of all chaperones because he was but the fourth son of one of the poorest peers in the United Kingdom, a fact which gave him an ægis from all assaults matrimonial, and a freedom from all smiles and wiles, traps and gins, which Goodwood was accustomed to tell him he bitterly envied him, and on which Cardonnel had fervently congratulated himself, till he came under the fire of the Hon. Val's large luminous eyes one night, when he was levelling his glass from his stall at Lady Marabout's box, to take a look at the new belle, as advised to do by that most fastidious female critic, Vane Steinberg. Valencia Valletort's luminous eyes had gleamed that night under their lashes, and pierced through the lenses of his lorgnon. He saw her, and saw nothing but her afterwards, as men looking on the sun keep it on their retina to the damage and exclusion of all other objects.

Physical beauty, even when it is a little bit soulless, is an admirable weapon for instantaneous slaughter, and the trained and pruned standard roses show a very effective mass of bloom; though, as Lady Marabout's floral tastes and experiences told her, they don't give one the lasting pleasure that a careless bough of wild rose will do, with its untutored grace and its natural fragrance. With the standard you see we keep in the artificial air of the horticultural tent, and are never touched out of it for a second; its perfume seems akin to a bouquet, and its destiny is, we are sure, to a parterre. The wild-rose fragrance breathes of the hill-side and the woodlands, and brings back to us soft touches of memory, of youth, of a fairer life and a purer air than that in which we are living now.

The Hon. Val did *not* have as many offers as her aunt and chaperone had on the first flush of her pride in her anticipated. Young ladies, educated on the "best systems," are apt to be a trifle wearisome, and *don't*, somehow or other, take so well as the sedulous efforts of their pruners and trainers—the rarefied moral atmosphere of the conservatories, in which they are carefully screened from ordinary air, and the anxiety evinced lest the flower should ever forget itself, and sway naturally in the wind—deserve. But Cardonnel had gone mad after her, that perfect face of hers had done for him; and whatever Goodwood might be, *he* was serious—he positively haunted the young beauty like her own shadow—he was leaning on the rails every morning of his life that she took her early ride —he sent her bouquets as lavishly as if he'd been a nursery gardener. By some species of private surveillance, or lover's clairvoyance, he knew beforehand where she would go, and was at the concert, fête, morning party, bazaar, or whatever it happened to be, as surely as was Lady Marabout herself. Poor Cardonnel was serious, and fiercely fearful of his all-powerful and entirely eligible rival; though greater friends than he and Goodwood had been, before this girl's face appeared on the world of Belgravia, never lounged arm-and-arm into Pratt's, or strolled down the "sweet shady side of Pall-Mall."

Goodwood's attentions were very marked, too, even to eyes less willing to construe them so than Lady Marabout's. Goodwood himself, if chaffed on the subject, vouchsafed nothing; laughed, stroked his moustaches, or puffed his cigar, if he happened to have that blessed resource in all difficulties, and comforter under all embarrassments, between his lips at the moment; but decidedly he sought Valencia Valletort more, or, to speak more correctly, he shunned her less, than he'd ever done any other young lady, and one or two Sunday mornings—*mirabile dictu!*—he was positively seen at St. Paul's, Knightsbridge, in the seat behind Lady Marabout's sittings—a fact which, combining as it did a brace of miracles at once, of early rising and unusual piety, set every Belgravienne in that fashionable sanctuary watching over the top of her illuminated prayer-book, to the utter destruction of her hopes and interruption of her orisons.

Dowagers began to tremble behind their fans, young ladies to quake over their bouquets; the topic was eagerly discussed by every woman from Clarges-street to Lowndes-square; their Graces of Doncaster smiled well pleased on Valencia — she was unquestionable blood, and they *so* wished dear Goodwood to settle! There was whispered an awful whisper to the whole female world; whispered over matutinal chocolate, and luncheon Strasbourg pâtés, ball-supper Moëts, and demi-monde-supper Silleri, over Vane Steinberg's cigar and Eulalie Rosière's cigarette, over the *Morning Post* in the clubs, and *Le Follet* in the boudoir, that—the Pet Eligible would—marry! That the Pet Prophecy of universal smash was going to be fulfilled could hardly have occasioned greater consternation.

The soul of Lady Marabout had been disquieted ever since her son's suggestions at Lady George Frangipane's morning party, and she began to worry: for herself, for Valencia, for Goodwood, for Cardonnel, for her responsibilities in general, and for her "dearest Adeliza's" alternate opinions of her duenna qualifications in particular. Lady Marabout had an intense wish, an innocent wish enough, as innocent and very similar in its way to that of an Eton boy to make a centre at a rifle-contest, viz., to win the Marquis of Goodwood; innocent, surely, for though neither the rifle prize nor the Pet Eligible could be won without mortification unspeakable to a host of unsuccessful aspirants, if we decree that sort of thing sinful and selfish, as everything natural seems to me to get decreed now-a-days, we may as well shut up at once; if

8*

we may not try for the top of the pole, why erect poles at all, monsieur? If we must not do our best to pass our friend and brother, we must give up climbing for ever, and go on all fours placably with Don and Pontos.

Everybody has his ambition: one sighs for the Woolsack, another for the Hunt Cup; somebody longs to be First Minister, somebody else pines to be first dancer; one man plumes himself on a new fish-sauce, another on a fresh reform bill; A. thirsts to get a single brief, B. for the time when he shall be worried with no briefs at all; C. sets his hopes on being the acrobat at Cremorne, D. on being the acrobat of the Tuileries; fat bacon is Hodge the hedger's *summum bonum*, and Johannisberg *pur* is mine; Empedocles thinks notoriety everything, and Diogenes thinks quiet everything—each has his own reading of ambition, and Lady Marabout had hers; the Duchess of Doncaster thirsted for the Garter for her husband, Lady Elmers's pride was to possess the smallest terrier that ever took daisy tea and was carried in a monkey-muff, her Grace of Amandine slaved night and day to bring her party in and throw the ministry out. Lady Marabout sighed but for one thing—to win the Pet Eligible of the season, and give éclat for once to one phase of her chaperone's existence.

Things were nicely in train. Goodwood was beginning to bite at that very handsome fly the Hon. Val, and promised to be hooked and landed without much difficulty before long, and placed, hopelessly for him, triumphantly for her, in the lime-basket of matrimony. Things were beautifully in train, and Lady Marabout was for once flattering herself she should float pleasantly through an unruffled and successful season, when Carruthers poured the one drop of *amari aliquid* into her champagne-cup by his suggestion of Cardonnel's doom. And then Lady Marabout began to worry.

She who could not endure to see a fly hurt or a flower pulled needlessly, had nothing for it but to worry for Cardonnel's destiny, and puzzle over the divided duties which Carruthers had hinted to her. To reject the one man because he was not well off did seem to her conscience, uncomfortably awakened by Phil's innuendoes, something more mercenary than she quite liked to look at; yet to throw over the other, future Duke of Doncaster, the eligible, the darling, the yearned-for of all May Fair and Belgravia, seemed nothing short of madness to inculcate to Valencia; a positive treason to that poor absent, trusting, "dearest Adeliza," who, after the visions epistolarily spread out before her, would utterly refuse to be comforted if Goodwood any way failed to become her son-in-law, and, moreover, the heaviest blow to Lady Marabout herself that the merciless axe of that brutal headsman Contretemps could deal her.

"I do not know really what to do or what to advise," would Lady Marabout say to herself over and over again (so disturbed by her onerous burden of responsibilities that she would let Despréaux arrange the most outrageous coiffures, and, never noticing them, go out to dinner with emeralds on blue velvet, or something as shocking to feminine nerves in her temporary aberration), forgetting one very great point, which, remembered, would have saved her all trouble, that nobody asked her to do anything, and not a soul requested her advice. "But Goodwood is decidedly won, and Goodwood must not be lost; in our position we owe something to Society," she would invariably conclude these mental debates; which last phase, being of a vagueness and obscure application that might have matched it with any Queen's speech or electional address upon record, was a mysterious balm to Lady Marabout's soul, and spoke volumes to *her*, if a trifle hazy to you and to me.

But Lady Marabout, if she was a little bit of a sophist, had not worn her eye-glass all these years without being keen-sighted on some subjects, and, though perfectly satisfied with her niece's conduct with Goodwood, saw certain symptoms which made her tremble lest the detrimental Lancer should have won greater odds than the eligible Marquis.

"Arthur Cardonnel is excessively handsome! Such very good style! Isn't it a pity they're all so poor! His father played away everything—literally everything. The sons have no more to marry upon, any one of them, than if they were three crossing-sweepers," said her ladyship, carelessly, driving home from St. Paul's one Sunday morning.

And, watching the effect of her stray arrow, she had beheld an actual flush on the beauty's fair, impassive cheek, and had positively heard a smothered sigh from an admirably brought-up heart, no more given ordinarily to such weaknesses than the diamond-studded heart pendent from her bracelet, the belle's heart and the bracelet's heart being both formed alike, to fetch their price, and bid to do no more:—power of volition would have been as inconvenient in, and interfered as greatly with, the sale of one as of the other.

"She does like him!" sighed Lady Marabout over that Sabbath's luncheon wines. "It's always my fate—always; and Goodwood, never won before, will be thrown—actually thrown—away, as if he were the younger son of a Nobody!" which horrible waste was so terrible to her imagination that Lady Marabout could positively have shed tears at the bare prospect, and might have shed them, too, if the Hon. Val, the butler, two footmen, and a page had not inconveniently happened to be in the room at the time, so that she was driven to restrain her feelings and drink some Amontillado instead. Lady Marabout is not the first person by a good many who has had to smile over sherry with a breaking heart. Ah! lips have quivered as they laughed over Chambertin, and trembled as they touched the bowl of a champagne-glass. Wine has assisted at many a joyous festa enough, but some that has been drunk in gaiety has caught gleams, in the eyes of the drinkers, of salt water brighter than its brightest sparkles: water that no other eyes can see. Because we may drink Badminton laughingly when the gaze of Society the Non-Sympathetic is on us, do you think we must never have tasted any more bitter dregs? *Va-t'en, bécasse!* where have you lived? Nero does not always fiddle while Rome is burning from utter heartlessness, believe me, but rather—sometimes, perhaps—because his heart is aching!

"Goodwood will propose to-night, I fancy, he is so very attentive," thought Lady Marabout, sitting with her sister chaperones on the cosey causeuses of a mansion in Carlton-terrace, at one of the last balls of the departing season. "I never saw dear Valencia look better, and certainly her waltzing is——Ah! good evening Major Cardonnel! Very warm to-night, is it not? I shall be so glad when I am down again at Fernditton. Town, in the first week of July, is really not habitable."

And she furled her fan, and smiled on him with her pleasant eyes, and couldn't help wishing he hadn't been on the Marchioness Rondeletia's visiting list, he *was* such a detrimental, and he was ten times handsomer than Goodwood!

"Will Miss Valletort leave you soon?" asked Cardonnel, sitting down by her.

"*Ah! monsieur, vous êtes là!*" thought Lady Marabout, as she answered, like a guarded diplomatist as she was, that it was not at all settled at present what her niece's post-season destiny would be, whether Devon or Fernditton, or the Spas, with her mother, Lady Honiton; and then unfurled her fan again, and chatted about Baden and her own indecision as to whether she should go there this September.

"May I ask you a question, and will you pardon me for its plainness?" asked Cardonnel, when she'd exhausted Baden's desirable and non-desirable points.

Lady Marabout shuddered as she bent her head, and thought, "The creature is never going to confide in me! He will win me over if he do, he looks so like his mother! And what shall I say to Adeliza!"

"Is your niece engaged to Goodwood or not?"

If ever a little fib was tempting to any lady, from Eve downward, it was tempting to Lady Marabout now. A falsehood would settle everything, send Cardonnel off the field, and clear all possibility of losing the "best match of the season." Besides, if not engaged to Goodwood actually to-night, Val would be, if she liked, to-morrow, or the next day, or before the week was over at the furthest—would it be such a falsehood after all? She coloured, she fidgeted her fan, she longed for the little fib!—how terribly tempting it looked! But Lady Marabout is a bad hand at prevarication, and she hates a lie, and she answered bravely, with a regretful twinge, "Engaged? No; not——"

"Not yet! Thank God!"

Lady Marabout stared at him, and at the words muttered under his moustaches:

"Really, Major Cardonnel, I do not see why you——"

"Should thank Heaven for it? Yet I do—it is a reprieve. Lady Marabout, you and my mother were close friends; will you listen to me for a second, while we are not overheard? That I have loved your niece —had the madness to love her, if you will—you cannot but have seen; that she has given me some reasonable encouragement it is no coxcombry to say, though I have known from the first what a powerful rival I had against me; but that Valencia loves me and does not love him, I believe—nay, I *know*. I have said nothing decided to her; when all hangs on a single die we shrink from hazarding the throw. But I must know my fate to-night. If she come to you—as girls will, I believe, sometimes—for countenance and council, will you stand my friend?—will you, for the sake of my friendship with your son, your friendship with my mother, support my cause, and uphold what I believe Valencia's heart will say in my favour?"

Lady Marabout was silent: no Andalusian ever worried her fan more ceaselessly in coquetry than she did in perplexity. Her heart was appealed to, and when that was enlisted Lady Marabout was lost!

"But—but—my dear Major Cardonnel, you are aware——" she began and stopped. I should suppose it may be a little awkward to tell a man to his face he is "not desirable!"

"I am aware that I cannot match with Goodwood? I am; but I know, also, that Goodwood's love cannot match with mine, and that your niece's affection is not his. That he may win her I know women too well not to fear, therefore I ask *you* to be my friend. If she refuse me, will you plead for me?—if she ask for counsel, will you give such as your own heart dictates (I ask no other)—and, will you remember that on Valencia's answer will rest the fate of a man's lifetime?"

He rose and left her, but the sound of his voice rang in Lady Marabout's ears, and the tears welled into her eyes: "Dear, dear! how like he looked to his poor dear mother! But what a position to place me in! Am I *never* to have any peace?"

Not at this ball, at any rate. Of all the worried chaperones and distracted duennas who hid their anxieties under pleasant smiles or affable lethargy, none were a quarter so miserable as Helena, Lady Marabout. Her heart and her head were enlisted on opposite sides; her wishes pulled one way, her sympathies another; her sense of justice to Cardonnel urged her to one side, her sense of duty to "dearest Adeliza" urged her to the other; her pride longed for one alliance, her heart yearned for the other. Cardonnel had confided in her and appealed to her; *sequitur*, Lady Marabout's honour would not allow her to go against him: yet, it was nothing short of grossest treachery to poor Adeliza, down there in Devon, expecting every day to congratulate her daughter on a prospective duchy won, to counsel Valencia to take one of these beggared Cardonnels, and, besides—to lose all her own laurels, to lose the capture of Goodwood!

No Guelphs and Ghibelines, no Royalists and Imperialists, ever fought so hard as Lady Marabout's divided duties.

"Valencia, Major Cardonnel spoke to me to-night," began that best-hearted and most badgered of ladies, as she sat before her dressing-room fire that night, alone with her niece.

Valencia smiled slightly, and a faint idea crossed Lady Marabout's mind that Valencia's smile was hardly a pleasant one, a trifle too much like the play of moonbeams on ice.

"He spoke to me about you."

"Indeed!"

"Perhaps you can guess, my dear, what he said?"

"I am no clairvoyante, aunt;" and Miss Val yawned a little, and held out one of her long slender feet to admire it."

"Every woman, my love, becomes half a clairvoyante when she is in love," said Lady Marabout, a little bit impatiently; she hadn't been brought up on the best systems herself, and though she admired the refrigeration (on principle), it irritated her just a little now and then. "Did he—did he say anything to *you* to-night?"

"Oh yes!"

"And what did you answer him, my love?"

"What would you advise me?"

Lady Marabout sighed, coughed, played nervously with the tassels of her peignoir, crumpled Bijou's ears with a reckless disregard to that priceless pet's feelings, and wished herself at the bottom of the Serpentine. Cardonnel had trusted her, she couldn't desert *him;* poor dear Adeliza had trusted her, she couldn't betray *her;* what was right to one would be wrong to the other, and to reconcile her divided duties with a Danaid's labour. For months she had worried her life out lest her advice should be asked, and now the climax was come, and asked it was.

"What a horrible position," thought Lady Marabout.

She waited and hesitated till the pendule had ticked off sixty seconds, then she summoned her courage and spoke:

"My dear, advice in such matters is often very harmful, and always very useless; plenty of people have asked my counsel, but I never knew any of them take it unless it chanced to chime in with their fancy. A woman's best adviser is her own heart, specially on such a subject as this. But before I give my opinion, may I ask if you have accepted him?"

Lady Marabout's heart throbbed quick and fast as she put the momentous question, with an agitation for which she would have blushed before her admirably nonchalante niece; but the tug of war was coming, and if Goodwood should be lost!

"You have accepted him?" she asked again.

"No! I—refused him."

The delicate rose went out of the Hon. Val's cheeks for once, and she breathed quickly and shortly.

Goodwood was *not* lost then!

Was she sorry—was she glad? Lady Marabout hardly knew; like Wellington, she felt the next saddest thing after a defeat is a victory.

"But you love him, Valencia?" she asked, half ashamed of suggesting such a weakness, to this glorious beauty.

The Hon. Val unclasped her necklet as if it were a chain choking her, and her face grew white and set: the coldest will feel on occasion, and all have *some* tender place that can wince at the touch.

"Perhaps; but such folly is best put aside at once. Certainly I prefer him to others, but to accept him would have been madness, absurdity. I told him so!"

"You told him so! If you had the heart to do so, Valencia, he has not lost much in losing you!" burst in Lady Marabout, her indignation getting the better of her judgment, and her heart, as usual, giving the coup de grace to her reason. "I am shocked at you! Every tender-hearted woman feels regret for affection she is obliged to repulse, even when she does not return it; and you who love this man——"

"Would you have had me accept him, aunt?"

"Yes," cried Lady Marabout, firmly, forgetting every vestige of "duty," and every possibility of dear Adeliza's vengeance, "if you love him, I would, decidedly. When I married my dear Philip's father he was what Cardonnel is, a cavalry man, as far off his family title then as Cardonnel is off his now."

"The more reason I should not imitate your imprudence, my dear aunt; death might not carry off the intermediate heirs quite so courteously in this case! No, I refused Major Cardonnel, and I did rightly; I should have repented it by now had I accepted him. There is nothing more silly than to be led away by romance. You De Boncœurs *are* romantic, you know; we Valletorts are happily free from the weakness. I am very tired, aunt, so good-night."

The Hon. Val went, the waxlight she carried shedding a paler shade on her handsome face, whiter and more set than usual, but held more proudly, as if it already wore the Doncaster coronet; and Lady Marabout sighed as she rang for her maid.

"Of course she acted wisely, and I ought to be very pleased; but that poor dear fellow!—his eyes *are* so like his mother's!"

"I congratulate you, mother, on a clear field. You've sent poor Arthur off very nicely," said Carruthers, the next morning, paying his general visit in her boudoir before the day began, which is much the same time in Town as in Greenland, and commences, whatever almanacks may say, about two or half-past P.M. "Cardonnel left this morning for Heaven knows where, and is going to exchange, Shelleto tells me, into the —th, which is ordered to Bengal, so *he* won't trouble you much more. When shall I be allowed to congratulate my cousin as the future Duchess of Doncaster?"

"Pray don't tease me, Philip. I've been vexed enough about your friend. When he came to me this morning, and asked me if there was no hope, and I was obliged to tell him there was none, I felt wretched," said Lady Marabout, as nearly pettishly as she ever said anything; "but I am really not responsible, not in the least. Besides, even you must admit that Goodwood is a much more desirable alliance, and if Valencia had accepted Cardonnel, pray what would all Belgravia have said? Why, that disappointed of Goodwood, she took the other out of pure pique! We owe something to Society, Philip, and something to ourselves!"

Carruthers laughed:

"Ah, my dear mother, you women will never be worth all you ought to be till you leave off kow-towing to 'what will be said,' and learn to defy that terrible oligarchy of the Qu'en dira-t-on?"

"When will Goodwood propose?" wondered Lady Marabout, fifty times a day, and Valencia Valletort wondered too. Whitebait was being eaten, and yachts being fitted, manned, and victualled, outstanding Ascot debts were being settled, and outstanding bills were being passed hurriedly through St. Stephen's; all the clockwork of the season was being wound up for the last time previous to a long standstill, and going at a deuce of a pace, as if longing to run down, and give its million wheels and levers peace; while everybody who'd anything to settle, whether monetary or matrimonial, personal or political, was making up his mind about it and getting it off his hands, and some men were being pulled up by wide-awake Jews to see what they were "made of," while others were pulled up by adroit dowagers to know what they had "meant," before the accounts of the season were scored out and settled. "Had Goodwood proposed?" asked all Belgravia. "Why hadn't Goodwood proposed?" asked Lady Marabout and Valencia. Twenty most favourable opportunities for the performance of that ceremony had Lady Marabout made for him "accidentally on purpose," the last fortnight; each of those times she had fancied the precious fish hooked and landed, and each time she had seen him, free from the hook, floating on the surface of society.

"He *must* speak definitely to-morrow," thought Lady Marabout. But the larvæ of to-morrow burst into the butterfly of to-day, and to-day passed into the chrysalis of yesterday, and Goodwood was always very nearly caught and never *quite!*

"Come up-stairs, Philip; I want to show you a little Paul Potter I bought the other day," said Lady Marabout one morning, returning from a shopping expedition to Regent-street, meeting her son at her own door just descending from his tilbury. "Lord Goodwood calling, did you say, Soames? Oh, very well."

And Lady Marabout floated up the staircase, but signed to her footman to open the door, not of the drawing-room, but of her own boudoir.

"The Potter is in my own room, Philip; you must come in here if you wish to see it," said that adroit lady, for the benefit of Soames. But when the door was shut Lady Marabout lowered her voice confidentially: "The Potter isn't here, dear; I had it hung in the little cabinet through the drawing-rooms, but I don't wish to go up there for a few moments—you understand."

Carruthers threw himself in a chair, and laughed till the dogs Bijou, Bonbon, and Pandore all barked in a furious concert.

"I understand! So Goody's positively coming to the point up there, is he?"

"No doubt he is," said Lady Marabout, reprovingly. "Why else should he come in when I was not at home? There is nothing extraordinary in it. The only thing I have wondered at is his having delayed so long."

"If a man had to hang himself, would you wonder he put off pulling the bolt?"

"I don't see any point in your jests at all!" returned Lady Marabout. "There is nothing ridiculous in winning such a girl as Valencia."

"No; but the question here is not of winning her, but of buying her. The price is a little high—a ducal coronet and splendid settlements, a wedding-ring and bondage for life; but he will buy her, nevertheless. Cardonnel couldn't pay the first half of the price, and so he was swept out of the auction-room. You are shocked, mother? Ah, truth *is* shocking sometimes, and always *maladroit;* one oughtn't to bring it into ladies' boudoirs."

"Hold your tongue, Philip! I will not have you so satirical. Where do you take it from? Not from me, I am sure! Hark! there is Goodwood going! That is his step on the stairs, I think! Dear me, Philip, I wish you sympathised with me a little more, for I *do* feel happy, and I can't help it; dear Adeliza will be so gratified."

"My dear mother, I'll do my best to be sympathetic; I'll go and congratulate Goodwood as he gets in his cab, if you fancy I ought; but you see, if I were in Dahomey, beholding the head of my best friend coming off, I couldn't quite get up the amount of sympathy in their pleasure at the refreshing sight the Dahomites might expect from me, and so——"

But Lady Marabout missed the comparison of herself to a Dahomite, for she had opened the door and was crossing to the drawing-rooms, her eyes bright, her step elastic, her heart exultant at the triumph of her manœuvres. The Hon. Val was playing with some ferns in an étagère at the bottom of the farthest room, and responded to the kiss her aunt bestowed on her about as much as if she had been one of the statuettes on the consoles.

"Well, love, *What did he say?*" asked Lady Marabout, breathlessly, with eager delight and confident anticipation.

Like drops of ice on warm rose-leaves fell each word of the intensely chill and slightly sulky response on Lady Marabout's heart.

"He said that he goes to Cowes to-morrow for the Royal Yacht Squadron dinner, and then on in the *Anadyomene* to the Spitzbergen coast for walruses. He left a P.P.C. card for you."

"*Walruses!*" shrieked Lady Marabout.

"Walruses," responded the Hon. Val.

"And said no more than that?"

"No more than that?"

The Pet Eligible had flown off uncaught after all! Lady Marabout needed no further explanation—*tout fut dit*. They were both silent and paralysed. Do you suppose Pompey and Cornelia had much need of words when they met at Lesbos after the horrible déroute of Pharsalia?

"I'm in your mother's blackest books for ever, Phil," said Goodwood to Carruthers in the express to Southampton for the R. Y. C. Squadron Regatta of that year, "but I can't help it. It's no good to badger us into marriage; it only makes us double, and run to earth. I *was* near compromising myself with your cousin, I grant, but the thing that chilled me was, she's too *studied*. It's all got up beforehand, and goes upon clockwork, and it don't interest one accordingly; the mechanism's perfect, but we know when it will raise its hand, and move its eyes, and bow its head, and when we've looked at its beauty once we get tired of it. That's the fault in Valencia, and in scores of them, and as long as they *won't* be natural, why, they can't have much chance with us!"

Which piece of advice Carruthers, when he next saw his mother, repeated to her, for the edification of all future débutantes, adding a small sermon of his own:

"My dear mother, I ask you, is it to be expected that we can marry just to oblige women and please the newspapers? Would you have me marched off to Hanover-square because it would be a kindness to take one of Lady Elmers's marriageable daughters, or because a leading journal fills up an empty column with farcical lamentation on our dislike to the bondage? Of course you wouldn't; yet, for no better reason, you'd have chained poor Goodwood, if you could have caught him. Whether a man likes to marry or not is certainly his own private business, though just now it's made a popular public discussion. Do you wonder that we shirk the institution? If we have not fortune, marriage cramps our energies, our resources, our ambitions, loads us with petty cares, and trebles our anxieties. To one who rises with such a burden on his shoulders, how many sink down in obscurity, who, but for the leaden weight of pecuniary difficulties with which marriage has laden their feet, might have climbed the highest round in the social ladder? On the other side, if we have fortune, if we have the unhappy happiness to be eligible, is it wonderful that we are not flattered by the worship of young ladies who love us for what we shall give them, that we don't feel exactly honoured by being courted for what we are worth, and that we're not over-willing to give up our liberty to oblige those who look on us only as good speculations? What think you, eh?"

Lady Marabout looked up and shook her head mournfully:

"My dear Philip, you are right. I see it—I don't dispute it; but when a thing becomes personal, you know philosophy becomes difficult. I have such letters from poor dear Adeliza—such letters! Of course she thinks it is all my fault, and I believe she will break entirely with me. It is so very shocking. You see all Belgravia coupled their names, and the very day that he went off to Cows in that heartless, abominable manner, if an announcement of the alliance as arranged did not positively appear in the *Court Circular!* It did indeed! I am sure Anne Hautton was at the bottom of it; it would be just like her. Perhaps poor Valencia cannot be pitied after her treatment of Cardonnel, but it is very had on *me*."

Lady Marabout is right: when a thing becomes personal, philosophy becomes difficult. When your gun misses fire, and a fine cock bird whirrs up from the covert and takes wing unharmed, never to swell the number of your triumph and the size of your game-bag, could you by any chance find it in your soul to sympathise with the bird's gratification at your mortification and its own good luck? I fancy not.

LADY MARABOUT'S TROUBLES;

OR,

THE WORRIES OF A CHAPERONE.

IN THREE SEASONS.

SEASON THE SECOND.—THE OGRE.

"IF there be one class I dislike more than another, it is that class; and if there be one person in town I utterly detest, it is that man!" said our friend Lady Marabout, with much unction, one morning, to an audience consisting of Bijou, Bonbon, and Pandore, a cockatoo, an Angora cat, and a young lady sitting in a rocking-chair, reading the magazines of the month. The dogs barked, the cockatoo screamed, the cat purred, a vehement affirmative, the human auditor looked up, and laughed:

"What is the class, Lady Marabout, may I ask?"

"Those clever, detestable, idle, good-for-nothing, fashionable, worthless men about town, who have not a penny to their fortune, and spend a thousand a year on gloves and scented tobacco — who are seen at everybody's house, and never at their own—who drive horses fit for a Duke's stud, and haven't money enough to keep a donkey on thistles—who have handsome faces and brazen consciences — who are positively leaders of ton, and yet are glad to write feuilletons before the world is up to pay their stall at the Opera—who give a guinea for a bouquet, and can't pay a shilling of their just debts—I detest the class, my dear!"

"So it seems, Lady Marabout. I never heard you so vehement. And who is the particular scapegoat of this type of sinners?"

"Chandos Cheveley."

"Chandos Cheveley? Isn't he that magnificent man Sir Philip introduced to me at the Amandines' breakfast yesterday? Why, Lady Marabout, his figure alone might outbalance a multitude of sins!"

"He is handsome enough. *Did* Philip introduce him to you, my dear? I wonder! It was very careless of him. But men *are* so thoughtless; they will know anybody themselves, and they think we may do the same. The man called here while we were driving this morning. I am glad we were out: he very seldom comes to *my* house."

"But why is he so dreadful? The Amandines are tremendously exclusive, I thought."

"Oh, he goes everywhere! No party is complete without Chandos Cheveley, and I have heard that at September or Christmas he has more invitations than he could possibly accept; but he is a most objectionable man, all the same—a man every one dreads to see come near her daughters. He has extreme fascination of manner, but he has not a farthing! How he lives, dresses, drives the horses he does, is one of those miracles of London men's lives which *we* can never hope to puzzle out. Philip says he likes him, but Philip never speaks ill of anybody, except a woman now and then, who teases him; but the man is my detestation—has been for years. I was annoyed to see his card: it is the first time he has called this season. He knows I can't endure his class or him."

With which Lady Marabout wound up a very unusually lengthy and uncharitable disquisition, length and uncharitableness being both out of her line; and Lady Cecil Ormsby rolled her handkerchief into a ball, threw it across the room for Bonbon, the spaniel puppy, and laughed till the cockatoo screamed with delight:

"Dear Lady Marabout, do forgive me, but it is such fun to hear you positively, for once, malicious! Who is your Orgre, genealogically speaking? this terrible—what's his name?—Chandos Cheveley?"

"The younger son of a younger son of one of the Marquises of Danvers, I believe, my dear; an idle man about town, you know, with not a sou to be idle upon, who sets the fashion, but never pays his tailor. I am never malicious, I hope, but I do consider men of that stamp very objectionable."

"But what is Sir Philip but a man about town?"

"My son! Of course he is a man about town. My dear, what else should he be? But if Philip likes to lounge all his days away in a club window, he has a perfect right; he has fortune. Chandos Cheveley is not worth a farthing, and yet yawns away his day in White's as if he were a millionnaire; the one can support his *far niente*, the other cannot. There are gradations in everything, my love, but in nothing more than among the men, of the same set and the same style, whom one sees in Pall-Mall."

"There are chesnut horses and horse-chesnuts,

chevaliers and chevaliers d'industrie, rois and rois d'Yvetot, Carrutherses and Chandos Cheveleys!" laughed Lady Cecil. "I understand, Lady Marabout. Il y a femmes et femmes—men about town and men about town. I shall learn all the classes and distinctions soon. But how is one to know the sheep that may be let into the fold from the wolves in sheep's clothing, that must be kept out of it? Your Ogre is really very distinguished-looking."

"Distinguished? Oh yes, my love; but the most distinguished men are the most objectionable sometimes. I assure you, my dear Cecil, I have seen an elder son whom sometimes I could hardly have told from his own valet, and a younger of the same family with the style of a D'Orsay. Why, did I not this very winter, when I went to stay at Rochdale, take Fitzbreguet himself, whom I had not chanced to see since he was a child, for one of the men out of livery, and bid him bring Bijou's basket out of the carriage. I did indeed—*I*, who hate such mistakes more than any one! And Lionel, his second brother, has the beauty of an Apollo and the *air noble* to perfection. One often sees it; it's through the doctrine of compensation, I suppose, but it's very perplexing, and causes endless *embrouillements*."

"When the mammas fall in love with Lord Fitz's coronet, and the daughters with Lord Lionel's face, I suppose?" interpolated Lady Cecil.

"Exactly so, dear. As for knowing the sheep from the wolves, as you call them," went on Lady Marabout, sorting her embroidery silks, "you may very soon know more of Chandos Cheveley's class—(this Magenta braid is good for nothing; it's a beautiful colour, but it fades immediately)—you meet them in the country at all fast houses, as they call them now-a-days, like the Amandines'; they are constantly invited, because they are so amusing, or so dead a shot, or so good a whip, and live on their invitations, because they have no *locale* of their own. You see, all the women worth nothing admire, and all the women worth anything shun, them. They have a dozen accomplishments, and not a single reliable quality; a hundred houses open to them, and not a shooting-box of their own property or rental. You will meet this Chandos Cheveley everywhere, for instance, as though he were somebody desirable. You will see him in his club window, as though he were born only to read the papers; in the Ride, mounted on a much better animal than Fitzbreguet, though the one pays treble the price he ought, and the other, I dare say, no price at all; at Ascot, on Amandine's or Goodwood's drag, made as much of among them all as if he were an heir-apparent to the throne; and yet, my love, that man hasn't a penny, lives Heaven knows where, and how he gets money to keep his cab and buy his gloves is, as I say, one of those mysteries of settling days, whist-tables, periodical writing, Baden *coups de bonheur*, and such-like fountains of such men's fortunes which *we* can never hope to penetrate—and very little we should benefit if we could! My dearest Cecil! if it is not ten minutes to five! We must go and drive at once."

Lady Ormsby was a great pet of Lady Marabout's; she had been so from a child; so much so, that when, the year after Valencia Valletort's discomfiture (a discomfiture so heavy and so public, that that young beauty was seized with a fit of filial devotion, attended her mamma to Nice, and figured not in Belgravia the ensuing season, and even Lady Marabout's temper had been slightly soured by it, as you perceive), another terrible charge was shifted on her shoulders by an appeal from the guardians of the late Earl of Rosediamond's daughter for her to be brought out under the Marabout wing, she had consented, and surrendered herself to be again a martyr to responsibility for the sake of Cecil and Cecil's lost mother. The young lady was a beauty; she was worse, she was an heiress; she was worse still, she was saucy, wayward, and notable for a strong will of her own—a more dangerous young thorough-bred was never brought to a gentler Rarey; and yet she was the first charge of this nature that Lady Marabout had ever accepted in the whole course of her life with no misgivings and with absolute pleasure. First, she was very fond of Cecil Ormsby; secondly, she longed to efface her miserable failure with Valencia by a brilliant success, which should light up all the gloom of her past of chaperonage; thirdly, she had a sweet and long-cherished diplomacy nestling in her heart to throw her son and Lord Rosediamond's daughter together, for the eventual ensnaring and fettering of Carruthers, which policy nothing could favour so well as having the weapon for that deadly purpose in her own house through April, May, and June.

Cecil Ormsby was a beauty and an heiress—spirited, sarcastic, brilliant, wilful, very proud; altogether, a more spirited young filly never needed a tight hand on the ribbons, a light but a firm seat, and a temperate though judicious use of the curb to make her endure being ridden at all, even over the most level grass countries of life. And yet, for the reasons just mentioned, Lady Marabout, who never had a tight hand upon anything, who is to be thrown in a moment by any wilful kick or determined plunge, who is utterly at the mercy of any filly that chooses to take the bit between her own teeth and bolt off, and is entirely incapable of using the curb, even to the most ill-natured and ill-trained Shetland that ever deserved to have its mouth sawed—Lady Marabout undertook the jockeyship without fear.

"I dare say you wonder, after my grief with Valencia, that I have consented to bring another girl out, but when I heard it was poor Rosediamond's wish— his dying wish, one may almost say—that Cecil should make her début with me, what *was* I to do, my dear?" she explained, half apologetically, to Carruthers, when the question was first agitated. Perhaps, too, Lady Marabout had in her heart been slightly sickened of perfectly trained young ladies brought up on the best systems, and admitted to herself that the pets of the foreign houses may *not* be the most attractive flowers after all.

So Lady Cecil Ormsby was installed in Lowndes-square, and though she was the inheritor of her mother's wealth, which was considerable, and possessor of her own wit and beauty, which were not inconsiderable either, and therefore a prize to fortune-hunters and a lure to misogamists, as Lady Marabout knew very well how to keep the first off, and had her pet project of numbering her refractory son among the converted second, she rather congratulated herself than otherwise in having the pleasure and éclat of introducing her; and men voted the Marabout Yearlings Sale of that season, since it comprised Rosediamond's handsome daughter, as dangerous as a horse-dealer's auction to a young greenhorn, as a draper's "sale without reserve, at enormous sacrifice," to a lady with a soul on bargains bent.

"How very odd! Just as we have been talking of him, there is that man again! I must bow to him, I suppose; though if there *be* a person I dislike——" said Lady Marabout, giving a frigid little bend of her head as her barouche, with its dashing roans, rolled from her door, and a tilbury passed them, driving slowly through the square.

Cecil Ormsby bowed to its occupant with less severity, and laughed under the sheltering shadow of her white parasol fringe.

"The Ogre has a very pretty trap, though, Lady Marabout, and the most delicious grey horse in it! Such good action!"

"If its action is good, my love, I dare say it is more than could be said of its master's actions. He is going to call on that Mrs. Maréchale, very probably; he was always there last season."

And Lady Marabout shook her head and looked grave, which, combined with the ever-damnatory demonstrative conjunction, blackened Mrs. Maréchale's moral character as much as Lady Marabout could blacken any one's, she loving as little to soil her own fingers and her neighbours' reputations with the indelible Italian chalk of scandal as any lady I know; being given, on the contrary, when compelled to draw any little social croquis of a backbiting nature, to sketch them in as lightly as she could, take out as many lights as possible, and rub in the shadows with a very chary and pitying hand, except, indeed, when she took the portrait of such an Ogre as Chandos Cheveley, when I can't say she was quite so merciful, specially when policy and prejudice combined to suggest that it would be best (and not unjust) to use the blackest Conté crayons obtainable.

The subject of it would not have denied the correctness of the silhouette Lady Marabout had snipped out for the edification of Lady Cecil, had he caught a glimpse of it: he had no habitation, nor was ever likely to have any, save a bachelor's suite in a back street; he had been an idle man for the last twenty years, with not a sou to be idle upon; the springs of his very precarious fortunes, his pursuits, habits, reputation, ways and means, were all much what she had described them; yet he set the fashion much oftener than Goodwood, and Dukes and millionnaires would follow the style of his tie, or the shape of his hat; he moved in the most brilliant circles as Court Circulars have it, and all the best houses were open to him. At his Grace of Amandine's, staying there for the shooting, he would alter the stud, find fault with the claret, arrange a Drive for deer in the forest, and flirt with her Grace herself, as though, as Lady Marabout averred, he had been Heir-Apparent or Prince Regent, who honoured the Castle by his mere presence, Amandine all the while swearing by every word he spoke, thinking nothing well done without Cheveley, and submitting to be set aside in his own Castle, with the greatest gratification at the extinction.

But that Chandos Cheveley was not worth a farthing, that he was but a Bohemian on a brilliant scale, that any day he might disappear from that society where he now glittered, never to reappear, everybody knew; how he floated there as he did, kept his cab and his man, paid for his stall at the Opera, his club fees, and all the other trifles that won't wait, was an eternal puzzle to every one ignorant of how expensively one may live upon nothing if one just gets the knack, and of how far a fashionable reputation, like a cake of chocolate, will go to support life when nothing more substantial is obtainable. Lady Marabout had sketched him correctly enough, allowing for a little politic bitterness thrown in to counteract Carruthers's thoughtlessness in having introduced him to Rosediamond's daughter (that priceless treasure for whom Lady Marabout would fain have had a guard of Janissaries, if they would not have been likely to look singular and come expensive); and ladies of the Marabout class did look upon him as an Ogre, guarded their daughters from his approach at a ball as carefully, if not as demonstratively, as any duck its ducklings from the approach of a water-rat, did not ask him to their dinners, and bowed to him chillily in the Ring. Others regarded him as harmless, from his perfect pennilessness; what danger was there in the fascinations of a man whom all Belgravia knew hadn't money enough to buy dog-skin gloves, though he always wore the best Paris lavender kid? While others, the pretty married women chiefly, from her Grace of Amandine downwards to Mrs. Maréchale, of Lowndes-square, flirted with him fearfully, and considered Chandos Cheveley what nobody ever succeeded in disproving him, the most agreeable man on town, with the finest figure, the best style, and the most perfect bow, to be seen in the Park any day between March and July.

But then, as Lady Marabout remarked on a subsequent occasion, a figure, a style, and a bow are admirable and enviable things, but they're not among the cardinal virtues, and don't do to live upon; and though they're very good buoys to float one on the smooth sparkling sea of society, if there come a storm one may go down, despite them, and become helpless prey to the sharks waiting below.

"Philip certainly admires her very much; he said the other day there was something in her, and that means a great deal from him," thought Lady Marabout, complacently, as she and Cecil Ormsby were wending their way through some crowded rooms. "Of course I shall not influence Cecil towards him; it would not be honourable to do so, since she might look for a higher title than my son's; still, if it should so fall out, nothing would give me greater pleasure, and really nothing would seem more natural with a little judicious manage——"

"May I have the honour of this valse with you?" was spoken in, though not to, Lady Marabout's ear. It was a soft, a rich, a melodious voice enough, and yet Lady Marabout would rather have heard the hiss of a Cobra Capella, for the footmen *might* have caught the serpent and carried it off from Cecil Ormsby's vicinity, and she couldn't very well tell them to rid the reception-chambers of Chandos Cheveley.

Lady Marabout vainly tried to catch Cecil's eye, and warn her of the propriety of an utter and entire repudiation of the valse in question, if there were no "engaged" producible to softly chill the hopes and repulse the advances of the aspirant; but Lady Cecil's soul was obstinately bent saltatory-wards; her chaperone's ocular telegram was lost upon her, and only caught by the last person who should have seen it, who read the message off the wires to his own amusement, but naturally was not magnanimous enough to pass it on.

"I ought to have warned her never to dance with that detestable man. If I could but have caught her eye even now!" thought Lady Marabout, restlessly. The capella *would* have been much the more endurable of the two; the serpent couldn't have passed its arm round Rosediamond's priceless daughter and whirled her down the ball-room to the music of Coote and Timney's band, as Chandos Cheveley was now doing.

"Why did *you* not ask her for that waltz, Philip?" cried the good lady, almost petulantly.

Carruthers opened his eyes wide.

"My dear mother, you know I never dance! I come to balls to oblige my hostesses and look at the women, but not to carry a seven-stone weight of tulle illusion and white satin, going at express pace, with the thermometer at 80 deg., and a dense crowd jostling one at every turn in the circle. *Bien obligé!* that's not my idea of pleasure; if it were the Pyrrhic dance, now, or the Tarantella, or the Bolero, under a Castilian chestnut-tree——"

"Hold your tongue! You might have danced for once, just to have kept her from Chandos Cheveley."

"From the best waltzer in London? Not so selfish. Ask Amandine's wife if women don't like to dance with that fellow!"

"I should be very sorry to mention his name to her, or any of her set," responded Lady Marabout, getting upon certain virtuous stilts of her own, which she was given to mount on rare occasions and at distant intervals, always finding them very uncomfortable and unsuitable elevations, and being as glad to cast them off as a traveller to kick off the *échasses* he has had to strap on over the sandy plains of the Landes.

"What could possess you to introduce him to Cecil, Philip? It was careless, silly, unlike you; you know how I dislike men of his—his—objectionable stamp," sighed Lady Marabout, the white and gold namesakes in her coiffure softly trembling a gentle sigh in the perfumy zephyr raised by the rotatory whirl of the waltzers, among whom she watched with a horrible fascination, as one watches a tiger being pugged out of its lair, or a deserter being led out to be shot, Chandos Cheveley waltzing Rosediamond's priceless daughter down the ball-room.

"He is so dreadfully handsome! I wonder why it is that men and women, who have no fortune but their faces, will be so dangerously, so obstinately, so provokingly attractive as one sees them so often!" thought Lady Marabout, determining to beat an immediate retreat from the present salons, since they were infested by the presence of her Ogre, to Lady Hautton's house in Wilton-crescent.

Lady Hautton headed charitable bazaars, belonged to the Cummingite nebulæ, visited Homes and Hospitals (floating to the bedside of luckless feminine patients to read out divers edifying passages, whose effect must have been somewhat neutralised to the hearers, one would imagine, by the envy-inspiring rustle of her silks, the flash of her rings, and the chimes of her bracelets, chains, and châtelaine), looked on the "Amandine set" as lost souls, and hence "did not know" Chandos

Cheveley—a fact which, though the Marabout and Hautton antagonism was patent to all Belgravia, served to endear her all at once to her foe; Lady Marabout, like a good many other people, being content to sink personal resentment, and make a truce with the infidels for the sake of enjoying a mutual antipathy—that closest of all links of union!

Lady Marabout and Lady Hautton were foes, but they were dear Helena and dear Anne, all the same; dined at each other's tables, and smiled in each other's faces. They might be private foes, but they were public friends; and Lady Marabout beat a discreet retreat to the Hautton's salons—"so many engagements" is so useful a plea!—and from the Hautton she passed on to a ball at the Duke of Doncaster's; and, as at both, if Lady Cecil Ormsby did not move "a goddess from above," she moved a brilliant, sparkling, nonchalante, dangerous beauty, with some of her sex's faults, all her sex's witcheries, and more than her sex's mischief, holding her own royally, saucily, and proudly, and Chandos Cheveley was encountered no more, but happily detained as a petit souper in a certain Section of the French Embassy. Lady Marabout drove homewards, in the grey of the morning, relieved, complacent, and gratified, dozing deliciously, till she was woke up with a start:

"Lady Marabout, what a splendid waltzer your Ogre, Chandos Cheveley, is!"

Lady Marabout opened her eyes with a jerk that set her feathers trembling, her diamonds scintillating, and her bracelets ringing an astonished little carillon.

"My love, how you frightened me!"

Cecil Ormsby laughed—a gay, joyous laugh, innocent of having disturbed a doze, a lapse into human weakness of which her chaperone never permitted herself to plead guilty.

"Frightened you, did I? Why your *bête noire* is as terrible to you as Cœur de Lion to the Saracen children, or Black Douglas to the Lowland! And, really I can't see anything terrible in him; he is excessively brilliant and agreeable, has something worth hearing to say to you, and his waltzing is——!"

Lady Cecil Ormsby had not a word in her repertory —though it was an enthusiastic and comprehensive one, and embraced five languages—sufficiently commendatory to finish her sentence.

"I dare say, dear! I never denied, or heard denied, his having every accomplishment under the sun. The only pity is, he has nothing more substantial!" returned Lady Marabout, a little bit tartly for *her* lips, only used to the softest (and most genuine) milk of roses.

Lord Rosediamond's daughter laughed a little mournfully, and played with her fan.

"Poor man! Brilliant and beggared, fashionable and friendless, courted and cashiered—a sad destiny! Do you know, Lady Marabout, I have half a mind to champion your Ogre!"

"My love, don't talk nonsense!" said Lady Marabout, hastily; at which Lady Cecil only laughed still more softly and gaily again, and sprang down as the carriage stopped in Lowndes-square.

"Rosediamond's daughter's deucedly handsome, eh, Cheveley? I saw you waltzing with her last night," said Goodwood at Lord's the next morning, watching a match between the Household Cavalry and the Zingari Eleven.

"Yes, she is the best thing we have seen for some time," said Cheveley, glancing round to see if the Marabout liveries were on the ground.

"Don't let the Amandine or little Maréchale hear you say so, or you'll have a deuce of a row," laughed Goodwood. "She's worth a good deal, too; she's all her mother's property, and that's something, I know. The deaths in her family have kept her back two years or more, but now she *is* out, I dare say Lady Tattersall will put her up high in the market."

"No doubt. Why don't *you* make the investment—she's much more attractive than that Valletort ice statue who hooked you so nearly last year? Fortescue's out! Well done, little Jimmy! Ah! there's the Marabout carriage. I am as unwelcome to that good lady, I know, as if I were Quasimodo or Quilp, and as much to be shunned, in her estimation, as Vidocq, armed to the teeth; nevertheless, I shall go and talk to them, if only in revenge for the telegraphic warning of 'dangerous' she shot at Lady Cecil last night when I asked her to waltz. Goodwood, don't you envy me my happy immunity from traps matrimonial?"

"There is that man again—how provoking! I wish we had not come to see Philip's return match. He is positively coming up to talk to us," thought Lady Marabout, restlessly, as her Ogre lifted his hat to her. In vain did she do her best to look severe, to look frigid, to chill him with a withering "good morning" (a little word, capable, if you notice, of expressing every gradation in feeling, from the nadir of delighted intimacy to the zero of rebuking frigidity); her coldest ice was as warm as a pine-apple ice that has been melting all day under a refreshment tent at a horticultural fête! Her *rôle* was *not* chilliness, and never could be; she would have beamed benign on a headsman who had led her out to instant decapitation, and been no more able to help it than a peach to help its bloom, or a claret its bouquet. She did her utmost to freeze Chandos Cheveley, but either she failed signally, or he, being blessed with the brazen conscience she had attributed to him, was steeled to all the tacit repulses of her looks, for he leaned against the barouche door, let her freeze him away as she might, and chatted to Cecil Ormsby, "positively," Lady Marabout remarked to that safest confidante, herself, "positively as if the man had been welcome at my house for the last ten years! If Cecil *would* but second me, he couldn't do it; but she *will* smile and talk with him just as though he were Goodwood or Fitzbreguet! It is very disagreeable to be forced against one's will like this into countenancing such a very objectionable person; and yet what *can* one do?"

Which query she could by no means satisfactorily answer herself, being a regular female Nerva for clemency, utterly incapable of the severity with which that stern Cataline, Lady Hautton, would have signed the unwelcome intruder out of the way in a brace of seconds. And under Nerva's gentle rule, though Nerva was longing with all her heart to have the courage to call the lictors, and say, "Away with him!" Cheveley leaned against the door of the carriage unmolested, though decidedly undesired by one of its occupants, talked to by Lady Cecil, possibly because she found him as agreeable as her Grace of Amandine and Lillia

Maréchale had done before her, possibly only from that rule of contrariety which is such a pet motor-power with her sex; and Lady Marabout reclined among her cushions, tucked up in her tiger-skin in precisely that state of mind in which Fuseli said to his wife, "Swear, my dear, you don't know how much good it will do you," dreading in herself the possible advent of the Hautton carriage, for that ancient enemy and rigid pietist, of whose keen tongue and eminent virtue she always stood secretly in awe, to see this worthless and utterly objectionable member of that fast, grace-less, and "very incorrect" Amandine set, absolutely *en sentinelle* at the door of her barouche!

Does your best friend *ever* come when you want him most? Doesn't your worst foe *always* come when you want him least? Of course, at that juncture, the Hautton carriage came on the ground (Hautton was one of the Zingari Club, and maternal interest brought her foe to Lord's as it had brought herself), and the Hautton eye-glass, significantly and surprisedly raised, said as distinctly to Lady Marabout, as though elfishly endowed with vocal powers, "You allow *that* man acquaintance with Rosediamond's daughter!" Lady Marabout was stung to the soul by the deserved rebuke, but she didn't know how on earth to get rid of the sinner! There he leaned, calmly, nonchalantly, deter-minedly, as if he were absolutely welcome; and Lady Cecil talked on to him as if he were absolutely wel-come too.

Lady Marabout felt branded in the eyes of all Belgravia to have Chandos Cheveley at her carriage door, the most objectionable man of all his most ob-jectionable class.

"It is very strange!" she thought. "I have seen that man about town the last five-and-twenty years—ever since he was a mere boy, taken up and petted by Adeline Patchouli for some piece of witty Brummelian impudence he said to her on his first introduction—and he has never sought my acquaintance before, but always seemed to be quite aware of my dislike to him and all his set. It is very grievous he should have chosen the very season I have poor dear Rosediamond's daughter with me; but it is always my fate—if a thing *can* happen to annoy me it always will!"

With which Lady Marabout, getting fairly distracted under the iron hand of adverse fate, and the ruthless surveillance of the Hautton glass, invented an impromptu necessity for immediate shopping at Lewis and Allonby's, and drove off the ground at the sole moment of interest the match possessed for her—viz. when Carruthers was rattling down Hautton's stumps, and getting innings innumerable for the Household.

"Mais ce n'est que le premier pas qui coûte;" the old proverb's so true we wear it threadbare with repeating it! Lady Marabout might as well have stayed on Lord's ground, and not lacerated her feelings by leaving at the very hour of the Household Cavalry's triumphs, for any good that she did thereby. The Hautton eye-glass had lighted on Chandos Cheveley, and Chandos Cheveley's eye-glass on Rosediamond's daughter;—and Cecil Ormsby arched her eyebrows, and gave her parasol a little impatient shake as they quitted Lord's.

"Lady Marabout, I never could have believed you ill natured; you interrupted my ball last night, and my conversation this morning! I shall scold you if you ever do so again. And now tell me (as curiosity is a weakness incidental to all women, no woman ought to refuse to relieve it in another) why *are* you so prejudiced against that very handsome, and very amusing person?"

"Prejudiced, my dear child! I am not in the least prejudiced," returned Lady Marabout. (Nobody ever admitted to a prejudice that *I* ever heard. It's a plant that grows in all gardens, and is sedulously matted up, watered, and strengthened; but invariably disavowed by its sturdiest cultivators.) "As for Chandos Cheveley, I merely mentioned to you what all town knows about him; and the dislike I have to his class is one of principle, not of prejudice."

Lady Cecil made a *moue mutine:*

"Oh, Lady Marabout! if you go to 'principle,' *tout est perdu!* 'Principle' has been made to bear the onus of every private pique since the world began, and has had to answer for more cruelties and injustice than any word in the language. The Romans flung the Christians to the lions 'on principle,' and the Europeans slew the Mahomedans 'on principle,' and 'principle' lighted the autos-da-fé, and signed to the tormentor to give a turn more to the rack! Please don't appeal to anything so severe and hypocritical. Come, what are the Ogre's sins?"

Lady Marabout laughed, despite the subject.

"Do you think I am a compiler of such catalogues, my love? Pray do not let us talk any more about Chandos Cheveley, he is very little worth it; all I say to you is, be as cool to him as you can, without rudeness, of course. I am never at home when he calls, and were I you I would be always engaged when he asks you to waltz; his acquaintance can in no way benefit you."

Lady Cecil gave a little haughty toss of her head, and lay back in the barouche.

"*I* will judge of that! I am not made for fetters of any kind, you know, and I like to choose my own acquaintance as well as to choose my own dresses. I cannot obey you either this evening, for he asked me to put him on my tablets for the first waltz at Lord Anisette's ball, and I consented. I had no 'engaged' ready, unless I had had a falsehood ready too, and *you* wouldn't counsel that, Lady Marabout, I am very sure?"

With that straightforward and perplexing question Cecil Ormsby successfully silenced her chaperone, by planting her in that disagreeable position known as between the horns of a dilemma; and Lady Marabout, shrinking alike from the responsibility of counselling a "necessary equivocation," as society politely terms its indispensable lies, and the responsibility of allowing Cecil acquaintance with the "very worst" of the Amandine set, sighed, wondered, envyingly how Anne Hautton would act in her place, and almost began to wish somebody else had had the onerous stewardship of that brilliant and priceless jewel, Rosediamond's daughter, now that the jewel threatened to be possessed with a will of its own:—the greatest possible flaw in a gem of pure water, which they only want to scintillate brilliantly among the bijouterie of society, and let itself be placed passively in the setting most suitable for it, that can be conceived in the eyes of lady lapidaries entrusted with its sale.

"It is very odd," thought Lady Marabout; "she

seems to have taken a much greater fancy to that odious man than to Philip, or Goodwood, or Fitz, or any one of the men who admire her so much. I suppose I always *am* to be worried in this sort of way! However, there can be no real danger; Chandos Cheveley is the merest butterfly flirt, and with all his faults none ever accused him of fortune-hunting. Still, they say he is wonderfully fascinating, and certainly he has the most beautiful voice I ever heard; and if Cecil should ever like him at all I could never forgive myself, and what *should* I say to General Ormsby?"

The General, Cecil's uncle and guardian, is one of the best-humoured, best-tempered, and most *laissez-faire* men in the Service, but was, for all that, a perpetual dead weight on Lady Marabout's mind just then, for was not he the person to whom, at the end of the season, she would have to render up account of the successes and the shortcomings of her chaperone's career?

"Do you think of proposing Chandos Cheveley as a suitable alliance for Cecil Ormsby, my dear Helena?" asked Lady Hautton, with that smile which was felt to be considerably worse than strychnine by her foes and victims, at a house in Grosvenor-place, that night.

"God forbid!" prayed Lady Marabout, mentally, as she joined in the Hautton laugh, and shivered under the stab of the Hautton sneer, which was an excessively sharp one, Lady Hautton being one of a rather numerous class of eminent Christians, so panoplied in the armour of righteousness that they can tread, without feeling it, on the tender feet of others.

The evening was spoiled to Lady Marabout; she felt morally and guiltily responsible for an unpardonable indiscretion:—with that man waltzing with Cecil Ormsby, her "graceful, graceless, gracious Grace" of Amandine visibly irritated with jealousy at the sight, and Anne Hautton whispering behind her fan with acidulated significance. Lady Marabout had never been more miserable in her life! She heard on all sides admiration of Rosediamond's daughter; she was gratified by seeing Goodwood, Fitzbreguet, Fulke Nugent, every eligible man in the room, suing for a place on her tablets; she had the delight of beholding Carruthers positively join the negligent beauty's train; and yet the night was a night of purgatory to Lady Marabout, for Chandos Cheveley had his first waltz, and several after it, and the Amandine set were there to gossip, and the Hautton clique to be shocked, at it.

"Soames, tell Mason, when Mr. Chandos Cheveley calls, I am not at home," said Lady Marabout, at breakfast.

"Yes, my lady," said Soames, who treasured up the order, and told it to Mr. Chandos Cheveley's man at the first opportunity, though, greatly to his honour, we must admit, he did *not* imitate the mild formula of fib, and tell his mistress her claret was not corked when it was so incontestably.

Cecil Ormsby lifted her head and looked across the table at her hostess, and the steady gaze of those violet eyes, which were Rosediamond's daughter's best weapons of war, so discomposed Lady Marabout, that she forgot herself sufficiently to proffer Bijou a piece of bread, an unparalleled insult, which that canine Sybarite did not forgive all day long.

"Not at home, sir," said Mason, as duly directed,

when Cheveley's cab pulled up, a week or two after the general order, at the door.

Cheveley smiled to himself as his grey had her head turned, and the wheel grated off the trottoir, while he lifted his hat to Cecil Ormsby, just visible between the amber curtains and above the balcony flowers of one of the windows of the drawing-room—quite visible enough for her return smile and bow to be seen in the street by Cheveley, in the room by Lady Marabout.

"Some of Lady Tattersall's generalship!" he thought, as the grey trotted out of the square. "Well! I have no business there. Cecil Ormsby is not her Grace of Amandine, nor little Maréchale, and the good lady is quite right to brand me 'dangerous' to her charge, and pronounce me 'inadmissible' to her footmen. I've very little title to resent her verdict."

"My dearest Cecil, whatever possessed you to bow to that man!" cried Lady Marabout, in direst distress.

"Is it not customary to bow to one's acquaintances—I thought it was?" asked Lady Cecil, with demure mischief.

"But, my dear, from a window!—and when Mason is saying we are not at home!"

"That isn't *Mason's* fib, or *Mason's* fault, Lady Marabout!" suggested Cecil, with wicked emphasis.

"There is no falsehood or fault at all anywhere—everybody knows well enough what 'not at home' means," returned Lady Marabout, almost pettishly.

"Oh yes," laughed the young lady, saucily. "It means 'I am at home and sitting in my drawing-room, but I shall not rise to receive you, because you are not worth the trouble.' It's a polite cut direct, and a honeyed rudeness—a bitter almond wrapped up in a sugar dragée, like a good many other bonbons handed about in society."

"My dear Cecil, you have some very strange ideas; you will get called satirical if you don't take care," said Lady Marabout, nervously.

Cecil Ormsby's tone worried her, and made her feel something as she felt when she had a restive, half-broken pair of horses in her carriage, for the direction of whose next plunge or next kick nobody could answer.

"And if I be—what then?"

"My dear child, you could not anyhow get a more disadvantageous reputation! It may amuse gentlemen, though it frightens half of *them;* but it offends all women irremediably. You see, there are so few whom it doesn't hit somewhere," returned Lady Marabout, quite innocent of the neat satire of her own last sentence.

Cecil Ormsby laughed, and threw herself down by her chaperone's side:

"Never mind: I can bear their enmity; it is a greater compliment than their liking. The women whom women love are always quiet, colourless, inoffensive—foils. Lady Marabout, tell me, why did you give that general order to Mason?"

"I have told you before, my dear. Because I have no wish to know Mr. Chandos Cheveley," returned Lady Marabout, as stiffly as she could say anything. "It is, as I said, not from prejudice, but from prin——"

"Lady Marabout, if you use that word again I will

drive to Uncle Ormsby's rooms in the Albany and stay with him for the season; I will, positively! I am sure all the gentlemen there will be delighted to have my society! Pray, what *are* your Ogre's crimes? Did you ever hear anything dishonourable, mean, ungenerous, attributed to him? Did you ever hear he broke his word, or failed to act like a gentleman, or was a defaulter at any settling day?"

Lady Marabout required some explanation of what a defaulter at a settling day might be, and, on receiving it, was compelled to confess that she never *had* heard anything of that kind imputed to Chandos Cheveley:

"Of course I have not, my dear. The man is a gentleman, everybody knows, however idle and improvident a one. If he could be accused of anything of that kind, he would not belong to such clubs, and associate with such men as he does. Besides, Philip would not know him; certainly would not think well of him, which I confess he does. But that is not at all the question."

"*Ne vous en déplaise*, I think it very much and very entirely the question," returned Lady Cecil, with a toss of her haughty little head. "If you can bring nothing in evidence against a man, it is not right to send him to the galleys and mark him 'Forçat.'"

"My dear Cecil, there is plenty in evidence against him," said Lady Marabout, with a mental back glance to certain stories told of the "Amandine set," "though not of that kind. A man may be perfectly unexceptionable in his conduct with his men friends, but very objectionable acquaintance for us to seek, all the same."

"Ah, I see! Lord Goodwood may bet, and flirt, and lounge his days away, and be as fast a man as he likes, and it is all right; but if Mr. Cheveley does the same it is all wrong, because he is not worth forgiving."

"Naturally it is," returned Lady Marabout, seriously and naïvely. "But how very oddly you put things, my love; and why you should interest yourself in this man, when everything I tell you is to his disadvantage, I cannot imagine."

A remark that showed Lady Marabout a skilful tactician, insomuch as it silenced Cecil—a performance rather difficult of accomplishment.

"I am very glad I gave the order to Mason," thought that good lady, "I only wish we did not meet the man in society; but it is impossible to help that. We are all cards of one pack, and get shuffled together, whether we like it or not. I wish Philip would pay her more attention; he admires her, I can see, and he can make any woman like him in ten days when he takes the trouble; but he is so tiresome! She would be exactly suited to him; she has all he would exact—beauty, talent, good blood, and even fortune, though that he would not need. The alliance would be a great happiness to me. Well, he dines here to-night, and he gives that concert at his barracks to-morrow morning, purely to please Cecil, I am sure. I think it may be brought about with careful management."

With which pleasant reflection she went to drive in the Ring, thinking that her maternal and duenna duties would be alike well fulfilled, and her chaperone's career well finished, if by any amount of tact, intrigue, finesses, and diplomacy she could live to see Cecil Ormsby sign herself Cecil Carruthers.

"If that man were only out of town!" she thought, as Cheveley passed them in Amandine's mail-phaeton at the turn.

Lady Marabout might wish Cheveley were out of town—and wish it devoutly she did—but she wasn't very likely to have her desire gratified till the general migration should carry him off in its tide to the deck of a yacht, a lodge in the Highlands, a German Kursaal, or any one of those myriad "good houses" where nobody was so welcome as he, the best shot, the best seat, the best wit, the best billiard player, the best whist player, and the best authority on all fashionable topics, of any man in England. Cheveley used to aver that he liked Lady Marabout, though she detested him; nay, that he liked her *for* her detestation; he said it was cordial, sincere, and refreshing, therefore a treat in the world of Belgravia; still, he didn't like her so well as to leave Town in the middle of May to oblige her; and though he took her hint as it was meant, and pulled up his hansom no more at her door, he met her and Rosediamond's daughter at dinners, balls, concerts, morning-parties innumerable. He saw them in the Ring; he was seen by them at the Opera; he came across them constantly in the gyration of London life. Night after night Lady Cecil persisted in writing his name in her tablets; evening after evening a bizarre fate worried Lady Marabout, by putting him on the left hand of her priceless charge at a dinner-party. Day after day all the harmony of a concert was marred to her ear by seeing her Ogre talking of Beethoven and Mozart, chamber music and bravura music in Cecil's: morning after morning gall was poured into her luncheon sherry, and wormwood mingled in her vol-au-vent, by being told, with frank mischief, by her desired daughter-in-law, that she "had seen Mr. Cheveley leaning on the rails, smoking," when she had taken her after-breakfast canter.

"Chandos Cheveley getting up before noon! He *must* mean something unusual!" thought her chaperone.

"Helena has set her heart on securing Cecil Ormsby for Carruthers. I hope she may succeed better than she did with poor Goodwood last season," laughed Lady Hautton, with her inimitable sneer, glancing at the young lady in question at a bazaar in Willis's Rooms, selling rosebuds for anything she liked to ask for them, and cigars tied up with blue ribbon a guinea the half-dozen, at the Marabout stall. Lady Hautton had just been paying a charitable visit to St. Cecilia's Refuge, of which she was head patroness, where, having floated in with much benignity, been worshipped by a select little toady troop, administered spiritual consolation with admirable condescension, and distributed illuminated texts for the adornment of the walls and refreshment of the souls, she was naturally in a Christian frame of mind towards her neighbours. Lady Marabout caught the remark—as she was intended to do—and thought it not quite a pleasant one; but, my good sir, did you ever know those estimable people, who spend all their time fitting themselves for another world, ever take the trouble to make themselves decently agreeable in the present one? The little pleasant courtesies, affabilities, generosities, and kindnesses, that rub the edge off the flint-stones of the Via Dolorosa, are quite beneath the attention of Mary the Saint, and only get attended to by Martha the Worldly, poor butterfly thing! who is fit for nothing more serviceable and profitable!

Lady Marabout *had* set her heart on Cecil Ormsby's filling that post of honour—of which no living woman was deserving in her opinion—that of "Philip's wife;" an individual who had been, for so many years, a fond ideal, a haunting anxiety, and a dreaded rival, en même temps, to her imagination. She *was* a little bit of a match-maker: she had, over and over again, arranged the most admirable and suitable alliances; alliances that would have shamed the scepticism of the world in general, as to the desirability of the holy bonds, and brought every refractory man to the steps of St. George's; alliances that would have come off with the greatest éclat, but for one trifling hindrance and difficulty—namely, the people most necessary to the arrangements could never by any chance be brought to view them in the same light, and were certain to give her diplomacy the *croc-en-jambe* at the very moment of its culminating glory and finishing finesses. She was a little bit of a match-maker—most kind-hearted women are; the tinder they play with is much better left alone, but *they* don't remember that! Like children in a forest they think they'll light a pretty bright fire, just for fun, and never remember what a seared, dreary waste that fire may make, or what a prairie conflagration it may stretch into before it's stopped.

"Cecil Ormsby is a terrible flirt," said Lady Hautton to another lady, glancing at the rapid sale of the rosebuds and cigars, the bunches of violets and the sprays of lilies of the valley, in which that brilliant beauty was doing such thriving business at such extravagant profits, while the five Ladies Hautton presided solemnly over articles of gorgeous splendour, which threatened to be left on hand, and go in a tombola, as ignominiously as a beauty after half a dozen seasons, left unwooed and unwon, goes to the pêle-mêle raffle of German Bad society, and is sold off at the finish to an unknown of the Line, or a Civil Service fellow, with five hundred a year.

"Was Cecil a flirt?" wondered Lady Marabout. Lady Marabout was fain to confess to herself that she thought she was—nay, that she hoped she was. If it wasn't flirting, that way in which she smiled on Chandos Cheveley, sold him cigarettes, laughed with him over the ices and nectarines he fetched her, and positively invested him with the cordon d'honneur of a little bouquet of Fairy roses for which twenty men sued, and he (give Satan his due) did not even ask— if it wasn't flirting, *what was it?* Lady Marabout shivered at the suggestion; and though she was, on principle, excessively severe on flirting, she could be very glad of what she didn't approve, when it aided her, on occasion—like most other people—and would so far have agreed with Talleyrand, as to welcome the worst crime (of coquetry) as far less a sin than the unpardonable blunder of encouraging an Ogre!

"I can't send Cecil away from the stall, as if she were a naughty child, and I can't order the man out of Willis's Rooms," thought that unhappy and fatally-worried lady, as she presided behind her stall, an emphatic witness of the truth of the poeticism that "grief smiles and gives no sign," insomuch as she looked the fairest, sunniest, best-looking, and best tempered Dowager that ever shrouded herself in Chantilly lace.

"I do think those ineligible, detrimental, objectionable persons ought not to be let loose on society as they are," she pondered; "let them have their clubs and their mess breakfasts, their Ascot and their Newmarket, their lansquenet parties and their handicap pigeon matches, if they like; but to have them come amongst *us* as they do, asked everywhere if they happen to have good blood and good style, free to waltz and flirt and sing, and show all sorts of attention to marriageable girls, while all the while they are no more available for anything serious than if they were club stewards or cabmen—creatures that live on their fashionable aroma, and can't afford to buy the very bottles of bouquets on their toilette-tables—fast men, too, who, knowing they can never marry themselves, make a practice of turning marriage into ridicule, and help to set all the rich men more dead against it than they are—to have them come promiscuously among the very best people, with nothing to distinguish them as dangerous, or label them as 'ought to be avoided,'—it's dreadful! it's a social evil! it *ought* to be remedied! They muzzle dogs in June, why can't they label Ogres in the season? I mustn't send poor little Bijou out for a walk in Kensington Gardens without a string, these men ought not to go about in society without restriction: a snap of Bijou's doesn't do half such mischief as a smile of theirs!"

And Lady Marabout chatted across the stall to his Grace of Doncaster, and entrapped him into purchases of fitting ducal prodigality, and smiled on scores of people she didn't know, in pleasant *pro tempore* expediency that had, like most expediency in our day, its ultimate goal in their purses and pockets, and longed for some select gendarmerie to clear Willis's Rooms of her Cobra Capella, and kept an eye all the while on Cecil Ormsby—Cecil, selling off everything on the stall by sheer force of her bright violet eyes, receiving ten-pound notes for guinea trifles, making her Bourse rise as high as she liked, courted for a spray of mignonette as entreatingly as ever Law was courted in the Rue Quincampoix for Mississippi scrip, served by a Corps d'Elite, in whom she had actually enlisted Carruthers, Goodwood, Fulke Nugent, Fitzbreguet, and plenty of the most desirable and most desired men in town, yet of which—oh the obstinacy of women!—she had actually made Chandos Cheveley, with those wicked little Fairy roses in his coat, positively the captain and the chief!

"It is enough to break one's heart!" thought Lady Marabout, wincing under the Hautton glance, which she saw only the plainer because she *wouldn't* see it at all, and which said with horrible distinctness, "There is that man, who can hardly keep his own cab, who floats on society like a pleasure boat, without rudder, ballast, or anchors, of whom I have told you, in virtuous indignation and Christian charity, fifty thousand naughty stories, who visits that wicked, notorious little Maréchale, who belongs to the Amandine set, who is everything that he ought not and nothing that he ought to be, who hasn't a penny he doesn't make by a well-made betting-book or a dashed-off magazine article,—there he is flirting all day at your own stall with Rosediamond's daughter, and you haven't the *savoir faire*, the strength of will, the tact, the proper feeling, to stop it!"

To all of which charges Lady Marabout humbly bent her head, metaphorically speaking, and writhed, in secret, under the glance of her ancient enemy, while she talked and laughed with the Duke of Doncaster. C. Petronius, talking epicureanisms and witticisms, while the life-blood was ebbing away at every breath, was nothing to the suffering and the fortitude of Helena, Lady Marabout, turning a smiling, sunny, tranquil countenance to the world in front of her stall, while that world could see Chandos Cheveley admitted behind it!

"I must do something to stop this!" thought Lady Marabout, with the desperation of a Charlotte Corday.

"Is Cheveley going in for the Ormsby tin?" said Amandine to Eyre Lee. "Best thing he could do, eh? But Lady Tattersall and the trustees would cut up rough, I am afraid."

"What does Chandos mean with that daughter of Rosediamond's?" wondered her Grace, annoyedly. She had had him some time in her own rose chains, and when ladies have driven a lover long in that sort of harness, they could double-thong him with all the might of their little hands, if they fancy he is trying to break away.

"Is Chandos Cheveley turning fortune-hunter? I suppose he would like Lady Cecil's money to pay off his Ascot losses," said Mrs. Maréchale, with a malin laugh. At Ascot, the day before, he had not gone near her carriage; the year before he had driven her down in her mail-phaeton: what would there be too black to say of him *now?*

"I must do something to stop this!" determined Lady Marabout, driving homewards, and glancing at Cecil Ormsby, as that young lady lay back in the carriage, a little grave and dreamy after her day's campaign—signs of the times terrifically ominous to her chaperone, skilled in reading such meteorological omens. But how was the drag to be put on the wheel? That momentous question absorbed Lady Marabout through her toilette that evening, pursued her to dinner, haunted her through two soirées, kept her wide awake all night, woke up with her to her early coffee, and flavoured the potted tongue and the volaille à la Richelieu she took for her breakfast. "I can't turn the man out of town, and I can't tell people to strike him off their visiting-lists, and I can't shut Cecil and myself up in this house as if it were a convent; and, as to speaking to her, it is not the slightest use. She has such a way of putting things that one can never deny their truth, or reason them away, as one can with other girls. Fond as I am of her, she's fearfully difficult to manage. Still I owe it as a sacred duty to poor Rosediamond and the General, who says he places such implicit confidence in me, to interfere. It is my duty; it can't be helped. I must speak to Chandos Cheveley himself. I have no right to consult my own scruples when so much is at stake," valorously determined Lady Marabout, resolved to follow stern moral rules, and, when right was right, to let "le diable prendre le fruit."

To be a perfect woman of the world, I take it, ladies must weed out early in life all such little contemptible weaknesses as a dislike to wounding other people; and a perfect woman of the world, therefore, Lady Marabout was not, and never would be. Nohow could she acquire Anne Hautton's invaluable sneer—nohow could she imitate that estimable pietist's delightful way of dropping little icybarbed sentences, under which I have known the bravest to shrink, frozen, out of her path. Lady Marabout was grieved if she broke the head off a flower needlessly, and she could not cure herself of the same lingering folly in disliking to say a thing that pained anybody; it is incidental to the De Boncœur blood—Carruthers inherits it—and I have seen fellows spared through it, whom he could else have withered into the depths of their boots by one of his satirical mots. So she did not go to her task of speaking to Chandos Cheveley, armed at all points for the encounter, and taking pleasure in feeling the edge of her rapier, as Lady Hautton would have done. The Cobra was dangerous, and must be crushed, but Lady Marabout did not very much relish setting her heel on it; it was a glittering, terrible, much-to-be-feared, and much-to-be-abused serpent,—but it might *feel* all the same, you see.

"I dislike the man on principle, but I don't want to pain him," she thought, sighing for the Hautton stern *savoir faire* and Achilles impenetrability, and goading herself on with the remembrance of duty and General Ormsby, when the opportunity she had resolved to seek presented itself accidentally at a breakfast of Lady George Frangipane's toy villa at Fulham, and she found herself comparatively alone in the rose-garden with Cheveley, for once without Cecil's terrible violet eyes upon her.

"Will you allow me a few words with you, Mr. Cheveley?" she asked, in her blandest manner—the kindly hypocrite!

The blow must be dealt, but it might as well be softened with a few chloroform fumes, and not struck savagely with an iron-spiked mace.

Cheveley raised his eyes.

"With me? With the greatest pleasure!"

"He is a mere fortune-hunter. I will *not* spare him, I am resolved," determined Lady Marabout, as she toyed with her parasol handle, remarked incidentally how unequalled Lady George was in roses, especially in the tea-rose, and dealt blow number one. "Mr. Cheveley, I am going to speak to you very frankly. I consider frankness in all things best, myself——"

Cheveley bowed, and smiled slightly.

"I wish he would answer, it would make it so much easier; he will only look at one with those eyes of his, and certainly they *are* splendid!" thought Lady Marabout, as she went on quickly, on the same principle as the Chasseurs Indiens approach an abattis at double-quick. "When Lord Rosediamond died last year he left, as probably you are aware, his daughter in my sole care; it was a great responsibility—very great—and I feel, of course, that I shall have to answer to him for my discharge of it."

Lady Marabout didn't say whether Rosediamond was accustomed to visit her per medium, and hear her account of her stewardship nightly through a table-claw; but we must suppose that he was. Cheveley bowed again, and didn't inquire, not being spiritually interested.

"Why *won't* he answer?" thought Lady Marabout. "That I have not been blind to your very marked attention to my dear Cecil, I think you must be aware,

Mr. Cheveley, and it is on that subject, indeed, that I——"

"Wished to speak to me? I understand!" said Cheveley, as she paused, with that faint smile, half sad, half proud, that perplexed Lady Marabout. "You are about to insinuate to me gently that those attentions have been exceedingly distasteful to you, exceedingly unacceptable in me; you would remind me that Lady Cecil Ormsby is a beauty and an heiress, and that I am a fortune-hunter, whose designs are seen through and motives found out; you would hint to me that our intercourse must cease: is it not so?"

Lady Marabout, cursed with that obstinate, ill-bred, unextinguishable weakness for truth incidental and ever fatal to the De Boncœurs, couldn't say that it was *not* what she was going to observe to him, but it was exceedingly unpleasant, now it was put in such plain, uncomplimentary terms, to admit to the man's face that she was about to tell him he was a mercenary schemer, whose attentions only sprang from a lawless passion for the *beaux yeux* of Cecil's *cassette*.

She would have told him all that, and much more, with greatest dignity and effect, if he hadn't anticipated her; but to have her weapon parried before it was fairly out of its sheath unnerved her arm at the outset.

"What *would* Anne Hautton do? Dear me! there never was anybody perpetually placed in such wretched positions as I am!" thought Lady Marabout, as she played with her parasol, and murmured something not very clear relative to "responsibility" and "not desirable," two words as infallibly a part of Lady Marabout's stock-in-trade as a sneer at the "swells" is of *Punch's*. How she sighed for some cold, nonchalant, bitter sentence, such as the Hautton répertoire could have supplied! how she scorned herself for her own weakness and lack of severity! But she would not have relished hurting a burglar's feelings, though she had seen him in the very act of stealing her jewel-boxes, by taxing him with the theft; and though the Ogre *must* be crushed, the crushing began to give Lady Marabout neuralgic twinges. She was no more able to say the stern things she had rehearsed and resolved upon, than she was able to stab him with her parasol, or strangle him with her handkerchief.

"I guessed rightly what you were about to say to me?" said Cheveley, who seemed somehow or other to have taken all the talk into his own hands, and to have become the master of the position. "I thought so. I do not wonder at your construction; I cannot blame you for your resolution. Lady Cecil has some considerable fortune, they say; it is very natural that you should have imagined a man like myself, with no wealth save a good name, which only serves to make lack of wealth more conspicuous, incapable of seeking her society for any better, higher, more disinterested motive than that of her money; it was not charitable, perhaps, to decide unhesitatingly that it was impossible I could be drawn to her by any other attraction, that it was imperative I must be dead to everything in her that gives her a nobler and a higher charm; but it was very natural, and one learns never to hope for the miracle of a charitable judgment, *even* from Lady Marabout!"

"My dear Mr. Cheveley, indeed you mistake!" began Lady Marabout, restlessly. That was a little bit of a story, he didn't mistake at all; but Lady Marabout, collapsing like an india-rubber ball under the prick of a sarcasm, shivered all over at his words, his voice, his slight, sad smile. "The man is as dreadful as Cecil," she thought; "he puts things so horribly clearly!"

"Mistake? I do not think I do. You have thought all this, and very naturally; but now hear me for a moment. I have sought Lady Cecil's society, that is perfectly true; we have been thrown together in society, very often accidentally; sometimes, I admit, through my own seeking. Few men could be with her and be steeled against her. I have been with her too much; but I sought her at first carelessly, then irresistibly and unconsciously, never with the motive you attribute to me. I am not as utterly beggared as you deem me, but neither am I entirely barren of honour. Believe me, Lady Marabout, my pride alone would be amply sufficient to raise a barrier between me and Cecil stronger than any that could be opposed to me by others. Yesterday I casually overheard words from Amandine which showed me that Society, like you, has put but one construction on the attention I have paid her—a construction I might have foreseen had I not been unconsciously fascinated, and forgetful for the time, of the infallible whispers of my kind friends. Her fortune, I know, was never numbered among her attractions for me; so little, that now that Amandine's careless words have reminded me of the verdict of Society, I shall neither seek her nor see her again. Scores of men marry women for their money, and their money alone, but I am not one of them; with my own precarious fortunes, only escaping ruin because I am not rich enough to tempt ruin, I would never take advantage of any interest I may have excited in her, to speak to her of a passion that the world would tell her was only another name for avarice and selfishness. I dare not trust myself with her longer, perhaps. I am no god to answer for my self-control; but you need not fear; I will never seek her love—never even tell her of mine. I shall leave town to-morrow; what *I* may suffer matters not. Lady Cecil is safe from me! Whatever you may have heard of my faults, follies, or vices, none ever told you, I think, that I broke my word?"

"And when the man said that, my dear Philip, I assure you I felt as guilty as if I had done him some horrible wrong; he stood there with his head up, looking at me with his sad proud eyes—and they are beautiful!—till, positively, I could almost have cried—I could, indeed, for though I don't like him on principle, I couldn't help pitying him," said Lady Marabout, in a subsequent relation of the scene to her son. "Wasn't it a terrible position? I was as near as possible forgetting everything due to poor Rosediamond, and saying to him that I believed Cecil liked him and would never like anybody else, but, thank Heaven! I remembered myself, and checked myself in time. If it had been anybody but Chandos Cheveley, I should really have admired him, he spoke so nobly! When he lifted his hat and left me, though I *ought* to have been glad (and I *was* glad, of course) that Cecil would be free from the society of anybody so objectionable and so dangerous, I felt wretched for him—I did indeed. It *is* so hard always to be placed in such miserable positions!"

By which you will perceive that the triumphant

crushing of Lady Marabout's Cobra didn't afford her the unmixed gratification she had anticipated.

"I have done what was my duty to poor Rosediamond, and what General Ormsby's confidence merited," she solaced herself that day, feeling uncomfortably and causelessly guilty, she hardly knew why, when she saw Chandos Cheveley keeping sedulously with the "Amandine set," and read in Cecil's tell-tale face wonder, perplexity, and regret thereat, till the Frangipane fête came to an end. She had appeased the manes of the late Rosediamond, who, to her imagination, always appeared sitting up aloft, keeping watch over the discharge of her chaperone's duties, but she had a secret and horrible dread that she had excited the wrath of Rosediamond's daughter. She had driven her Ogre off the scene, it is true, but she could not feel that she had altogether come off the best in the contest. Anne Hautton had congratulated her, indeed, on having "acted with decision *at last*," but then she had marred it all by asking if Carruthers was likely to be engaged to Cecil? And Lady Marabout had been forced to confess he was not; Philip, when pressed by her that very morning to be a little attentive to Cecil, having shaken his head and laughed:

"She's a bewitching creature, mother, but she don't bewitch *me!* You know what Shakspeare says of wooing, wedding, and repentance. I've no fancy for the inseparable trio!"

Altogether, Lady Marabout was far from peace and tranquillity, though the Cobra *was* crushed, as she drove away from the Frangipane breakfast, and she was little nearer them when Cecil turned her eyes upon her with a question worse to Lady Marabout's ear than the roar of a Lancaster battery:

"What have you said to him?"

"My dear Cecil! What have I said to whom?" returned Lady Marabout, with Machiavelian surprise.

"You know well enough, Lady Marabout! What have you said to him—to Mr. Cheveley?"

Cecil's impetuosity invariably knocked Lady Marabout down at one blow, as a ball knocks down the pegs at lawn billiards. She rallied after the shock, but not successfully, and tried at coldness and decision, as recommended by Hautton prescriptions.

"My dear Cecil, I have said to him what I think it my duty to say to him. Responsible as I am for you——"

"Responsible for me, Lady Marabout? Indeed you are not. I am responsible for myself!" interrupted Lady Cecil, with that haughty arch of her eyebrows and that flush on her face before which Lady Marabout was powerless. "What have you said to him? I *will* know!"

"I said very little to him, indeed, my dear; he said it all himself."

"What did he say himself?"

"I *must* tell her—she is so dreadfully persistent," thought the unhappy and badgered Peeress; and tell her she did, being a means of lessening the young lady's interest in the subject of discussion as little judicious as she could well have hit upon.

Lady Cecil listened, silent for once, shading her face with her parasol, shading the tears that gathered on her lashes and rolled down her delicate flushed cheeks, at the recital of Chandos Cheveley's words, from her chaperone's sight.

Lady Marabout gathered courage from the tranquillity with which her recital was heard.

"You see, my love, Chandos Cheveley's own honour points in the same direction with my judgment," she wound up, in conclusion. "He has acted rightly at last, I allow, and if you—if you have for the moment felt a tinge of warmer interest in him—if you have been taken by the fascination of his manner, and invested him with a young girl's romance, you will soon see with us how infinitely better it is that you should part, and how impossible it is that——"

Lady Cecil's eyes flashed such fire through their tears, that Lady Marabout stopped, collapsed and paralysed.

"It is by such advice as that you repay his nobility, his generosity, his honour!—it is by such words as those you reward him for acting as not one man in a hundred would have acted! Hush, hush, Lady Marabout, I thought better of you!"

"Good Heavens! *where will it end?*" thought Lady Marabout, distractedly, as Rosediamond's wayward daughter sprang down at the door with a flush in her face, and a contemptuous anger in her eyes, that made Bijou, jumping on her, stop, stare, and whine in canine dismay.

"And I fancied she was listening passively!" thought Lady Marabout.

"Well! the man is gone to-day, that is one comfort. I am very thankful I acted as I did," reasoned that ever-worried lady in her boudoir the next morning. "I am afraid Cecil is really very fond of him, there were such black shadows under her eyes at breakfast, poor child! But it is much better as it is—much better. I should never have held up my head again if I had allowed her to make such a disadvantageous alliance. I can hardly bear to think of what would have been said, even now the danger is over!"

While Lady Marabout was thus comforting herself over her embroidery silks, Cecil Ormsby was pacing into the Park, with old Twitters, the groom, ten yards behind her, taking her early ride before the world was up—it was only eleven o'clock; Cecil had been used to early rising, and would never leave it off, having discovered some recipe that made her independent of ordinary mortals' quantum of sleep.

"Surely he will be here this morning to see me for the last time," thought that young lady, as she paced up the New Ride under the Kensington Gardens trees, with her heart beating quickly under the gold aiglettes of her riding-jacket.

"I must see her once more, and then——" thought Chandos Cheveley, as he leaned against the rails, smoking, as he had done scores of mornings before. His man had packed his things; his hansom was waiting at the gates to take him to the station, and his portmanteau was lettered "Ischl." He had only come to take one last look of the face that haunted him as no other had ever succeeded in doing. The ring of a horse's hoof fell on his ear. There she came, on her roan hack, with the sun glancing off her chestnut hair. He looked up to bow to her as she passed on, for the Ride had never been a rendezvous for more than a bow (Cecil's insurrectionary tactics had always been carried on before Lady Marabout's face), but the roan was pulled up by him that morning for the very first time, and Cecil's eyes fell on him through their lashes.

"Mr. Cheveley—is it true you are going out of town?"

"Quite true."

If her voice quivered as she asked the question, he barely kept his own from doing the same as he answered it.

"Will you be gone long?"

"Till next season, at earliest."

His promise to Lady Marabout was hard to keep! He would not have trusted his strength if he had known she would have done more than canter on with her usual bow and smile.

Cecil was silent. The groom waited like a statue his ten yards behind them. She played with her reins nervously, the colour coming and going painfully in her face.

"Lady Marabout told me of—of some conversation you had with her yesterday?"

Low as the words were, Cheveley heard them, and his hand, as it lay on the rails, shook like a girl's.

Cecil was silent again; she looked at him, her eyes full of unshed tears, as the colour burned in her face, and she drooped her head almost to a level with her hands as they played with the reins.

"She told me—you——"

She stopped again. Cecil was new to making proposals, though not to rejecting them. Cheveley set his teeth to keep in the words that rushed to his lips, and Cecil saw the struggle as she bent her head lower and lower to the saddle, and twisted the reins into a Gordian knot.

"Do you—must we—why should——"

Fragmentary monosyllables enough, but sufficient to fell his strength.

"For God's sake do not tempt me!" he muttered. "You little know!"

"I know all!" she whispered, softly.

"You cannot! My worthless life!—my honour! I could not take such a sacrifice, I would not!——"

"But if my peace——"

She could not end her phrase, yet it said enough;—his hand closed on hers.

"Your peace! Good God! in *my* hands! I stay, then—let the world say what it likes!"

"Drive back; I have changed my mind about going abroad to-day," said Cheveley, as he got into his hansom at Albert-gate.

"How soon she has got over it! Girls do," thought Lady Marabout, as Cecil Ormsby came in from her ride with the brighest bloom on her cheeks a June breeze ever fanned there. She laid her hat on the table, flung her gauntlets at Bijou, and threw herself on her knees by Lady Marabout, a saucy smile on her face, though her lashes were wet.

"Dear Lady Marabout, I can forgive you now, but you will never forgive me!"

Lady Marabout turned white as her point-lace cap, gave a little gasp of paralysed terror, and pushed back her chair as though a shell had exploded on the hearth-rug.

"Cecil! Good Heaven!—you don't mean——"

"Yes I do," said Cecil, with a fresh access of colour, and a low, soft laugh.

Lady Marabout gasped again for breath.

"General Ormsby!" was all she could ejaculate.

"General Ormsby? What of him? Did you ever know Uncle Johnnie refuse to please *me?* And if my money be to interfere with my happiness, and not promote it, as I conceive it its duty and purpose to do, why, I am of age in July, you know, and I shall make a deed of gift of it all to the Soldiers' Home or the Wellington College, and there is only one person who will care for me *then*."

Lady Cecil was quite capable of carrying her threat into execution, and Lady Cecil had her own way accordingly, as she had had it from her babyhood.

"I shall never hold up my head again! And what a horrible triumph for Anne Hautton! I am always the victim—always!" said Lady Marabout, that day two months, when the last guest at Cecil Ormsby's wedding déjeûner had rolled away from the house. "A girl who might have married anybody, Philip; she refused twenty offers this season—she did, indeed! It is heart-breaking, say what you like; you needn't laugh, it *is*. Why did I offer them Fernditton for this month, you say, if I didn't countenance the alliance? Nonsense! that is nothing to the purpose. Of course, I seemed to countenance it to a degree, for Cecil's sake, and I admire Chandos Cheveley, I confess (at least I should do, if I didn't dislike his class on principle); but, say what you like, Philip, it is the most terrible thing that could have happened for *me*. Those men *ought* to be labelled, or muzzled, or done something with, and not be let loose on society as they are. He has a noble nature, you say. I don't say anything against his nature! She worships him? Well, I know she does. What is that to the point? He will make her happy? I am sure he will. He has the gentlest way with her possible. But how does that console *me?* Think what *you* feel when an outsider, as you call it, beats all the favourites, upsets all your betting-books, and carries off the Doncaster Cup, and then realise, if you've any humanity in you, what *we* feel under such a trial as this is to me! Only to think what Anne Hautton will always say!"

Lady Marabout is not the only person to whom the first thought, the most dreaded ghost, the ghastliest skeleton, the direst aggravation, the sharpest dagger-thrust, under all troubles, is the remembrance of that one omnipotent ogre—"QU'EN DIRA-T-ON?"

"Laugh at her, mother," counselled Carruthers; and, *ami lecteurs*, I pass on his advice to you as the best and sole bowstring for strangling the ogre in question, which is the grimmest we have in all Bogeydom.

LADY MARABOUT'S TROUBLES;

OR,

THE WORRIES OF A CHAPERONE.

IN THREE SEASONS.

SEASON THE THIRD.—THE CLIMAX.

"My dear Philip, the most unfortunate thing has happened," said Lady Marabout, one morning; "really the greatest contretemps that could have occurred. I suppose I never *am* to be quiet!"

"What's the row *now*, madre carissima?" asked her son.

"It is no row, but it is an annoyance. You have heard me speak of my poor dear friend Mrs. Montolieu; you know she married unhappily, poor thing, to a dreadful creature, something in a West India regiment—nobody at all. It is very odd and it is very wrong, and there must be a great mistake somewhere, but certainly most marriages *are* unhappy."

"And yet you are always recommending the institution! What an extraordinary obstinacy and opticism, my dear mother! I suppose you do it on the same principle as nurses recommend children nasty medicines, or as old Levett used to tender me dry biscuit *sans confiture:* "'Tisn't so nice as marmalade, I know, Master Philip, but then, dear, it's *so* wholesome!'"

"Hold your tongue, Philip," cried Lady Marabout; "I don't mean it in that sense at all, and you know I don't. If poor Lilla Montolieu is unhappy, I am sure it is all her abominable odious husband's fault; she is the sweetest creature possible. But she has a daughter, and concerning that daughter she wrote to me about a month ago, and—I never was more vexed in my life —she wants me to bring her out this season."

"A victim again! My poor dear mother, you certainly deserve a Belgravian testimonial; you shall have a statue set up in Lowndes-square commemorative of the heroic endurance of a chaperone's existence, subscribed for gratefully by the girls you married well, and penitentially by the girls you couldn't marry at all."

Lady Marabout laughed a little, but sighed again:
"'It is fun to you, but it is death to me'——"

"As the women say when we flirt with them," interpolated Carruthers.

"You see, poor dear Lilla didn't know what to do. There she is, in that miserable island with the unpronounceable name that the man is governor of; shut out of all society, with nobody to marry this girl to if she had her there, except their secretary, or a West Indian planter. Of course, no mother would ruin her daughter's prospects, and take her into such an out-of-the-world corner. She knew no one so well as myself, and so to me she applied. She is the sweetest creature! I would do anything to oblige or please her, but I can't help being very sorry she has pounced upon me. And I don't the least know what this girl is like, not even whether she is presentable. I dare say she was petted and spoiled in that lazy, luxurious, tropical life when she was little, and she has been brought up the last few years in a convent in France, the very last education *I* should choose for a girl. Fancy, if I should find her an ignorant, unformed hoyden, or a lethargic, overgrown child, or an artificial French girl, who goes to confession every day, and carries on twenty undiscoverable love affairs—fancy, if she should be ugly, or awkward, or brusque, or gauche, as ten to one she will be—fancy, if I find her utterly unpresentable!—what in the world shall I do!"

"Decline her," suggested Carruthers. "I wouldn't have a horse put in my tilbury that I'd never seen, and risk driving a spavined, wall-eyed, underbred brute through the Park; and I suppose the ignominy of the début would be to you much what the ignominy of such a turn-out would be to me."

"Decline her? I can't, my dear Philip! I agreed to have her a month ago. I have never seen you to tell you till now, you know; you've been so sworn to Newmarket all through the Spring Meetings. Decline her? she comes to-night!"

"Comes to-night?" laughed Carruthers. "All is lost, then. We shall see the Countess of Marabout moving through London society with a West Indian, who has a skin like Othello; has as much idea of manners as a housemaid that suddenly turns out an heiress, and is invited by people to whom she yesterday carried up their hot water; reflects indelible disgrace on her chaperone by gaucheries unparalleled; throws glass or silver missiles at Soames's head when he doesn't wait upon her at luncheon to her liking, as she has been accustomed to do at the negroes———"

"Philip, pray don't!" cried Lady Marabout, piteously.

"Or, we shall welcome under the Marabout wing a young lady fresh from convent walls and pensionnaire flirtations, who astonishes a dinner-party by only taking the first course, on the score of jours maigres and conscientious scruples; who is visited by révérends pères from Farmstreet, and fills your drawing-room with High Church curates, whom she tries to draw over from their 'mother's' to their 'sister's' open arms; who goes every day to early morning mass instead of taking an early morning canter, and who, when invited to sing at a soirée musicale, begins 'Sancta Maria adorata!'"

"Philip, *don't!*" cried Lady Marabout. "Bark at him, Bijou, the heartless man! It is as likely as not little Montolieu may realise one of your horrible sketches. Ah, Philip, you don't know what the worries of a chaperone are!"

"Thank Heaven, no!" laughed Carruthers.

"It is easy to make a joke of it, and very tempting, I dare say—one's woes always *are* amusing to other people, they don't feel the smart themselves, and only laugh at the grimace it forces from one—but I can tell you, Philip, it is anything but a pleasant prospect to have to go about in society with a girl one may be ashamed of!—I don't know anything more trying; I would as soon wear paste diamonds as introduce a girl that is not perfectly good style."

"But why not have thought of all this in time?"

Lady Marabout sank back in her chair, and curled Bijou's ears with a sigh.

"My dear Philip, if everybody always thought of things in time, would there be any follies committed at all? It's precisely because repentance comes too late, that repentance is such a horrible wasp, with such a merciless sting. Besides, *could* I refuse poor Lilla Montolieu, unhappy as she is with that bear of a man?"

"I never felt more anxious in my life," thought Lady Marabout, as she sat before the fire in her drawing-room—it was a chilly April day—stirring the cream into her preprandial cup of tea, resting one of her small satin-slippered feet on Bijou's back, while the firelight sparkled on the Dresden figures, the statuettes, the fifty thousand costly trifles, in which the Marabout rooms equalled any in Belgravia. "I never felt more anxious—not on any of Philip's dreadful yachting expeditions, nor even when he went that perilous exploring tour into Arabia Deserta, I do think. If she *should* be unpresentable—and then poor dear Lilla's was not much of a match, and the girl will not have a sou, she tells me frankly; I can hardly hope to do anything for her. There is one thing, she will not be a responsibility like Valencia or Cecil, and what would have been a bad match for *them* will be a good one for her. She must accept the first offer made her, if she have any at all, which will be very doubtful; few Benedicts bow to Beatrices now-a-days, unless Beatrice is a good 'investment,' as they call it. She will soon be here. That is the carriage now stopped, I do think. How anxious I feel! Really it can't be worse for a Turkish bridegroom never to see his wife's face till after the ceremony than it is for one not to have seen a girl till one has to introduce her. If she shouldn't be good style!"

And Lady Marabout's heart palpitated, possibly prophetically, as she set down her little Sèvres cup and rose out of her arm-chair, with Bijou shaking his silver collar and bells, to welcome the new inmate of Lowndes-square, with her sunny smile and her kindly voice, and her soft beaming eyes, which, as I have often stated, would have made Lady Marabout look amiable at an Abruzzi bandit who had demanded her purse, or an executioner who had led her out to capital punishment, and now made her radiate, warm and bright, on a guest whose advent she dreaded. Hypocrisy, you say. Not a bit of it! Hypocrisy may be eminently courteous, but, take my word for it, it's never *cordial!* There are natures who throw such golden rays around them naturally, as there are others who think brusquerie and acidity cardinal virtues, and deal them out as points of conscience; are there not sunbeams that shine kindly alike on fragrant violet tufts and barren brambles, velvet lawns and muddy trottoirs? are there not hail-clouds that send jagged points of ice on all the world pêle-mêle, as mercilessly on the broken rose as on the granite boulder?

"She *is* good style, thank Heaven!" thought Lady Marabout, as she went forward, with her white soft hands, their jewels flashing in the light, outstretched in welcome. "My dear child, how much you are like your mother! You must let me be fond of you for her sake, first, and then—for your own!"

The conventional thought did not make the cordial utterance insincere. The two ran in couples—we often drive such pairs, every one of us—and if *they* entail insincerity, *Veritas, vale!*

"Madre mia, I called to inquire if you have survived the anxiety of last night, and to know what *jeune sauvage* or fair *religieuse* you may have had sent you for the galvanising of Belgravia?" said Carruthers, paying his accustomed visit in his mother's boudoir, and throwing macaroons at Bijou's nose.

"My dear Philip, I hardly know; she puzzles me. She's what, if she were a man, I should classify as a detrimental."

"Is she awkward?"

"Not in the least. Perfect manners, wherever she learned them."

"Brusque?"

"Soft as a gazelle. Very like her mother."

"Brown?"

"Fair as that statuette, with a beautiful bloom; lovely gold hair, too, and hazel eyes."

"What are the short-comings, then?"

"There are none; and it's that that puzzles me. She's been six years in that convent, and yet, I do assure you, her style is perfect. She's hardly eighteen, but she's the air of the best society. She is—a—well, *almost* nobody, as people rank now, you know, for poor dear Lilla's marriage was not what she should have made, but the girl might be a royal duke's daughter for manner."

"A premature artificial *femme du monde?* Bah! nothing more odious," said Carruthers, poising a macaroon on Pandore's nose. "Make ready!—present!—fire! There's a good dog!"

"No, nothing of that sort: very natural, frank, vivacious. Nothing artificial about her; very charming indeed! But she might be a young Countess, the queen of a *monde*, rather than a young girl just out of a French convent; and, you know, my dear Philip, that sort of wit and nonchalance may be admirable for Cecil Cheveley, assured of her position, but they're dangerous to a girl like this Flora Montolieu: they will make people remark her and ask who she is, and try to pull her to pieces, if they don't find her somebody they *dare* not hit. I would much rather she were of the general ordinary pattern, pleasing, but nothing remarkable, well-bred, but nothing to envy, thoroughly educated, but monosyllabic in society; such a girl as that passes among all the rest, suits mediocre men (and the majority of men *are* mediocre, you know, my dear Philip), and pleases women because she is a nice girl, and no rival; but this little Montolieu——"

And Lady Marabout sighed with a prescience of coming troubles, while Carruthers laughed and rose.

"Will worry your life out! I must go, for I have to sit in court-martial at two (for a mere trifle, a deuced bore to us, but *le service oblige!*), so I shall escape introduction to your little Montolieu to-day. Why *will* you fill your house with girls, my dear mother?—it is fifty times more agreeable when you are reigning alone. Henceforth, I can't come in to lunch with you without going through the formula of a mild flirtation—women think you so ill-natured if you don't flirt a little with them, that amiable men like myself haven't strength of mind to refuse. You should keep *your* house an open sanctuary for me, when you know I've no other in London except when I retreat into White's and the U. S.!"

"She puzzles me!" pondered Lady Marabout, as Despréaux disrobed her that night. "I always *am* to be puzzled, I think! I never *can* have one of those quiet, mediocre, well-mannered, remarkable-for-nothing girls, who have no idiosyncrasies and give nobody any trouble; one marries them safely to some second-rate man; nobody admires them, and nobody dislikes them; they're to society what neutral tint is among body-colours, or rather what greys are among dresses, inoffensive, unimpeachable, always look ladylike, but never look brilliant; colourless dresses are very useful, and so are characterless girls; and I dare say the draper would tell us the greys in the long run are the easiest to sell, as the girls are to marry; they please the commonplace taste of the generality, and do for everyday wear! Flora Montolieu puzzles me; she is very charming, very striking, very lovable, but she puzzles me! I have a presentiment that that child will give me a world of anxiety, an infinitude of trouble!"

And Lady Marabout laid her head on her pillow, not the happier that Flora Montolieu was lying asleep in the room next her, dreaming of the wild-vine shadows and the night-blooming flowers of her native tropics, under the rose-curtains of her new home in Lowndes-square, already a burden on the soul and a responsibility on the mind of that home's most genial and generous mistress.

"If she were a man I should certainly call her a detrimental," said Lady Marabout, after a more deliberate study of her charge. "You know, my dear Philip, the sort of man one calls detrimental; attractive enough to do a great deal of damage, and ineligible enough to make the damage very unacceptable: handsome and winning, but a younger son, or a something nobody wants; a delightful flirtation, but a terrible alliance; you know what I mean! Well, that is just what this little Montolieu is in our sex; I am quite sure it is what she will be considered; and if it be bad for a man, it is very much worse for a woman! Everybody will admire her, and nobody will marry her; I have a presentiment of it!"

With which prophetical mélange of the glorious and the inglorious for her charge's coming career, Lady Marabout sighed, and gave a little shiver, such as

Sur des maux ignorés nous fait gémir d'avance,

as Delphine Gay well phrased it. And she floated out of her boudoir to the dining-room for luncheon, at which unformal and pleasant meal Carruthers chanced to stay, criticise a new dry sherry, and take a look at this unsalable young filly of the Marabout Yearling Sales.

"I don't know about her being detrimental, mother, nor about her being little; she is more than middle height," laughed he; "but I vow she is the prettiest thing you've had in your list for some time. You've had much greater beauties, you say? Well, perhaps so; but I bet you any money she will make a sensation."

"I am sure she will," reiterated Lady Marabout, despairingly. "I have no doubt she will have a brilliant season; there is something very piquante, taking, and uncommon about her; but who will marry her at the end of it?"

Carruthers shouted with laughter.

"Heaven forbid that I should attempt to prophesy!

I would undertake as readily to say who'll be the owner of the winner of the Oaks ten years hence! I can tell you who *won't*——"

"Yourself; because you'll never marry anybody at all," cried Lady Marabout. "Well! I must say I should not wish you to renounce your misogamistic notions here. The Montolieus are not at all what *you* should look for; and a child like Flora would be excessively ill suited to you. If I could see you married, as I should desire, to some woman of weight and dignity, five or six-and-twenty, fit for you in every way——"

"*De grace, de grace!* My dear mother, the mere sketch will kill me, if you insist on finishing it! Be reasonable! Can anything be more comfortable, more tranquil, than I am now? I swing through life in a rocking-chair; if I'm a trifle bored now and then, it's my heaviest trial. I float as pleasantly on the waves of London life, in my way, as the lotus-eaters of poetry on the Ganges in theirs; and *you'd* have the barbarity to introduce into my complacent existence the sting of matrimony, the phosphorus of Hymen's torch, the symbolical serpent of a wedding-ring?—for shame!"

Lady Marabout laughed despite herself, and the solemnity, in *her* eyes, of the subject.

"I *should* like to see you happily married, for all that, though I quite despair of it now; but perhaps you are right."

"Of course I am right! Adam was tranquil and unworried till fate sent him a wife, and he was typical of the destinies of his descendants. Those who are wise take warning; those who are not, neglect it and repent. Lady Hautton et Cie are very fond of twisting scriptural obscurities into 'types.' *There's* a type plain as day, and salutary to mankind, if detrimental to women!"

"Philip, you are abominable! don't be so wicked!" cried Lady Marabout, enjoying it all the more because she was a little shocked at it, as your best women will on occasion; human nature is human nature everywhere, and the female heart gives pleasurable little pulses at the sight of forbidden fruits now, as in the days of Eve.

"Who's that Miss Montolieu with your mother this year, Phil?" dozens of men asked Carruthers, that season, across the mess-table, in the smoking-room of the Guards, in the Ride or the Ring, in the doorways of ball-rooms, or anywhere where such-like questions are asked and new pretty women discussed.

"What is it in her that takes so astonishingly?" wondered Lady Marabout, who is, like most women, orthodox on all points, loving things by rule, worrying if they go out of the customary routine, and was, therefore, quite incapable of reconciling herself to so revolutionary a fact as a young lady being admired who was not a beauty, and sought while she was detrimental in every way. It was "out of the general rule," and your orthodox people hate anything "out of the general run," as they hate their prosperous friends: the force of hatred can no further go! Flora Montolieu's crime in Belgravia was much akin to the Bonapartes' crimes to the Bourbons. Thrones must be filled legitimately, if not worthily, in the eyes of the orthodox people, and this Petit Caporal of Lady Marabout's had no business to reign where the hereditary

Princesses and all the other noble lines failed to sway the sceptre. Lady Marabout, belonging to the noble lines herself, agreed in her heart with them, and felt a little bit guilty to have introduced this democratic and unwelcome element into society.

Flora Montolieu "took," as people say of bubble companies, meaning that they will pleasantly ruin a million or two: or of new fashions, meaning that they will become general with the many and, *sequitur*, unwearable with the few. She had the brilliance and grace of one of her own tropical flowers, with something piquante and attractive about her that one had to leave nameless, but that was all the more charming for that very fact perhaps; full of life and animation, but soft as a gazelle, as her chaperone averred; not characterless, as Lady Marabout fondly desired (on the same principle, I suppose, as a timid whip likes a horse as spiritless as a riding-school hack), but gifted with plenty of very marked character, so much, indeed, that it rather puzzled her *camériste*.

"Girls shouldn't have marked character; they should be clay that one can mould, not a self-chiselled statuette, that will only go into its own niche, and won't go into any other. This little Montolieu would make just such a woman as Vittoria Colonna or Madame de Sablé, but one doesn't want *those* qualities in a girl who is but a single little ear in the wheat-sheaf of society, and whom one wants to marry off, but can't expect to marry well. Her poor mother, of course, will look to me to do something advantageous for her, and I verily believe she is that sort of girl that will let me do nothing," thought Lady Marabout, already beginning to worry, as she talked to Lady George Frangipane at a breakfast in Palace Gardens, and watched Flora Montolieu, with Carruthers on her left and Goodwood on her right, amusing them both, to all semblance, and holding her own to the Lady Hauttons' despite, who held *their* own so excessively chillily and loftily that no ordinary mortals cared to approach them, but, beholding them, thought involuntarily of the stately icebergs off the Spitzbergen coast, only that the icebergs *could* melt or explode when their time came, and the time was never known when the Hautton service could be moved to anger or melt to any sunshine whatever. At least, whether their maids or their mother ever beheld the first of the phenomena, far be it from me to say, but the world never saw either.

"Well, Miss Montolieu, how do you like our life here?" Carruthers was asking. "Which is preferable —Belgravia or St. Denis?"

"Oh, Belgravia, decidedly," laughed Lady Marabout's charge. "I think your life charming. All change, excitement, gaiety, who would not like it?"

"Nobody—that is not fresh to it!"

"Fresh to it? Ah! are you one of the class who find no beauty in anything unless it is new? If so, do not charge the blame on to the thing, as your tone implies; take it rather to yourself and your own fickleness."

"Perhaps I do," smiled Carruthers. "But whether oneself or 'the thing' is to blame, the result's much the same—satiety! Wait till you have had two or three seasons, and then tell me if you find this mill-wheel routine, these circus gyrations, so delightful! We are the performing stud, who go round and round in the hippodrome, day after day for show, till we are sick of the whole programme, knowing our white stars are but a daub of paint, and our gay spangles only tinfoil. You are a little pony just joined to the troupe, and just pleased with the glitter of the arena. Wait till you've had a few years of it before you say whether going through the same hoops and passing over the same sawdust is so very amusing."

"If I do not, I shall desert the troupe, and form a circus of my own less mechanical and more enjoyable."

"*Il faut souffrir pour être belle, il faut souffrir encore plus pour être à la mode!*" said Goodwood, on her right, while Lady Egidia Hautton thought, "How bold that little Montolieu is!" and her sister, Lady Feodorowna, wondered what her cousin Goodwood *could* see there.

"I do not see the necessity," interrupted Flora, "and I certainly would never bow to the 'il faut.' I would make fashion follow me; I would not follow fashion." ("That child talks as though she were the Duchess of Amandine," thought Lady Marabout, catching fragmentary portions across the table, the Marabout oral and oracular organs being always conveniently multiplied when she was armed cap-à-pie as a chaperone.) "Sir Philip, you talk as if you belonged to the 'nothing-is-new, and nothing-is-true, and it-don't-signify' class. I should have thought you were above the nil admirari affectation."

"He admires, as we all do, when we find something that compels our homage," said Goodwood, with an emphasis that would have made the hearts of any of the Hereditary Princesses palpitate with gratification, but at which the ungrateful Petit Caporal only glanced at him a little surprisedly with her large hazel eyes, as though she by no means saw the point of the speech.

Carruthers laughed:

"Nil admirari? Oh no. I enjoy life, but then it is thanks to the clubs, my yacht, my cigar-case, my stud, a thousand things,—not thanks at all to Belgravia."

"Complimentary to the Belgraviennes!" cried Flora, with a shrug of her shoulders. "They have not known how to amuse you, then?"

"Ladies never *do* amuse us!" sighed Carruthers. "*Tant pis pour nous!*"

"Are you going to Lady Patchouli's this evening?" asked Goodwood.

"I believe we are. I think Lady Marabout said so."

"Then I shall exert myself, and go too. It will be a terrible bore—balls always are. But to waltz with *you* I will try to encounter it!"

Flora Montolieu arched her eyebrows, and gave him a little disdainful glance.

"Lord Goodwood, do not be so sure that I shall waltz at all with you. If *you* take vanity for wit, *I* cannot accept discourtesy as compliment!"

"Well hit, little lady!" thought Carruthers, with a mental bravissima.

"What a speech!" thought Lady Marabout, across the table, as shocked as though a footman had dropped a cascade of iced hock over her.

"You got it for once, Goodwood," laughed Carruthers, as they drove away in his tilbury. "You never had such a sharp brush as that."

"By Jove, no! Positively it was quite a new sensation—refreshing, indeed! One grows so tired of the women who agree with one eternally. She's charming, on my word. Who *is* she, Phil? In an heraldic sense, I mean."

"My dear child, what could possess you to answer Lord Goodwood like that?" cried Lady Marabout, as her barouche rolled down Palace Gardens.

"Possess me? The Demon of Mischief, I suppose."

"But, my love, it was a wonderful compliment from him!"

"Was it? I do not see any compliment in those vain impertinent, Brummelian amour-propreisms. I must coin the word, there is no good one to express it."

"But, my dear Flora, you know he is the Marquis of Goodwood, the Duke of Doncaster's son! It is not as if he were a boy in the Lancers, or an unfledged *petit maître* from the Foreign Office——"

"Were he her Majesty's son, he should not gratify his vanity at my expense! If he expected me to be flattered by his condescension, he mistook me very much. He has been allowed to adopt that tone, I suppose; but from a man to a woman a chivalrous courtesy is due, though the man be an emperor."

"Perhaps so—of course; but that *is* their tone now-a-days, my love, and you cannot alter it. I always say the Regency-men inaugurated it, and their sons and grandsons out-Herod Herod. But to turn a tide, or to be a wit with impunity, a woman wants to occupy a prominent and unassailable position. Were you the Duchess of Amandine you might say that sort of thing, but a young girl just out *must not*—indeed she must not! The Hauttons heard you, and the Hauttons are very merciless people; perfectly bred themselves, and pitiless on the least infringement of the convenances. Besides, ten to one you may have gained Goodwood's ill will; and he is a man whose word has immense weight, I assure you."

"I do not see anything remarkable in him to give him weight," said the literal and unimpressible little Montolieu. "He is a commonplace person to my taste, neither so brilliant nor so handsome by a great deal as many gentlemen I see—as Philip, for instance, Lady Marabout?"

"As my son? No, my love, he is not; very few men have Philip's talents and person," said Lady Marabout, consciously mollified and propitiated, but going on, nevertheless with a Spartan impartiality highly laudable. "Goodwood's rank, however, is much higher than Philip's (at least it stands so, though really the Carruthers are by far the older, dating as far back as Ethelbert II., while the Doncaster family are literally unknown till the fourteenth century, when Gervaise d'Ascotte received the acolade before Ascalon from Godfrey de Bouillon); Goodwood *has* great weight, my dear, in the best circles. A compliment from him is a great compliment to any woman, and the sort of answer you gave him——"

"Must have been a great treat to him, dear Lady Marabout, if every one is in the habit of kow-towing before him. Princes, you know, are never so happy as when they can have a little bit of nature; and my speech must have been as refreshing to Lord Goodwood as the breath of his Bearnese breezes and the freedom of his Pyrenean forests were to Henri Quatre after the court etiquette and the formal ceremonial of Paris."

"I don't know about its being a treat to him, my dear; it was more likely to be a shower-bath. And your illustration isn't to the point. The Bearnese breezes were Henri Quatre's native air, and might be pleasant to him; but the figurative ones are not Goodwood's, and I am sure cannot please him."

"But, Lady Marabout, I do not want to please him!" persisted the young lady, perversely. "I don't care in the least what he thinks, or what he says of me!"

"Dear me, how oddly things go!" thought Lady Marabout. "There was Valencia, one of the proudest girls in England, his equal in every way, an acknowledged beauty, who would have said the dust on the trottoir was diamonds, and worn turquoises on azureline, or emeralds on rose, I verily believe, if such opticisms and gaucheries had been Goodwood's taste; and here is this child—for whom the utmost one can do will be to secure a younger son out of the Civil Service, or a country member—cannot be made to see that he is of an atom more importance than Soames or Mason, and treats him with downright nonchalant indifference. What odd anomalies one sees in everything!"

"Who *is* that young lady with you this season?" Lady Hautton asked, smiling that acidulated smile with which that amiable saint always puts long questions to you of which she knows the answer would be *peine forte et dure.* "Not the daughter of that horrid John Montolieu, who did all sorts of dreadful things, and was put into a West India regiment! Indeed! that man? Dear me! Married the sister of your incumbent at Fernditton? Ah, really!—very singular! But how do you come to have brought out the daughter?"

At all of which remarks Lady Marabout winced, and felt painfully guilty of a gross democratic dereliction from legitimate and beaten paths, conscious of having sinned heavily in the eyes of the world and Lady Hautton, by bringing within the sacred precincts of Belgravia the daughter of a *mauvais sujet* in a West India corps, and a sister of a perpetual curate. The world was a terrible dragon to Lady Marabout; to her imagination it always appeared an incarnated and omniscient bugbear, Argus-eyed, and with all its hundred eyes relentlessly fixed on her, spying out each item of her short-comings, every little flaw in the Marabout diamonds, any spur-made tear in her Honiton flounces, any crease in her train at a Drawing-room, any lèse-majesté against the royal rule of conventionalities, any glissade on the polished oak floor of society, though like a good many other people she often worried herself needlessly; the flaws, tears, creases, high treasons, and false glissades being fifty to one too infinitesimal or too unimportant to society for one of the hundred eyes (vigilant and unwinking though I grant they are) to take note of them. The World was a terrible bugbear to Lady Marabout, and its special impersonation was Anne Hautton. She disliked Anne Hautton; she didn't esteem her; she knew her to be a narrow, censorious, prejudiced, and strongly malicious lady; but she was the personification of the World to Lady Marabout, and had weight and terror in consequence. Lady Marabout is not the first person who has burnt incense and bowed in fear before a little miserable clay image she cordially despised, for no better reason—for the self-same reason, indeed.

"She evidently thinks I ought not to have brought Flora out; and perhaps I shouldn't; though, poor little thing, it seems very hard she may not enjoy society—fitted for society, too, as she is—just because her father is in a West India regiment, and poor Lilla was only a clergyman's daughter. Goodwood really seems to admire her. I can never forgive him for his heartless flirtation with Valencia; but if he *were* to be won by a Montolieu, what would the Hauttons say?"

And sitting against the wall, with others of her sisterhood, at a ball, a glorious and golden vision rose up before Lady Marabout's eyes.

If the unknown, unwelcome, revolutionary little Montolieu should go in and win where the Lady Hauttons had tried and failed through five seasons—if this little tropical flower should be promoted to the Doncaster conservatory, where all the stately stephanotises of the peerage had vainly aspired to bloom—if this Petit Caporal should be crowned with the Doncaster diadem, that all the legitimate rulers had uselessly schemed to place on their brows! The soul of Lady Marabout rose elastic at the bare prospect—it would be as great a triumph for a chaperone as for a general to conquer a valuable position with a handful of boy recruits.

If it *should* be! Anne Hautton would have nothing to say after *that!*

And Lady Marabout, though she was the most amiable lady in Christendom, was not exempt from a feeling of longing for a stone to roll to the door of her enemy's stronghold, or a flourish of trumpets to silence the boastful and triumphant *fanfare* that was perpetually sounding at sight of her defeats, from her opponent's ramparts.

Wild, visionary, guiltily scheming, sinfully revolutionary seemed such a project in her eyes. Still, how tempting! It would be a terrible blow to Valencia, who'd tried for Goodwood fruitlessly, to be eclipsed by this unknown Flora; it would be a terrible blow to their Graces of Doncaster, who held nobody good enough, heraldically speaking, for their heir-apparent, to see him give the best coronet in England to a bewitching little interloper, sans money, birth, or rank. "They wouldn't like it, of course; I shouldn't like it for Philip, for instance, though she's a very sweet little thing; all the Ascottes would be very vexed, and all the Valletorts would never forgive it; but it would be *such* a triumph over Anne Hautton!" pondered Lady Marabout, and the last clause carried the day. Did you ever know private pique fail to carry the day over public charity?

And Lady Marabout glanced with a glow of prospective triumph, which, though erring to her Order, was delicious to her individuality, at Goodwood waltzing with the little Montolieu a suspicious number of times, while Lady Egidia Hautton was condemned to his young brother, Seton Ascotte, and Lady Feodorowna danced positively with nobody better than their own county member, originally a scion of Goodwood's bankers! Could the force of humiliation further go? Lady Hautton sat smiling and chatting, but the tiara on her temples was a figurative thorn crown, and Othello's occupation was gone. When a lady's daughters are dancing with an unavailable *cadet* of twenty, and a parvenu, only acceptable in the last extremities of despair, what good is it for her to watch the smiles and construe the attentions?

"We shall see who triumphs now," thought Lady Marabout, with a glow of pleasure, for which her heart reproached her a moment afterwards. "It is very wrong," she thought; "if those poor girls don't marry, one ought to pity them; and as for her—going through five seasons, with a fresh burden of responsibility leaving the school-room, and added on your hands each year, *must* sour the sweetest temper; it would do mine, I am sure. I dare say, if I had had daughters, I should have been ten times more worried even than I am."

Which she would have been, undoubtedly, and the eligibles on her visiting-list ten times more too! Men wouldn't have voted the Marabout dinners and soirée's so pleasant as they did, under the sway of that sunshiny hostess, if there had been Lady Maudes and Lady Marys to exact attention, and lay mines under the Auxerre carpets, and man-traps among the épergne flowers of Lowndes-square. Nor would Lady Marabout have been the same; the sunshine couldn't have shone so brightly, nor the milk of roses flowed so mildly under the weight and wear of marriageable but unmarried daughters; the sunshine would have been fitful, the milk of roses curdled at best. And no wonder! Those poor women! they have so much to go through in the world, and play but such a monotonous rôle, taken at its most brilliant and best, from first to last, from cradle to grave, from the berceaunettes in which they commence their existence to the mausoleum in which they finish it. If they *do* get a little bit soured when they have finished their own game, and have to sit at the card-tables, wide awake, however weary, vigilant however drowsy, alert however bored to death, superintending the hands of the fresh players, surreptitiously suggesting means for securing the tricks, keeping a dragon's eye out for revokes, and bearing all the brunt of the blame if the rubber be lost—if they do get a little bit soured, who can, after all, greatly wonder?

"That's a very brilliant little thing, that girl Montolieu," said Goodwood, driving over to Hornsey Wood, the morning after, with Carruthers and some other men, in his drag.

"A deuced pretty waltzer!" said St. Lys, of the Bays; "turn her round in a square foot."

"And looks very well in the saddle; sits her horse better than any woman in the Ride, except Rosalie Rosière, and as she came from the Cirque Olympique originally, one don't count *her*," said Fulke Nugent. "I *do* like a woman to ride well, I must say. I promised your mother to take a look at the Marabout Yearlings Sale, Phil, if ever I wanted the never-desirable and ever-burdensome article she has to offer, and if anything could tempt me to pay the price she asks, I think it would be that charming Montolieu."

"She's the best thing Lady Tattersall ever had on hand," said Goodwood, drawing his whip over his off-wheeler's back. "You know, Phil—gently, gently,

Coronet!—what spoilt your handsome cousin was, as I said, that it was all mechanism; perfect mechanism, I admit, but all artificial, prearranged, put together, wound up to smile in this place, bow in that, and frown in the other; clockwork every inch of it! Now —so-ho, Zouave! confound you, *won't* you be quiet? —little Montolieu hasn't a bit of artifice about her: 'tisn't only that you don't know what she's going to say, but that *she* doesn't either; and whether it's a smile or a frown, a jest or a reproof, it's what the moment brings out, not what's planned beforehand."

"The hard hit you had the other day seems to have piqued your interest," said Carruthers, smoothing a loose leaf of his Manilla."

"Naturally. The girl didn't care a button about my compliment (I only said it to try her), and the plucky answer she gave me amused me immensely. Anything unartificial and frank is as refreshing as hock-and-seltzer after a field-day—one likes it, don't you know?"

"Wonderfully eloquent you are, Goody. If you come out like that in St. Stephen's, we shan't know you, and the ministerialists will look down in the mouth with a vengeance!"

"Don't be satirical, Phil! If I admire Mademoiselle Flora, what is it to you, pray?"

"Nothing at all," said Carruthers, with unnecessary rapidity of enunciation.

"My love, what are you going to wear to-night? The Bishop of Bonviveur is coming. He was a college friend of your poor uncle's; knew your dear mother before she married. I want you to look your very best and charm him, as you certainly do most people," said Lady Marabout. Adroit intriguer! The bishop was going, sans doute; the bishop loved good wine, good dinners, and good society, and found all three in Lowndes-square, but the bishop was entirely unavailable for purposes matrimonial, having had three wives, and being held tight in hand by a fourth; however, a bishop is a convenient piece to cover your king, in chess, and the bishop served admirably just then in Lady Marabout's moves as a *locum tenens* for Goodwood. Flora Montolieu, in her innocence, made herself look her prettiest for her mother's old friend, and Flora Montolieu was conveniently ready, looking her prettiest, for her chaperone's Pet Eligible, when Goodwood—who hated to dine anywhere in London except at the clubs, the Castle, or the Guards' mess, and was as difficult to get for your dinners as birds'-nests soup or Tokay pur—entered the Marabout drawing-rooms.

"Anne Hautton will see he dined here to-night, in the *Morning Post* to-morrow morning, and she will know Flora must attract him very unusually. What *will* she, and Egidia, and Feodorowna say?" thought Lady Marabout, with a glow of pleasure, which she was conscious was uncharitable and sinful, and yet couldn't repress, let her try how she might.

In scheming for the future Duke of Doncaster for John Montolieu's daughter, she felt much as democratically and treasonably guilty to her order as a Prince of the blood might feel heading a Chartist émeute; but then, suppose the Chartist row was that Prince's sole chance of crushing an odious foe, as it was the only chance for her to humiliate the Hautton, don't you think it might look tempting? Judge nobody, my good sir, till you've been in similar circumstances yourself—a golden rule, which might with advantage employ those illuminating colours with which ladies employ so much of their time just now. Remembering it, they might hold their white hands from flinging those sharp flinty stones, that surely suit them so ill, and that soil their fingers in one way quite as much as they soil the victim's bowed head in another? Illuminate the motto, mesdames and demoiselles! Perhaps you *will* do that —on a smalt ground, with a gold Persian arabasque round, and impossible flowers twined in and out of the letters; but, *remember* it!—pardon! It were asking too much.

"My dear Philip, did you notice how very marked Goodwood's attentions were to Flora last night?" asked Lady Marabout, the morning after, in one of her most sunshiny and radiant moods, as Carruthers paid her his general matutinal call in her boudoir.

"Marked?"

"Yes, marked! Why do you repeat it in that tone? If they *were* marked, there is nothing to be ridiculed that I see. They were very marked indeed, especially for him; he's such an unimpressible, never-show-anything man. I wonder you did not notice it!"

"My dear mother!" said Carruthers, a little impatiently, brushing up the Angora cat's ruff the wrong way with his cane, "do you suppose I pass my evenings noticing the attentions other men may see fit to pay to young ladies?"

"Well—don't be impatient. You never used to be," said Lady Marabout. "If you were in my place just for a night or two, or any other chaperone's, you'd be more full of pity. But people never *will* sympathise with anything that doesn't touch themselves. The only chord that strikes the key-note in anybody is the chord that sounds 'self;' and that is the reason why the world is as full of crash and tumult as Beethoven's 'Storm.'"

"Quite right, my dear mother!"

"Of course it's quite right. I always think you have a great deal of sympathy for a man, Philip, even for people you don't harmonise with—(you could sympathise with that child Flora, yesterday, in her rapturous delight at seeing that Coccoloba Uvifera in the Patchouli conservatory, because it reminded her of her West Indian home, and you care nothing whatever about flowers, nor yet about the West Indies, I should suppose)—but you never will sympathise with me. You know how many disappointments and grievances and vexations of every kind I have had the last ten, twenty, ay, thirty, forty seasons—ever since I had to chaperone your Aunt Eleanore, almost as soon as I was married, and was worried, more than anybody ever *was* worried, by her coquetries and her inconsistencies and her vacillations—so badly as she married, too, at the last! Those flirting beauties so often do; they throw away a hundred admirable chances and put up with a wretched *dernier ressort;*—let a thousand salmon break away from the line out of their carelessness, and end by being glad to land a little minnow. I don't know when I *haven't* been worried by chaperoning. Flora Montolieu is a great anxiety, a great difficulty, little detrimental that she is!"

"Detrimental! What an odd word you choose for her."

"I don't choose it for her; she *is* it," returned Lady Marabout, decidedly.

"How so?"

"How so! Why, my dear Philip, I told you the very first day she came. How so! when she is John Montolieu's daughter, when she has no birth to speak of, and not a farthing to her fortune."

"If she were Jack Ketch's daughter you could not speak much worse. Her high-breeding might do credit to a Palace; I only wish one found it in all Palaces! and I never knew you before measure people by their money."

"My dear Philip, no more I do. I can't bear you when you speak in that tone; it's so hard and sarcastic, and unlike you. *I* don't know what you mean either. I should have thought a man of the world like yourself knew well enough what I intend when I say Flora is a detrimental. She has a sweet temper, very clever, very lively, very charming, as any one knows by the number of men that crowd about her, but a detrimental she is——"

"Poor little heart!" muttered Carruthers in his beard, too low for his mother to hear.

"——And yet I am quite positive that if she herself act judiciously, and it is well managed for her, Goodwood may be won before the season is over," concluded Lady Marabout.

Carruthers, not feeling much interest, it is presumed, in the exclusively feminine pursuit of matchmaking, returned no answer, but played with Bijou's silver bells, and twisted his own tawny moustaches.

"I am quite positive it *may be*, if properly managed,"

reiterated Lady Marabout. "You might second me a little, Philip."

"*I?* Good Heavens! my dear mother, what are you thinking of? I would sooner turn torreador, and throw lassos over bulls at Madrid, than help you to fling nuptial cables over poor devils in Belgravia. Twenty to one! I'm going to the Yard to look at a bay filly of Cope Fielden's, and then on to a mess-luncheon of the Bays."

"Must you go?" said his mother, looking lovingly on him. "You look tired, Philip. Don't you feel well?"

"Perfectly; but Cambridge had us out over those confounded Wormwood Scrubs this morning, and three hours in this June sun, in our harness, makes one swear. If it were a sharp brush, it would put life into one; as it is, it only inspires one with an intense suffering from boredom, and an intense desire for hock-and-seltzer."

"I am very glad you haven't a sharp brush, as you call it, for all that," said Lady Marabout. "It might be very pleasant to you, Philip, but it wouldn't be quite so much so to me. I wish you would stay to luncheon."

"Not to-day, thanks; I have so many engagements."

"You have been very good in coming to see me this season—even better than usual. It *is* very good of you, with all your amusements and distractions. You have given me a great many days this month," said Lady Marabout, gratefully. "Anne Hautton sees nothing of Hautton, she says, except at a distance in Pall-Mall or the Park, all the season through. Fancy if I saw no more of you! Do you know, Philip, I am almost reconciled to your never marrying. I have never seen anybody I should like at all for you, unless you had chosen Cecil Ormsby—Cecil Cheveley I mean; and I am sure I should be very jealous of your wife if you had one. I couldn't help it."

"Rest tranquil, my dear mother; you will never be put to the test!" said Carruthers, with a laugh, as he bid her good morning.

"Perhaps it *is* best he shouldn't marry: I begin to think so," mused Lady Marabout, as the door closed on him. "I used to wish it very much for some things. He is the last of his name, and it seems a pity; there ought to be an heir for Deepdene; but still marriage *is* such a lottery (he is right enough there, though I don't admit it to him: it's a tombola where there is one prize to a million of blanks; one can't help seeing that, though, on principle, I never allow it to him or any of his men), and if Philip had any woman who didn't appreciate him, or didn't understand him, or didn't make him happy, how wretched *I* should be! I have often pictured Philip's wife to myself, I have often idealised a sort of woman I should like to see him marry, but it's very improbable I shall ever meet my ideal realised; one never does! And, after all, whenever I have fancied, years ago, he *might* be falling in love, I have always felt a horrible dread lest she shouldn't be worthy of him—a jealous fear of her that I could not conquer. It's much better as it is; there is no woman good enough for him."

With which compliment to Carruthers at her sex's expense Lady Marabout returned to weaving her pet projected toils for the ensnaring of Goodwood, for whom also, if asked, I dare say the Duchess of Doncaster would have averred on *her* part, looking through *her* maternal Claude glasses, no woman was good enough either. When ladies have daughters to marry, men always present to their imaginations a battalion of worthless, decalogue-smashing, utterly unreliable individuals, amongst whom there is not one fit to be trusted or fit to be chosen; but when their sons are the candidates for the holy bond, they view all women through the same foggy and non-embellishing medium, which, if it does not speak very much for their unprejudiced discernment, at least speaks to the oft-disputed fact of the equality of merit in the sexes, and would make it appear that, in vulgar parlance, there must be six of the one and half a dozen of the other.

"Flora, soft and careless, and rebellious as she looks, *is* ambitious, and has set her heart on winning Goodwood, I do believe, as much as ever poor Valencia did. True she takes a different plan of action, as Philip would call it, and treats him with gay, nonchalante indifference, which certainly seems to pique him more than ever my poor niece's beauty and quiet deference to his opinions did; but that is because she reads him better, and knows more cleverly how to rouse him. She has set her heart on winning Goodwood, I am certain, ambitious as it seems. How eagerly she looked out for the Blues yesterday at that Hyde Park inspection—though I am sure Goodwood does not look half so handsome as Philip does in harness, as they call it; Philip is so much the finer man! I will just sound her to-day—or to-night as we come back from the Opera," thought Lady Marabout, one morning.

Things were moving to the very best of her expectations. Learning experience from manifold failures, Lady Marabout had laid her plans this time with a dexterity that defied discomfiture: seconded by both the parties primarily necessary to the accomplishment of her manœuvres, with only a little outer-world opposition to give it piquancy and excitement, she felt that she might defy the fates to checkmate her here. This should be her Marathon and Lemnos, which, simply reverted to, should be sufficient to secure her immunity from the attacks of any feminine Xantippus who should try to rake up her failures and tarnish her glory. To win Goodwood with a nobody's daughter would be a feat as wonderful in its way as for Miltiades to have passed "in a single day and with a north wind," as Oracle exacted, to the conquest of the Pelasgian Isles; and Lady Marabout longed to do it, as you, my good sir, may have longed in your day to take a king in check with your only available pawn, or win one of the ribands of the turf with a little filly that seemed to general judges scarcely calculated to be in the first flight at the Chester Consolation Scramble.

Things were beautifully in train; it even began to dawn on the perceptions of the Hauttons, usually very slow to open to anything revolutionary and unwelcome. Her Grace of Doncaster, a large, lethargic, somnolent dowager, rarely awake to anything but the interests and restoration of the old ultra-Tory party in a Utopia always dreamed of and never realised, like many other Utopias political and poetical, public and personal, had turned her eyes on Flora Montolieu, and asked her son the question inevitable, "*Who* is she?" to which Goodwood had replied with a devil-may-care recklessness and a headlong indefiniteness which grated on her Grace's ears, and imparted her no information whatever: "One of Lady Tattersall's yearlings, and the most charming creature *I* ever met. You know that? Why did you ask me, then? You know all I do, and all I care to do!"—a remark that made the Duchess wish her very dear and personal friend, Lady Marabout, were comfortably and snugly interred in the mausoleum at Fernditton, rather than alive in the flesh in Belgravia, chaperoning young ladies whom nobody knew, and who were not to be found in any of Sir E. Burke's triad of volumes.

Belgravia, and her sister Mayfair, wondered at it, and talked over it, raked the parental Montolieu lineage mercilessly, and found out, from the Bishop of Bonviveur and Sauceblanche, that the uncle on the distaff side had been only a Tug at Eton, and had lived and died at Fernditton a perpetual curate and nothing else—not even a dean, not even a rector! Goodwood *couldn't* be serious, settled the coteries. But the more hints, innuendoes, questions, and adroitly concealed but simply suggested animadversion Lady Marabout received, the greater was her glory, the warmer her complacency, when she saw her Little Montolieu, who was not little at all, leading, as she undoubtedly did lead, the most desired eligible of the day captive in her chains, sent bouquets by him, begged for waltzes by him, followed by him at the Ride, riveting his lorgnon at the Opera, monopolising his attention —though, clever little intriguer, she knew too well how to pique him ever to let him monopolise hers.

"She certainly makes play, as Philip would call it,

admirably with Goodwood," said Lady Marabout, admiringly, at a morning party, stirring a cup of Orange Pekoe, yet with a certain irrepressible feeling that she should almost prefer so very young a girl not to be quite so adroit a schemer at seventeen. "That indifference and nonchalance is the very thing to pique and retain such a courted fastidious creature as Goodwood; and she knows it, too. Now a clumsy casual observer might even fancy that she liked some others—even you, Philip, for instance—much better; she talks to you much more, appeals to you twice as often, positively teases you to stop and lunch or come to dinner here, and really told you the other night at the Opera she missed you when you didn't come in the morning; but to anybody who knows anything of the world, it is easy enough to see which way her inclinations (yes, I *do* hope it is inclination as well as ambition—I am not one of those who advocate pure *mariages de convenance;* I don't think them right, indeed, though they are undoubtedly very expedient sometimes) turn. I do not think *anybody* ever could prove me to have erred in my quick-sightedness in those affairs. I may have been occasionally mistaken in other things, or been the victim of adverse and unforeseen circumstances which were beyond my control, and betrayed me; but I know no one can read a girl's heart more quickly and surely than I, or a man's either, for that matter."

"Oh, we all know you are a clairvoyante in heart episodes, my dear mother; they are the one business of your life!" smiled Carruthers, sitting down his ice, and lounging across the lawn to a group of cedars, where Flora Montolieu stood playing at croquet, and who, like a scheming adventuress as she was, immediately verified Lady Marabout's words, and piqued Goodwood à outrance by avowing herself tired of the game, and entering with animated verve into the prophecies for Ascot with Carruthers, whose bay filly Sunbeam, sister to Wild-Falcon, was entered to run for the Queen's Cup.

"What an odd smile that was of Philip's," thought Lady Marabout, left to herself and her Orange Pekoe. "He has been very intimate with Goodwood ever since they joined the Blues, cornets together, three-and-twenty years ago; surely he can't have heard him drop anything that would make him fancy he was *not serious?*"

An idle fear, which Lady Marabout dismissed contemptuously from her mind when she saw how entirely Goodwood—in defiance of the Hautton's sneer, the drowsy Duchess's unconcealed frown, all the comments sure to be excited in feminine minds, and all the chaff likely to be elicited from masculine lips at the mess-table, and in the U. S., and in the Guards' box before the curtain went up for the ballet—vowed himself to the service of the little detrimental throughout that morning party, and spoke a temporary adieu, whose tenderness, if she did not exactly catch, Lady Marabout could at least construe, as he pulled up the tiger-skin over Flora's dainty dress, before the Marabout carriage rolled down the Fulham-road to town. At which tenderness of farewell Carruthers—steeled to all such weaknesses himself—gave a disdainful glance and a contemptuous twist of his moustaches, as he stood by the door talking to his mother.

"You too, Phil?" said Goodwood, with a laugh, as the carriage rolled away.

Carruthers stared at him haughtily, as he will stare at his best friends if they touch his private concerns more nearly than he likes; a stare which said disdainfully, "I don't understand you," and thereby told the only lie to which Carruthers ever stooped in the whole course of his existence.

Goodwood laughed again.

"If you poach on my manor *here*, I shall kill you, Phil; so *gare à vous!*"

"You are in an enigmatical mood to-day! I can't say I see much wit in your riddles," said Carruthers, with his grandest and most contemptuous air, as he lit his Havannah.

"Confound that fellow! I'd rather have had any other man in London for a rival! Twenty and more years ago how he cut me out with that handsome Virginie Pcauderose, that we were both such mad boys after in Paris. However, it will be odd if *I* can't win the day here. A Goodwood rejected—pooh! There isn't a woman in England that would do it!" thought Goodwood, as he drove down the Fulham-road.

"'*His* manor!' Who's told him it's his? And if it be, what is that to me?" thought Carruthers, as he got into his tilbury. "Philip, *you're* not a fool, like the rest of them, I hope? You've not forsworn yourself surely? Pshaw!—nonsense!—impossible!"

"Certainly she *has* something very charming about her. If I were a man I don't think I could resist her," thought Lady Marabout, as she sat in her box in the grand tier, tenth from the Queen's, moving her fan slowly, lifting her lorgnon now and then, listening vaguely to the music of the second act of the "Barbiere," for probably about the two hundredth time in her life, and looking at Flora Montolieu, sitting opposite to her.

"The women are eternally asking me who she is. I don't care a hang *who*, but she's the prettiest thing in London," said Fulke Nugent, which was the warmest praise that any living man about town remembered to have heard fall from his lips, which limited themselves religiously to one legitimate laudation, which is a superlative now-a-days, though Mr. Lindley Murray, if alive, wouldn't, perhaps, receive or recognise it as such: "Not bad-looking."

"It isn't *who* a woman is, it's *what* she is, that's the question, I take it," said Goodwood, as he left the Guards' box to visit the Marabout.

"By George!" laughed Nugent to Carruthers, "Goody must be serious, eh, Phil? He don't care a button for little Bibi; he don't care even for Zerlina. When the ballet begins I verily believe he's thinking less of the women before him than of the woman who has left the house; and if a fellow can give more ominous signs of being 'serious,' as the women phrase it, I don't know 'em, do you?"

"I don't know much about that sort of thing at all!" muttered Carruthers, as he went out to follow Goodwood to the Marabout box.

That is an old, old story, that of the fair Emily stirring feud between Palamon and Arcite. It has been acted out many a time since Beaumont and Fletcher lived and wrote their twin-thoughts and won their twin-laurels; but the bars that shut the kinsmen in their prison-walls, the ivy-leaves that filled in the rents of their prison-stones, were not more entirely and blissfully innocent of the feud going on within, and the battle foaming near them, than the calm, complacent soul of Lady Marabout was of the rivalry going on close beside her for the sake of little Montolieu.

She certainly thought Philip made himself specially brilliant and agreeable that night; but then that was nothing new, he was famous for talking well, and liked his mother enough not seldom to shower out for her some of his very best things; certainly she thought Goodwood did not shine by the contrast, and looked, to use an undignified word, rather cross than otherwise; but then nobody *did* shine beside Philip, and she knew a reason that made Goodwood pardonably cross at the undesired presence of his oldest and dearest chum. Even *she* almost wished Philip away. If the presence of her idolised son could have been unwelcome to her at any time, it was so that night.

"It isn't like Philip to monopolise her so, he who has so much tact usually, and cares nothing for girls himself," thought Lady Marabout; "he must do it for mischief, and yet *that* isn't like him at all; it's very tiresome, at any rate."

And with that skilful diplomacy in such matters, on which, if it was sometimes overthrown, Lady Marabout not unjustly plumed herself, she dexterously entangled Carruthers in conversation, and during the crash of one of the choruses, whispered, as he bent forward to pick up her fan, which she had let drop,

"Leave Flora a little to Goodwood; he has a right —he spoke decisively to her to-day."

Carruthers bowed his head, and stooped lower for the fan.

He left her accordingly to Goodwood till the curtain fell after the last act of the "Barbiere;" and Lady Marabout congratulated herself on her own adroitness. "There is nothing like a little tact," she thought; "what would society be without the guiding genius of tact, I wonder? One dreadful Donnybrook Fair!"

But, someway or other, despite all her tact, or because her son inherited that valuable quality in a triple measure to herself, someway, it was Goodwood who led her to her carriage, and Carruthers who led the little Montolieu.

"Terribly *bête* of Philip; how very unlike him!" mused Lady Marabout, as she gathered her burnous round her.

Carruthers talked and laughed as he led Flora Montolieu through the passages, more gaily, perhaps, than usual.

"My mother has told me some news to-night, Miss Montolieu," he said, carelessly. "Am I premature in proffering you my congratulations? But even if I be so, you will not refuse the privilege to an old friend—to a very sincere friend—and will allow me to be the first to wish you happiness?"

Lady Marabout's carriage stopped the way. Flora Montolieu coloured, looked full at him, and went to it, without having time to answer his congratulations, in which the keenest-sighted hearer would have failed to detect anything beyond every-day friendship and genuine indifference. The most truthful men will make the most consummate actors when spurred up to it.

"My dear child, you look ill to-night; I am glad you have no engagements," said Lady Marabout, as she sat down before the dressing-room fire, toasting her little satin-shod foot—she has a weakness for fire even in the hottest weather—while Flora Montolieu lay back in a low chair, crushing the roses mercilessly. "You *do* feel well? I should not have thought so, your face looks so flushed, and your eyes so preternaturally dark. Perhaps it is the late hours; you were not used to them in France, of course, and it must be such a change to this life from your unvarying conventual routine at St. Denis. My love, what was it Lord Goodwood said to you to-day?"

"Do not speak to me of him, Lady Marabout, I hate his name!"

Lady Marabout started with an astonishment that nearly upset the cup of coffee she was sipping.

"Hate his name? My dearest Flora, why, in Heaven's name?"

Flora did not answer; she pulled the roses off her hair as though they had been infected with Brinvilliers' poison.

"What has he done?"

"*He* has done nothing!"

"Who has done anything, then?"

"Oh, no one—no one has done anything, but—I am sick of Lord Goodwood's name—tired of it!"

Lady Marabout sat almost speechless with surprise.

"Tired of it, my dear Flora?"

Little Montolieu laughed:

"Well, tired of it, perhaps from hearing him praised so often, as the Athenian trader grew sick of Aristides, and the Jacobin of Washington's name. Is it unpardonably heterodox to say so?"

Lady Marabout stirred her coffee in perplexity:

"My dear child, pray don't speak in that way; that's like Philip's tone when he is enigmatical and sarcastic, and worries me. I really cannot in the least understand you about Lord Goodwood, it is quite incomprehensible to me. I thought I overheard him to-day at Lady George's concert speak very definitely to you indeed, and when he was interrupted by the Duchess before you could give him his reply, I thought I heard him say he should call to-morrow morning to know your ultimate decision. Was I right?"

"Quite right."

"He really proposed marriage to you to-day?"

"Yes."

"And yet you say you are sick of his name?"

"Does it follow, imperatively, Lady Marabout, that because the Sultan throws his handkerchief it must be picked up with humility and thanksgiving?" asked Flora Montolieu, furling and unfurling her fan with an impatient rapidity that threatened entire destruction of its ivory and feathers, with their Watteau-like group elaborately painted on them—as pretty a toy of the kind as could be got for money, which had been given her by Carruthers one day in payment of some little bagatelle of a bet.

"Sultan!—Humility!" repeated Lady Marabout, scarcely crediting her senses. "My dear Flora, do you know what you are saying? You must be jesting! There is not a woman in England who would be insensible to the honour of Goodwood's proposals. You are jesting, Flora!"

"I am not, indeed!"

"You mean to say, you could positively think of *rejecting* him?" cried Lady Marabout, rising from her chair in the intensity of her amazement, convinced that she was the victim of some horrible hallucination.

"Why should it surprise you if I did?"

"*Why?*" repeated Lady Marabout, indignantly. "Do you ask me *why?* You must be a child indeed, or a consummate actress, to put such a question; excuse me, my dear, if I speak a little strongly: you perfectly bewilder me, and I confess I cannot see your motives or your meaning in the least. You have made a conquest such as the proudest women in the peerage have vainly tried to make; you have one of the highest titles in the country offered to you; you have won a man whom everybody declared would never be won; you have done this, pardon me, without either birth or fortune on your own side, and then you speak of rejecting Goodwood—Goodwood, of all the men in England! You cannot be serious, Flora, or, if you are, you must be mad!"

Lady Marabout spoke more hotly than Lady Marabout had ever spoken in all her life. Goodwood absolutely won—Goodwood absolutely "come to the point"—the crowning humiliation of the Hauttons positively within her grasp—her Marathon and Lemnos actually gained! and all to be lost and flung away by the unaccountable caprice of a wayward child! It was sufficient to exasperate a saint, and a saint Lady Marabout never pretended to be.

Flora Montolieu toyed recklessly with her fan.

"You told Sir Philip this evening, I think of——"

"I hinted it to him, my dear—yes. Philip has known all along how much I desired it, and as Goodwood is one of his oldest and most favourite friends, I knew it would give him sincere pleasure both for my sake and Goodwood's, and yours too, for I think Philip likes you as much as he ever does any young girl—better, indeed; and I could not imagine—I could not dream for an instant—that there was any doubt of your acceptation, as, indeed, there *cannot* be. You have been jesting to worry me, Flora!"

Little Montolieu rose, threw her fan aside, as if its ivory stems had been hot iron, and leaned against the mantelpiece.

"You advise me to accept Lord Goodwood, then, Lady Marabout?"

"My love, if you need my advice, certainly!—such an alliance will never be proffered to you again; the brilliant position it will place you in I surely have no need to point out!" returned Lady Marabout. "The little hypocrite!" she mused, angrily, "as if her own mind were not fully made up—as if any girl in Europe would hesitate over accepting the Doncaster coronet—as if a nameless Montolieu could doubt for a moment her own delight at being created Marchioness of Goodwood! Such a triumph as *that*—why I wouldn't credit *any* woman who pretended she wasn't dazzled by it!"

"I thought you did not approve of marriages of convenience?"

Lady Marabout played a tattoo—slightly perplexed tattoo—with her spoon in her Sèvres saucer.

"No more I do, my dear—that is, under some circumstances; it is impossible to lay down a fixed rule for everything! Marriages of convenience—well, perhaps not; but as *I* understand these words, they mean a mere business affair, arranged as they are in France, without the slightest regard to the inclinations of either;

merely regarding whether the incidents of fortune, birth, and station are equal and suitable. Marriages *de convenance* are when a parvenu barters his gold for good blood, or where an *ancienne princesse* mends her fortune with a *nouveau riche*, profound indifference, meanwhile, on each side. I do not call this so; decidedly not! Goodwood must be very deeply attached to you to have forgotten his detestation of marriage, and laid such a title as his at your feet. Have you any idea of the weight of the Dukes of Doncaster in the country? Have you any notion of what their rent-roll is? Have you any conception of their enormous influence, their very high place, the magnificence of their seats? Helmsley almost equals Windsor! All these are yours if you will; and you affect to hesitate——"

"To let Lord Goodwood buy me!"

"Buy you? Your phraseology is as strange as my son's!"

"To accept him only for his coronet and the rent-roll, his position and his Helmsley, seems not a very grateful and flattering return for his preference?"

"I do not see that at all," said Lady Marabout, irritably. Is there anything more annoying than to have unwelcome truths thrust in our teeth? "It is not as though he were odious to you—a hideous man, a coarse man, a cruel man, whose very presence repelled you. Goodwood is a man quite attractive enough to merit some regard, independent of his position, you have an affectionate nature, you would soon grow attached to him——"

Flora Montolieu shook her head.

"And, in fact," she went on, warming with her subject, and speaking all the more determinedly because she was speaking a little against her conscience, and wholly for her inclinations, "my dear Flora, if you need persuasion—which you must pardon me if I doubt your doing in your heart, for I cannot credit any woman as being insensible to the suit of a future Duke of Doncaster, or invulnerable to the honour it does her—if you need persuasion, I should think I need only refer to the happiness it will afford your poor dear mother, amidst her many trials, to hear of so brilliant a triumph for you. You are proud—Goodwood will place you in a position where pride may be indulged with impunity, nay, with advantage. You are ambitious—what can flatter your ambition more than such an offer? You are clever—as Goodwood's wife you may lead society like Madame de Rambouillet, or immerse yourself in political intrigue like the Duchess of Devonshire. It is an offer which places within your reach everything most dazzling and attractive, and it is one, my dear Flora, which you must forgive me if I say a young girl of obscure rank, as rank goes, and no fortune whatever, should pause before she lightly rejects. You cannot afford to be fastidious as if you were an heiress or a lady-in-your-own-right."

That was as ill-natured a thing as the best-natured lady in Christendom ever said on the spur of self-interest, and it stung Flora Montolieu more than her hostess dreamed.

The colour flushed into her face and her eyes flashed:

"You have said sufficient, Lady Marabout. I accept the Marquis to-morrow."

And taking up her fan and her opera-cloak, leaving

the discarded roses unheeded on the floor, she bade her chaperone good night, and floated out of the dressing-room, while Lady Marabout sat stirring the cream in a second cup of coffee, a good deal puzzled, a little awed by the odd turn affairs had taken, with a slight feeling of guilt for her own share in the transaction, an uncomfortable dread lest the day should ever come when Flora should reproach her for having persuaded her into the marriage, a comfortable conviction that nothing but good *could* come of such a brilliant and enviable alliance, and, above all other conflicting feelings, one delicious, dominant, glorified security of triumph over the Hauttons, *mère et filles.*

But when morning dawned, Lady Marabout's horizon seemed cleared of all clouds, and only radiant with unshadowed sunshine. Goodwood was coming, and coming to be accepted.

She seemed already to read the newspaper paragraphs announcing his capture and Flora's conquest, already to hear the Hauttons' enforced congratulations, already to see the nuptial party gathered round the altar-rail of St. George's. Lady Marabout had never felt in a sunnier, more light-hearted mood, never more completely at peace with herself and all the world as she sat in her boudoir at her writing-table, penning a letter which began:

"My dearest Lilla,—What happiness it gives me to congratulate you on the brilliant future opening to your sweet Flora——"

And which would have continued, no doubt, with similar eloquence if it had not been interrupted by

Soames opening the door and announcing "Sir Philip Carruthers," who walked in, touched his mother's brow with his moustaches, and went to stand on the hearth with his arm on the mantelpiece.

"My dear Philip, you never congratulated me last night; pray do so now!" cried Lady Marabout, delightedly, wiping her pen on the pennon, which a small ormolu knight obligingly carried for that useful purpose. Ladies always wipe their pens as religiously as they bolt their bedroom doors, believe in cosmetics, and go to church on a Sunday.

"Was your news of last night true, then?" asked Carruthers, bending forwards to roll Bijou on its back with his foot.

"That Goodwood had spoken definitely to her? Perfectly. He proposed to her yesterday at the Frangipane concert—not *at* the concert of course, but afterwards, when they were alone for a moment in the conservatories. The Duchess interrupted them—did it on purpose—and he had only time to whisper hurriedly he should come this morning to hear his fate. I dare say he felt tolerably secure of it. Last night I naturally spoke to Flora about it. Oddly enough, she seemed positively to think at first of rejecting him—*rejecting* him!—only fancy the madness! Between ourselves, I don't think she cares anything about him, but with such an alliance as that, of course I felt it my bounden duty to counsel her as strongly as I could to accept the unequalled position it proffered her. Indeed, it could have been only a girl's waywardness, a child's caprice to pretend to hesitate, for she *is* very ambitious and very clever, and I would never believe that any woman—and she less than any—would be proof against such dazzling prospects. It would be absurd, you know, Philip. Whether it was hypocrisy or a real reluctance, because she doesn't feel for him the idealic love she dreams of, I don't know, but I put it before her in a way that plainly showed her all the brilliance of the proffered position, and before she bade me good night I had vanquished all her scruples, if she had any, and I am able to say——"

"Good God, what have you done?"

"Done?" re-echoed Lady Marabout, vaguely terrified. "Certainly I persuaded her to accept him. She *has* accepted him probably; he is here now! I should have been a strange person indeed to let any young girl in my charge rashly refuse such an offer."

"You induced her to accept him! God forgive you!"

Lady Marabout turned pale as death, and gazed at him with undefinable terror:

"Philip! You do not mean——"

"Great Heavens! have you never seen, mother——"

He leaned his arms on the marble, with his forehead bowed upon them, and Lady Marabout gazed at him still, as a bird at a basilisk.

"Philip, Philip! what have I done? How could I tell?" she murmured, distractedly, tears welling into her eyes. "If I had only known! But how could I dream that child had any fascination for you? How could I fancy——"

"Hush! No, you are in no way to blame. You could not know it. *I* barely knew it till last night," he answered, gently.

"Philip loves her, and *I* have made her marry Goodwood!" thought Lady Marabout, agonised, remorseful, conscience-struck, heart-broken in a thousand ways at once. The climax of her woes was reached, life had no greater bitterness for her left; her son loved, and loved the last person in England she would have had him love; that woman was given to another, and *she* had been the instrument of wrecking the life to save or serve which she would have laid down her own in glad and instant sacrifice! Lady Marabout bowed her head under a grief, before which the worries so great before, the schemes but so lately so precious, the small triumphs just now so all-absorbing, shrank away into their due insignificance. Philip suffering, and suffering through her! Self glided far away from Lady Marabout's memory then, and she hated herself, more fiercely than the gentle-hearted soul had ever hated any foe, for her own criminal share in bringing down this unforeseen terrific blow on her beloved one's head.

"Philip, my dearest, what *can* I do?" she cried, distractedly; "if I had thought—if I had guessed——"

"Do nothing. A woman who could give herself to a man whom she did not love should be no wife of mine, let me suffer what I might."

"But *I* persuaded her, Philip! Mine is the blame!"

His lips quivered painfully:

"Had she cared for me as—I may have fancied, she had not been so easy to persuade! She has not much force of character, where she wills. He is here now you say; I cannot risk meeting him just yet. Leave me for a little while; leave me—I am best alone."

Gentle though he always was to her, his mother knew him too well ever to dispute his will, and the most bitter tears Lady Marabout had ever known, ready as she was to weep for other people's woes, and rarely as she had had to weep for any of her own, choked her utterance and blinded her eyes as she obeyed and closed the door on his solitude. Philip—her idolised Philip—that ever her house should have sheltered this creature to bring a curse upon him! that ever she should have brought this tropical flower to poison the air for the only one dear to her!

"I am justly punished," thought Lady Marabout, humbly and penitentially—"justly. I thought wickedly of Anne Hautton. I did not do as I would be done by. I longed to enjoy their mortification. I advised Flora against my own conscience and against hers. I am justly chastised! But that *he* should suffer through me, that my fault has fallen on his head, that my Philip, my noble Philip, should love and not be loved, and that *I* have brought it on him——Good Heaven! what is that?"

"That" was a man whom her eyes, being misty with tears, Lady Marabout had brushed against, as she ascended the staircase, ere she perceived him, and who, passing on with a muttered apology, was down in the hall and out of the door Mason held open before she had recovered the shock of the rencontre, much before she had a possibility of recognising him through the mist aforesaid.

A fear, a hope, a joy, a dread, one so woven with another there was no disentangling them, sprang up like a ray of light in Lady Marabout's heart—a possibility dawned in her: to be rejected as an impossibility? Lady Marabout crossed the ante-room, her heart throbbing tumultuously, spurred on to noble atonement and reckless self-sacrifice, if fate allowed them.

She opened the drawing-room door; Flora Montolieu was alone.

"Flora, you have seen Goodwood?"

She turned, her own face as pale and her own eyes as dim as Lady Marabout's.

"Yes."

"You have refused him?"

Flora Montolieu misconstrued her chaperone's eagerness, and answered haughtily enough:

"I have told him that indifference would be too poor a return for his affections to insult him with it, and that I would not do him the injury of repaying his trust by falsehood and deception. I meant what I said to you last night; I said it on the spur of pain, indignation, no matter what; but I could not keep my word when the trial came."

Lady Marabout bent down and kissed her, with a fervent gratitude that not a little bewildered the recipient.

"My dear child! thank God! little as I thought to say so. Flora, tell me, you love some one else?"

"Lady Marabout, you have no right——"

"Yes, I have a right—the strongest right! Is not that other my son?"

Flora Montolieu looked up, then dropped her head and burst into tears—tears that Lady Marabout soothed then, tears that Carruthers soothed, yet more effectually still, five minutes afterwards.

"That *I* should have sued that little Montolieu, and sued to her for Philip!" mused Lady Marabout. "It is very odd. Perhaps I get used to being crossed and disappointed and trampled on in every way and by everybody; but certainly, though it is most contrary to my wishes, though a child like that is the last person I should ever have chosen or dreamt of as Philip's wife, though it is a great pain to me, and Anne Hautton of course will be delighted to rake up everything she can about the Montolieus; and it *is* heart-breaking when one thinks how a Carruthers *might* marry, how the Carruthers always *have* married, rarely any but ladies-in-their-own-right for countless generations, still it *is* very odd, but I certainly feel happier than ever I did in my life, annoyed as I am and grieved as I am. It *is* heart-breaking (that horrid John Montolieu! I wonder what relation one stands in legally to the father of one's son's wife; I will ask Sir Fitzroy Kelly; not that the Montolieus are likely to come to England)—it is very sad when one thinks who Philip might have married; and yet she certainly is infinitely charming, and she really appreciates and understands him. If it were not for what Anne Hautton will always say, I could really be pleased! To think what an anxious hope, what a dreadful ideal, Philip's wife has always been to me; and now, just as I had got reconciled to his determined bachelor preferences, and had grown to agree with him that it was best he shouldn't marry, he goes and falls in love with this child! Everything is at cross-purposes in life, I think! There is only one thing I am resolved upon—I will NEVER chaperone anybody again."

And she kept her vow. None can christen her Lady Tattersall any longer with point, for there are no yearling sales in that house in Lowndes-square, whatever there be in the other domiciles of that fashionable quarter. Lady Marabout has shaken that burden off her shoulders, and moves in blissful solitude and tripled serenity through Belgravia, relieved of responsibility, and wearing her years as lightly, losing the odd trick at her whist as sunnily, and beaming on the world in general as radiantly as any dowager in the English Peerage.

That she was fully reconciled to Carruthers's change of resolve was shown in the fact that when Anne Hautton turned to her, on the evening of his marriage-day, after the dinner to which Lady Marabout had bidden all her friends, and a good many of her foes, with an amiable murmur:

"I am *so* grieved for you, dearest Helena—I know what your disappointment must be!—what should *I* feel if Hautton——Your *belle-fille* is charming, certainly, very lovely; but then—such a connexion! You have my deepest sympathies! I always told you how wrong you were when you fancied Goodwood admired little Montolieu—I beg her pardon, I mean Lady Carruthers—but you *will* give your imagination such reins!"

Lady Marabout smiled, calmly and amusedly, felt no pang, and—thought of Philip.

I take it things must be very rose-coloured with us when we can smile sincerely on our enemies, and defeat their stings simply because we feel them not.

A STUDY A LA LOUIS QUINZE;

or,

PENDANT TO A PASTEL BY LA TOUR.

I HAVE, among others hanging on my wall, a pastel of La Tour's; of the artist-lover of Julie Fel, of the monarch of pastellistes, the touch of whose crayons was a "brevet of wit and of beauty," and on whose easel bloomed afresh the laughing eyes, the brilliant tints, the rose-hued lips of all the loveliest women of the "Règne Galant," from the princesses of the Blood of the House of Bourbon to the princesses of the green-room of the Comédie-Française. Painted in the days of Louis Quinze, the light of more than a century having fallen on its soft colours to fade and blot them with the icy brush of time, my pastel is still fresh, still eloquent. The genius that created it is gone—gone the beauty that inspired it—but the picture is deathless! It shows me the face of a woman, of a beautiful woman, else, be sure she would not have been honoured by the crayons of La Tour; her full southern lips are parted with a smile of triumph; a chef-d'œuvre of coquetry, a headdress of lace and pearls and little bouquets of roses is on her unpowdered hair, which is arranged much like Julie Fel's herself in the portrait that hangs, if I remember right, at the

Musée de Saint Quentin; and her large eyes are glancing at you with languor, malice, victory, all commingled. At the back of the picture is written "Mlle. Thargélie Dumarsais;" the letters are faded and yellow, but the pastel is living and laughing yet, through the divine touch of the genius of La Tour. With its perfume of dead glories, with its odour of the Beau Siècle, the pastel hangs on my wall, living relic of a buried age, and sometimes in my mournful moments the full laughing lips of my pastel will part, and breathe, and speak to me of the distant past, when Thargélie Dumarsais saw all Paris at her feet, and was not humbled then as now by being only valued and remembered for the sake of the talent of La Tour. My beautiful pastel gives me many confidences. I will betray one to you —a single leaf from a life of the eighteenth century.

I.

THE FIRST MORNING.

In the heart of Lorraine, nestled down among its woods, stood an old château that might have been the château of the Sleeping Beauty of fairy fame, so sequestered it stood amidst its trees chained together by fragrant fetters of honeysuckle and wild vine, so undisturbed slept the morning shadows on the wild thyme that covered the turf, so unbroken was the silence in which the leaves barely stirred, and the birds folded their wings and hushed their song till the heat of the noonday should be passed. Beyond the purple hills stretching up in the soft haze of distance in the same province of laughing, luxurious, sunlit Lorraine, was Lunéville, the Lunéville of Stanislaus, of Montesquieu, of Voltaire, of Hénault, of Boufflers, a Versailles in miniature, even possessing a perfect replica of Pompadour in its own pretty pagan of a Marquise. Within a few leagues was Lunéville, but the echo of its mots and madrigals did not reach over the hills, did not profane the sunny air, did not mingle with the vintage-song of the vine-dressers, the silver babble of the woodland brook, the hushed chant of the Ave Maria, the vesper bells chimed from the churches and monasteries, which made the sole music known or heard in this little valley of Lorraine.

The château of Grande Charmille stood nestled in its woods, grey, lonely, still, silent as death, yet not gloomy, for white pigeons circled above its pointed towers, brilliant dragon-flies fluttered above the broken basin of the fountain that sang as gaily as it rippled among the thyme as though it fell into a marble cup, and bees hummed their busy happy buzz among the jessamine that clung to its ivy-covered walls — walls built long before Lorraine had ceased to be a kingdom and a power, long before a craven and effeminated Valois had dared to kick the dead body of a slaughtered Guise. Not gloomy with the golden light of a summer noon playing amidst the tangled boughs and on the silvered lichens; not gloomy, for under the elm-boughs on the broken stone steps that led to the fountain, her feet half buried in violet-roots and wild thyme, leaning her head on her hand, as she looked into the water, where the birds flew down to drink, and fluttered their wings fearless of her presence, was a young girl of sixteen—and if women sometimes darken lives, it must be allowed that they always illumine landscapes!

Aline, when Boufflers saw her in the spring morning, in all the grace of youth and beauty, unconscious of themselves, made not a prettier picture than this young dreamer under the elm-boughs of the Lorraine woods, as she bent over the water, watching it bubble and splash from the fountain-spout, and hide itself with a rippling murmur under the broad green reeds and the leaves of the waterlily. She was a charming picture: a brunette with long ebon tresses, with her lashes drooping over her back, languid, almond-shaped eyes, a smile on her half-pouted lips, and all the innocence and dawning beauty of her sixteen years about her, while she sat on the broken steps, now brushing the water-drops off the violets, now weaving the reeds into a pretty, useless toy, now beckoning the birds that came to peck on the rose-sprays beside her.

"Favette! where are your dreams?"

Favette, the young naïad of the Lorraine elm-woods, looked up, the plait of rushes dropping from her hands, and a warm sudden blush tinging her cheeks and brow with a tint like that on the damask rose-leaves that had fallen into the water, and floated there like delicate shells.

"Mon Dieu, Monsieur Léon! how you frightened me!"

And like a startled fawn, or a young bird glancing round at a rustle amidst the leaves, Favette sprang up, half shy, half smiling, all her treasures gathered from the woods— of flowers, of mosses, of berries, of feathery grasses, long ivy-sprays—falling from her lap on to the turf in unheeded disorder.

"*I* frightened you, Favette! Surely not. Are you sorry to see me, then?"

"Sorry? Oh no, Monsieur Léon!" and Favette

glanced through her thick curled lashes, slyly yet archly, and began to braid again her plait of rushes.

"Come, tell me, then, what and whom were you dreaming of, ma mie, as you looked down into the water? Tell me, Favette. You have no secrets from your playmate, your friend, your brother?"

Favette shook her head, smiling, and plaited her rushes *à tort et à travers*, the blush on her cheeks as bright as that on the cups of the rose-leaves that the wind shook down in a fresh shower into the brook.

"Come, tell me, mignonne. Was it—of me?"

"Of you? Well, perhaps—yes!"

It was first love that whispered in Favette's pretty voice those three little words; it was first love that answered in his, as he threw himself down on the violet-tufted turf at her feet, as Boufflers at Aline's.

"Ah, Favette, so should it be! for every hope, every dream, every thought of *mine*, is centred in and coloured by you."

"Yet you can leave me to-day," pouted Favette, with a sigh and a *moue mutine*, and gathering tears in her large gazelle eyes.

"Leave you? Would to Heaven I were not forced! But against a king's will what power has a subject? None are too great, none are too lowly, to be touched by that iron hand if they provoke its grasp. Vincennes yawns for those who dare to think, For-l'Evêque for those who dare to jest. Monsieur de Voltaire was sent to the Bastille for merely defending a truth and his own honour against De Rohan-Chabot. Who am I, that I should look for better grace?"

Favette struck him with her plaited rushes, a reproachful little blow.

"Monsieur Vincennes—Monsieur Voltaire—who are they? I know nothing of those stupid people!"

He smiled, and fondly stroked her hair.

"Little darling! The one is a prison that manacles the deadly crimes of Free Speech and Free Thought; the other a man who has suffered for both, but loves both still, and will, sooner or later, help to give both to the world——"

"Ah, you think of your studies, of your ambitions, of your great heroes! You think nothing of me, save to call me a little darling. You are cruel, Monsieur Léon!"

And Favette twisted her hand from his grasp with petulant sorrow, and dashed away her tears—the tears of sixteen—as bright and free from bitterness as the water drops on the violet bells.

"*I* cruel—and to you! My heart must indeed be badly echoed by my lips, if you have cause to fancy so a single moment. Cruel to you? Favette, Favette! is a man ever cruel to the dearest thing in his life, the dearest name in his thoughts? If I smiled I meant no sneer; I love you as you are, mignonne; the picture is so fair, one touch added, or one touch effaced, would mar the whole in *my* eyes. I love you as you are! with no knowledge but what the good sisters teach you in their convent solitude, and what the songs of the birds, the voices of the flowers, whisper to you of their woodland lore. I love you as you are! Every morning when I am far away from you, and from Lorraine, I shall think of you gathering the summer roses, calling the birds about you, bending over the fountain to see it mirror your own beauty; every evening I shall think of you leaning from the window, chanting softly to yourself the Ora pro nobis, while the shadows deepen, and the stars we have so often watched together come out above the pine-hills. Favette, Favette! exile will have the bitterness of death to me: to give me strength to bear it, tell me that you love me more dearly than as the brother you have always called me; that you will so love me when I shall be no longer here beside you, but shall have to trust to memory and fidelity to guard for me in absence the priceless treasure of your heart?"

Favette's head drooped, and her hands played nervously with the now torn and twisted braid of rushes: he saw her heart beat under its muslin corsage, like a bee caught and caged in the white leaves of a lily; and she glanced at him under her lashes with a touch of naïve coquetry.

"If I tell you so, what gage have I, Monsieur Léon, that, a few months gone by, you will even remember it? In those magnificent cities you will soon forget Lorraine; with the *grandes dames* of the courts you will soon cease to care for Favette?"

"Look in my eyes, Favette, they alone can answer you as I would answer! Till we meet again none shall supplant you for an hour, none rob you of one thought; you have my first love, you will have my last. Favette, you believe me?"

"Yes—I believe!" murmured Favette, resting her large eyes fondly on him. "We will meet as we part, though you are the swallow, free to take flight over the seas to foreign lands, and I am the violet, that must stay where it is rooted in the Lorraine woods!"

"Accept the augury," he whispered, resting his lips upon her low smooth brow. "Does not the swallow ever return to the violet, holding it fairer than all the gaudy tropical flowers that may have tempted him to rest on the wing and delay his homeward flight? Does not the violet ever welcome him the same, in its timid winning spring-tide loveliness, when he returns to, as when he quitted, the only home he loves? Believe the augury, Favette; we shall meet as we part!"

And they believed the augury, as they believed in life, in love, in faith; they who were beginning all, and had proved none of the treacherous triad!

What had he dreamed of in his solitary ancestral woods fairer than this Lorraine violet, that had grown up with him, side by side, since he, a boy of twelve, gathered heaths from the clefts of the rocks that the little child of six years old cried for and could not reach? What had she seen that she loved half so well as M. le Chevalier from the Castle, whom her uncle, the Curé, held as his dearest and most brilliant pupil, whose eyes always looked so lovingly into hers, and whose voice was always lavishing fond names on his petite Favette?

They believed the augury, and were happy even in the sweet sorrow of parting—sorrow that they had never known before—as they sat together in the morning sunlight, while the water bubbled among the violet tufts, among the grasses and wild thyme, and the dragon-flies fluttered their green and gold and purple wings amidst the tendrils of the vines, and the rose-leaves, drifted gently by the wind, floated down the brook, till they were lost in deepening shadow under the drooping boughs.

II.

THE SECOND MORNING.

"Savez-vous que Favart va écrire une nouvelle comédie—La Chercheuse d'Esprit?"

"Vraiment? Il doit bien écrire cela, car il s'occupe toujours à le *chercher*, et n'arrive jamais à le trouver!"

The mot had true feminine malice, but the lips that spoke it were so handsome, that had even poor Favart himself, the poet-pastrycook who composed operas and comedies while he made méringues and fanfreluches, and dreamed of libretti while he whisked the cream for a supper, been within hearing, they would have taken the smart from the sting; and, as it was, the hit only caused echoes of softly-tuned laughter, for the slightest words of those lips it was the fashion through Paris just then to bow to, applaud, and re-echo.

Before her Psyche, shrouded in cobweb lace, powdered by Martini, gleaming with pearls and emeralds, scented with most delicate amber, making her morning toilette, and receiving her morning levee according to the fashion of the day, sat the brilliant satirist of poor Favart. The *ruelle* was crowded; three marshals, De Richelieu, Lowendal, and Maurice de Saxe; a prince, De Soubise; a poet, Claude Dorat; an abbé, Voisenon; a centenarian, Saint-Aulaire; peers uncounted, De Bièvre, De Caylus, De Villars, D'Etissac, Duras, D'Argenson—a crowd of others—surrounded and superintended her toilette, in a glittering troop of courtiers and gentlemen. Dames d'atours (for she had her maids of honour as well as Marie Leczinska) handed her her flacons of perfume, or her numberless notes on gold salvers, chased by Réveil; the ermine beneath her feet, humbly sent by the Russian ambassador—far superior to what the Czarina sent to Madame de Mailly—had cost two thousand louis; her bedroom outshone in luxury any at Versailles, Choisy, or La Muette, with its Venetian glass, its medallions of Fragonard, its plaques of Sèvres, its landscapes of Watteau, framed in the carved and gilded wainscoting; its Chinese lamps, swinging by garlands of roses; its laughing Cupids, buried under flowers, painted in fresco above the alcove; its hangings of velvet, of silk, of lace; its cabinets, its screens, its bonbonnières, its jewel-boxes, were costly as those of the Marquises de Pompadour or De Prie.

Who was she?—a Princess of the Blood, a Duchess of France, a mistress of the King?

Lords of the chamber obeyed her wishes, ministers signed lettres de cachet, at her instance; "*ces messieurs*," la Queue de la Régence, had their rendezvous at her suppers; she had a country villa that eclipsed Trianon; she had fêtes that outshone the fêtes at Versailles; she had a "*droit de chasse*" in one of the royal districts; she had the first place on the easels of Coypel, Lancret, Pater, Vanloo, La Tour; the first place in the butterfly odes of Crébillon le Gai, Claude Dorat, Voisenon.

Who was she?—the Queen of France? No; much more—the Queen of Paris!

She was Thargélie Dumarsais; matchless as Claire Clairon, beautiful as Madeleine Gaussin, resistless as Sophie Arnould, great as Adrienne Lecouvreur. She was a Power in France—for was she not the Empress of the Comédie? If Madame Lenormand d'Etioles ruled the government at Versailles, Mademoiselle Thargélie Dumarsais ruled the world at Paris; and if the King's favourite could sign her enemies, by a smile, to the Bastille, the Court's favourite could sign hers, by a frown, to For-l'Evêque.

The *foyer* was nightly filled while she played in *Zaïre*, or *Polyeucte*, or *Les Folies Amoureuses*, with a court of princes and poets, marshals and marquises, beaux esprits and abbés galants; and mighty nobles strewed with bouquets the path from her carriage to the coulisses; bouquets that she trod on with nonchalant dignity, as though flowers only bloomed to have the honour of dying under her foot. Louis Quinze smilingly humoured her caprices, content to wait until it was her pleasure to play at his private theatre; dukes, marquises, viscounts, chevaliers, vied who should ruin himself most magnificently and most utterly for her; and lovers the most brilliant and the most flattering, from Richelieu, Roi de Ruelles, to Dorat, poet of boudoir-graces and court-Sapphos, left the titled beauties of Versailles for the self-crowned Empress of the Français. She had all Paris for her clientela, from Versailles to the Caveau; for even the women she deposed, the actors she braved, the journalists she consigned to For-l'Evêque, dared not raise their voice against the idol of the hour. A Queen of France? Bah! Pray what could Marie Leczinska, the pale, dull pietist, singing canticles in her private chapel, compare for power, for sway, for courtiers, for brilliant sovereignty, for unrivalled triumph, with Thargélie Dumarsais, the Queen of the Theatre?

Ravishingly beautiful looked the matchless actress as she sat before her Psyche, flashing *œillades*, on the brilliant group who made every added aigrette, every additional bouquet of the coiffure, every little *mouche*, every touch to the already perfect toilette, occasion for flattering simile and soft-breathed compliment; ravishingly beautiful, as she laughed at Maurice de Saxe, or made a disdainful *moue* at an impromptu couplet of Dorat's, or gave a blow of her fan to Richelieu, or asked Saint-Aulaire what he thought of Vanloo's portrait of her as *Rodugune;* ravishingly beautiful, with her charms that disdained alike rouge and maréchale powder, and were matchless by force of their own colouring, form, and voluptuous languor, when, her toilette finished, followed by her glittering crowd, she let Richelieu lead her to his carriage.

There was a review of Guards on the plain at Sablons that morning, a fête afterwards, at which she would be surrounded by the most brilliant staff of an Army of Noblesse, and Richelieu was at that moment the most favoured of her troop of lovers. M. le Duc, as every one knows, never sued at court or coulisse in vain, and the love of Thargélie Dumarsais, though perhaps with a stronger touch of romance in it than was often found in the atmosphere of the foyer, was, like the love of her time and her class, as inconstant and vivacious, now settling here, now lighting there, as any butterfly that fluttered among the limes at Trianon. Did not the jest-loving *parterre* ever salute with gay laughter two lines in a bagatelle-comedy of the hour—

> Oui l'Amour papillonne, sans entraves, à son gré;
> Chargé longtemps de fers, de soie même, il mourrait!—

when spoken by Thargélie Dumarsais—laughter that hailed her as head-priestess of her pleasant creed, in a city and a century where the creed was universal?

"Ah, bonjour! You have not seen her before, have you, semi-Englishman? You have found nothing like her in the foggy isles, I wager you fifty louis!" cried one of Thargélie Dumarsais's court, the Marquis de la Thorillière, meeting a friend of his who had arrived in Paris only the day before, M. le Chevalier de Tallemont des Réaux, as Richelieu's cortége rolled away, and the Marquis crossed to his own carriage.

"Her? Whom? I have not been in Paris for six years, you know. What can I tell of its idols, as I remember of old that they change every hour?"

"True! but, bon Dieu! not to know La Dumarsais! What it must be to have been buried in those benighted Britannic Isles! Did you not see her in Richelieu's carriage?"

"No. I saw a carriage driving off with such an escort and such fracas, that I thought it could belong to nobody less than to Madame Lenormand d'Etioles; but I did not observe it any further. Who is this beauty I ought to have seen?"

"Thargélie Dumarsais, for whom we are all ruining ourselves with the prettiest grace in the world, and for whom you will do the same when you have been once to the Français; that is, if you have the good fortune to attract her eyes and please her fancy, which you may do, for the fogs have agreed with you, Léon!—I should not wonder if you become the fashion, and set the women raving of you as 'leur zer zevalier!'"

"Thanks for the prophecy, but I shall not stay long enough to fulfil it, and steal your myrtle crowns. I leave again to-morrow."

"*Leave?* Sapristi! See what it is to have become half English, and imbibed a taste for spleen and solitude! Have you written another satire, or have you learned such barbarism as to dislike Paris?"

"Neither; but I leave for Lorraine to-morrow. It is five years since I saw my old pine-woods."

"Dame! it is ten years since *I* saw the wilds of Bretagne, and I will take good care it shall be a hundred before I see them again. *Hors de Paris, c'est hors du monde.* Come with me to La Dumarsais's *petit souper* to-night, and you will soon change your mind."

"My good Armand, you have not been an exile, as I have; you little know how I long for the very scent of the leaves, the very smell of the earth at Grande Charmille! But bah! I talk in Hebrew to you. You have been lounging away your days in titled beauties' *petits salons*, making butterfly verses, learning their broidery, their lisp, and their perfumes, talking to their parrots, and using their cosmétiques, till you care for no air but what is musk-scented! But what of this Dumarsais of yours—does she equal Lecouvreur?"

"Eclipses her!—with Paris as with Maurice de Saxe. Thargélie Dumarsais is superb, mon cher— unequalled, unrivalled! We have had nothing like her for beauty, for grace, for talent, nor pardieu! for extravagance! She ruined *me* last year in a couple of months. Richelieu is in favour just now—with what woman is he not? Thargélie is very fond of the

Marshals of France! Saxe is fettered to her hand and foot, and the Duchesse de Bouillon hates her as rancorously as she does Adrienne. Come and see her play *Phèdre* to-night, and you will renounce Lorraine. I will take you to supper with her afterwards; she will permit any friend of mine entry, and then, generous man that I am, I shall have put you *en chemin* to sun yourself in her smiles and ingratiate yourself in her favour. Don't give me too much credit for the virtue though, for I confess I should like to see Richelieu supplanted."

"Does his reign threaten to last long, then?"

The Marquis shrugged his shoulders, and gave his badine an expressive whisk.

"Dieu sait! we are not prophets in Paris. It would be as easy to say where that weathercock may have veered to-morrow, as to predict where La Dumarsais's love may have lighted ere a month! Where are you going, may I ask?"

"To see Lucille de Vaudreuil. I knew her at Lunéville; she and Madame de Boufflers were warm friends till Stanislaus, I believe, found Lucille's eyes lovelier than Madame la Marquise deemed fit, and then they quarrelled, as women ever do, with virulence in exact proportion to the ardour of their friendship."

"As the women quarrel at Choisy for *notre maître!* They will be friends again when both have lost the game, like Louis de Mailly and the Duchesse de Châteauroux. The poor Duchess! Fitz-James and Maurepas, Châtillon and Bouillon, Rochefoucauld and Le Père Pérussot, all together, were too strong for her. All the gossip of that Metz affair reached you across the water, I suppose? Those pests of Jesuits! if they want him to be their Very Christian King, and to cure him of his worship of Cupidon, they will have to pull down all the stones of La Muette and the Parc aux Cerfs! What good is it to kill *one* poor woman when women are as plentiful as roses at Versailles? And now let me drive you to Madame de Vaudreuil; if *she* do not convert you from your fancy for Lorraine this morning, Thargélie Dumarsais will to-night."

"*Mon zer zevalier, Paris est ado'able! Vous n'êtes pas sé'ieux en voulant le quitter, z'en suis sûre!*" cried the Comtesse de Vaudreuil, in the pretty lisp of the day, a charming little blonde, patched and powdered, nestled in a chair before a fire of perfumed wood, teasing her monkey Zulmé with a fan of Pater's, and giving a pretty little sign of contempt and disbelief with some sprays of jessamine employed in the chastisement of offenders more responsible and quite as audacious as Zulmé.

Her companion, her "zer zevalier," was a young man of seven-and-twenty, with a countenance frank, engaging, nobly cast, far more serious, far more thoughtful in its expression, than was often seen in that laughing and mocking age. Exiled when a mere boy for a satirical pamphlet which had provoked the wrath of the Censeur Royal, and might have cost him the Bastille but for intercession from Lunéville, he had passed his youth less in pleasure than in those philosophical and political problems then beginning to agitate a few minds; which were developed later on in the "Encyclopédie," later still in the Assemblée Nationale. Voltaire and Helvetius had spoken well of him at Madame de Geoffrin's; Claudine de Tencin had introduced him the night before in her brilliant salons; the veteran Fontenelle had said to him; "*Monsieur, comme censeur royal je refusai mon approbation à votre brochure; comme homme libre je vous en félicite*"—all that circle was prepared to receive him well, the young Chevalier de Tallemont might make a felicitous season in Paris if he chose, with the romance of his exile about him, and Madame de Vaudreuil smiling kindly on him.

"The country!" she cried; "the country is all very charming in eclogues and pastorals, but out of them it is a desert of ennui! What *can* you mean, Léon, by leaving Paris to-morrow? Ah, méchant, there must be something we do not see, some love besides that of the Lorraine woods!"

"Madame, is there not my father?"

"*Bien zoli!* But at your age men are not so filial. There is some other reason—but what? Any love you had there five years ago has hardly any attractions now. Five years! Ma foi, five months is an eternity that kills the warmest passion!"

"May there not be some love, madame, that time only strengthens?"

"I never heard of it if there be. It would be a very dreary affair, I should fancy, smouldering, smouldering on and on like an ill-lit fire. Nobody would thank you for it, mon cher, *here!* Come, what is your secret? Tell it me."

Léon de Tallemont smiled; the smile of a man who has happy thoughts, and is indifferent to ridicule.

"Madame, one can refuse you nothing! My secret? It is a very simple one. The greatest pang of my enforced exile was the parting from one I loved; the greatest joy of my return is that I return to her."

"*Bon Dieu! comme c'est drôle!* Here is a man talking to me of love, and of a love not felt for *me!*" thought Madame la Comtesse, giving him a soft glance of her beautiful blue eyes. "You are a very strange man. You have lived out of France till you have grown wretchedly serious and eccentric. Loved this woman for five years? Léon! Léon! you are telling me a fairy tale. Who is she, this enchantress? She must have some mysterious magic. Tell me—quick!"

"She is no enchantress, madame, and she has no magic save the simple one of having ever been very dear to me. We grew up together at Grande Charmille; she was the orphan niece of the Priest, a fond, innocent, laughing child, fresh and fair, and as untouched by a breath of impure air as any of the violets in the valley. She was scarcely out of the years of childhood when I left her, with beauty whose sweetest grace of all was its own unconsciousness. Through my five long years of exile I have remembered Favette as I saw her last under the elm-boughs in the summer light, her eyes dim with the tears of our parting, her young heart heaving with its first grief. I have loved her too well for others to have power to efface or to supplant her; of her only have I thought, of her only have I dreamed, holding her but the dearer as the years grew further from the hour of our separation, nearer to the hour of our reunion. I have heard no word of her since we parted; but of what value is love without trust and fidelity in trial? The beauty of her childhood may have merged into the beauty of womanhood, but I fear no other change in Favette. As we parted so we vowed to meet, and I believe in her love as in my own. I know that I shall find my Lorraine violet, without stain or soil. Madame, Favette is still dearer to me now, Heaven help me, than five years ago. Five years—five years—true! it *is* an eternity! Yet the bitterness of the past has faded for ever from me *now*, and I only see—the future!"

Madame de Vaudreuil listened in silence; his words stirred in her chords long untouched, never heard amidst the mots, the madrigals, the laughter of her world of Paris, Versailles, and Choisy. She struck him a little blow with her jessamine-sprays, with a mist gathering over her lovely blue eyes.

"Hush, hush, Léon! you speak in a tongue unknown here. A word of the heart amongst us sounds a word of a *Gaulois* out of fashion—forbidden."

III.

MIDNIGHT.

The Français was crowded. Thargélie Dumarsais, great in *Electre, Chimène, Inès*, as in "*Ninette à la Cour*," "*Les Moissonneurs*," or "*Annette et Lubin*," was playing in "*Phèdre*." Louis Quinze was present, with all the powdered marquises, the titled wits, the glittering gentlemen of the Court of Versailles; but no presence stayed the shout of adoration with which the parterre welcomed the idol of the hour, and Louis le Bien-aimé (des femmes!) himself added his royal quota to the ovation, and threw at her feet a diamond, superb as any in his regalia. It was whispered that the Most Christian King was growing envious of his favourite's favour with La Dumarsais, and would, ere long, supersede him.

The foyer was filled with princes of the blood, marshals of France, dukes, marquises, the élite of her troop of lovers; lords and gentlemen crowded the passages, flinging their bouquets for her carpet as she passed; and poor scholars, young poets, youths without a sou—amongst them Diderot, Gilbert, Jean-Jacques Rousseau—pressed forward to catch a glimpse, by the light of the links, of this beauty, on which only the eyes of grands seigneurs who could dress Cupidon in a court habit *parfilé d'or* were allowed to gaze closely, as she left the Français, after her unmatched and uninterrupted triumphs, and went to her carriage with Richelieu. The suppers of Thargélie Dumarsais were renowned through Paris; they equalled in magnificence the suppers of the Regency, rivalled them for licence, and surpassed them for wit. All the world might flock to her fêtes, where she undisguisedly sought to surpass the lavishness of Versailles, even by having showers of silver flung from her windows to the people in the streets below; but to her *soupers à huis clos* only a chosen few were admitted, and men would speak of having supped with La Dumarsais as boastfully as women of having supped with the King at Choisy.

"What you have lost in not seeing her play *Phèdre!* Helvetius would have excused you; all the talk of his salons is not worth one glance at La Dumarsais. Mon ami! you will be converted to Paris when once you have seen her," said the Marquis de la Thorillière, as his carriage stopped in the Chaussée d'Antin.

Léon de Tallemont laughed, and thought of the eyes that would brighten at his glance, and the heart that would beat against his own once more under the vine shadows of Lorraine. No new magic, however seductive, should have strength to shake his allegiance to that Memory: and, true to his violet in Lorraine, he defied the Queen of the Foyer.

"We are late, but that is always a more pardonable fault than to be too early," said the Marquis as they were ushered across the vestibule, through several salons, into the supper-room, hung with rich tapestries of "Les Nymphes au Bain," "Diane Chasseresse," and "Apollon et Daphné;" with gilded consoles, and rosewood buffets, enamelled with medallion groups, and crowded with Sèvres and porcelaine de Saxe, while Venetian mirrors at each end of the salle reflected the table, with its wines, and fruits, and flowers, its gold dishes and Bohemian glass. The air was heavily perfumed, and vibrating with laughter. The guests were Richelieu, Bièvre, Saxe, D'Etissac, Montcrif, and lovely Marie Camargo, the queen of the coulisses who introduced the "short skirts" of the ballet, and upheld her innovation so staunchly amidst the outcries of scandalised Jansenists and journalist. But even Marie Camargo herself paled—and would have paled even had she been, what she was not, in the first flush of her youth—before the superb beauty, the languid voluptuousness, the sensuous grace, the southern eyes, the full lips, like the open leaves of a damask rose, melting yet mocking, of the most beautiful and most notorious woman of a day in which beauty and notoriety were rife, the woman with the diamond of Louis Quinze sparkling in the light upon her bosom, whom Versailles and Paris hailed as Thargélie Dumarsais.

The air, scented with amber, rang with the gay echoes of a stanza of Dorat's, chanted by Marie Camargo; the "Cupids and Bacchantes," painted in the panels of Sèvres, seemed to laugh in sympathy with the revel over which they presided: the light flashed on the King's diamond, to which Richelieu pointed, with a wicked whisper; for the Marshal was getting tired of his own reign, and his master might pay his court when he would. Thargélie Dumarsais, more beautiful still at her *petit souper* than at her *petit lever*, with her hair crowned with roses, true flowers of Venus that might have crowned Aspasia, looked up laughingly as her lacqueys ushered in le Marquis de la Thorillière and Le Chevalier de Tallemont.

"M. le Marquis," cried the actress, "you are late! It is an impertinence forbidden at my court. I shall sup in future with barred doors, like M. d'Orléans; then all you late-comers———"

Through the scented air, through the echoing laughter, stopping her own words, broke a startled bitter cry:

"*Mon Dieu, c'est Favette!*"

Thargélie Dumarsais shrank back in her rose velvet fauteuil as though the blow of a dagger had struck her; the colour fled from her lips, and underneath the delicate rouge on her cheeks; her hand trembled as it grasped the King's aigrette.

"Favette—Favette! Who calls me that?"

It was a forgotten name, the name of a bygone life, that fell on her ear with a strange familiar chime, breaking in on the wit, the licence, the laughter of her midnight supper, as the subdued and mournful sound of vesper bells might fall upon the wild refrains and noisy drinking-songs of bacchanalian melody.

A surprised silence fell upon the group, the laughter hushed, the voices stopped; it was a strange interruption for a midnight supper. Thargélie Dumarsais involuntarily rose, her lips white, her eyes fixed, her hand clasped convulsively on the King's diamond. A vague, speechless terror held mastery over her, an awe she could not shake off had fastened upon her, as though the dead had risen from their graves, and come thither to rebuke her for the past forgotten, the innocence lost. The roses in her hair, the flowers of revel, touched a cheek blanched as though she beheld some unearthly thing, and the hand that lay on the royal jewel shook and trembled.

"Favette? Favette?" she echoed again. "It is so many years since I heard that name!"

Her guests sat silent still, comprehending nothing of this single name which had such power to move and startle her. Richelieu alone, leaning back in his chair, leisurely picked out one of his brandy-cherries, and waited as a man waits for the next scene at a theatre:

"Is it an unexpected tragedy, or an arranged comedy, ma chère? Ought one to cry or to laugh? Give me the *mot d'ordre!*"

His words broke the spell, and called Thargélie Dumarsais back to the world about her. Actress by profession and by nature, she rallied with a laugh, putting out her jewelled hand with a languid glance from her long almond-shaped eyes.

"A friend of early years, my dear Duc, that is all. Ah, Monsieur de Tallemont, what a strange rencontre! When did you come to Paris? I scarcely knew you at the first moment: you have so long been an exile, one may pardonably be startled by your apparition, and take you for a ghost! I suppose you never dreamed of meeting Favette Fontanie under my *nom de théâtre!* Ah! how we change, do we not, Léon? Time is so short, we have no time to stand still! Marie, ma chère, give Monsieur le Chevalier a seat beside you—he cannot be happier placed!"

Léon de Tallemont heard not a word that she spoke; he stood like a man stunned and paralysed by a sudden and violent blow, his head bowed, a mortal pallor changing his face to the hues of death, the features that were a moment before bright, laughing, and careless, now set in mute and rigid anguish.

"Favette! Favette!" he murmured, hoarsely, in the vague dreamy agony with which a man calls wildly and futilely on the beloved dead to come back to him from the silence and horror of the grave.

"Peste!" laughed Richelieu. "This cast-off lover seems a strange fellow! Does he not know that absent people have never the presumption to dream of keeping their places, but learn to give them graciously up!—shall I teach him the lesson? If he have his sixteen quarterings, a prick of my sword will soon punish his impudence!"

The jeer fell unheeded on Léon de Tallemont's ear; had he heard it, the flippant sneer would have had no power to sting him then. Regardless of the men around the supper-table, he grasped Thargélie Dumarsais's hands in his:

"This is how we meet!"

She shrank away from his glance, terrified, she scarce knew why, at the mute anguish upon his face.

Perhaps for a moment she realised how utterly she had abused the love and wrecked the life of this man; perhaps with his voice came back to her thronging thoughts of guileless days, memories ringing through the haze of years, as distant chimes ring over the water from lands we have quitted, reaching us when we have floated far away out to sea—memories of an innocent and untroubled life, when she had watched the woodland flowers open to the morning sun, and listen to the song of the brooks murmuring over the violet roots, and heard the sweet evening song of the birds rise to heaven under the deep vine shadows of Lorraine.

One moment she was silent, her eyes falling, troubled and guilty, beneath his gaze; then she looked up, laughing gaily, and flashing on him her languid, lustrous glance.

"You look like a somnambulist, *mon ami!* Did nobody ever tell you, then, how Mme. de la Vrillière carried me off from Lorraine, and brought me in her train to Paris, till, when Favette Fontanie was tired of being petted like the spaniel, the monkey, and the parrot, she broke away from Madame la Marquise, and made, after a little probation at the Foire St. Laurent, her appearance at the Français as Thargélie Dumarsais? *Allons donc!* have I lost my beauty, that you look at me thus? You should be reminding me of the proverb, '*On revient toujours à ses premiers amours!* Surely, Thargélie Dumarsais will be as attractive to teach such a lesson as that little peasant girl, Favette, used to be? Bah, Léon! Can I not love you as well again in Paris as I once loved you at Grande Charmille! And—who knows?—perhaps I will!"

She leaned towards him; her breath fanning his cheek, her scented hair brushing his lips, her eyes meeting his with eloquent meaning, her lips parted with the resistless witchery of that melting and seductive *sourire d'amour* to which they were so admirably trained. He gazed down on her, breathless, silence-stricken—gazed down on the sorceress beauty to which the innocent loveliness of his Lorraine flower had changed. Was this woman, with the rouge upon her cheeks, the crimson roses in her hair, the mocking light in her eyes, the wicked laugh on her lips, the diamond glittering like a serpent's eye in her bosom—was she the guileless child he had left weeping, on the broken steps of the fountain, tears as pure as the dew in the violet-bells, with the summer sunlight streaming round her, and no shade on her young brow darker than the fleeting shadow flung from above by the vine-leaves? A cry broke once more from his lips:

"Would to God I had died before to-night!"

Then he lifted his head, with a smile upon his face—a smile that touched and vaguely terrified all those who saw it—the smile of a breaking heart.

"I thank you for your proffered embraces, but *I* am faithful. I love but one, and I have lost her; Favette is dead! I know nothing of Thargélie Dumarsais, the Courtesan."

He bowed low to her and left her—never to see her face again.

A silence fell on those he had quitted, even upon Richelieu; perhaps even he realised that all beauty, faith, and joy were stricken from this man's life; and—reality of feeling was an exile so universally banished from the gay salons of the Dix-huitième Siècle, that its intrusion awed them, as by the unwonted presence of some ghostly visitant.

Thargélie Dumarsais sat silent—her thoughts had flown away once more from her brilliant supper-chamber to the fountain at Grande Charmille; she was seeing the dragon-flies flutter among the elm-boughs, and the water ripple over the wild thyme; she was feeling the old priest's good-night kiss upon her brow, and her own hymn rise and mingle with the chant of the vesper choir; she was hearing the song of the forest birds echo in the Lorraine woods, and a fond voice whisper to her, "Fear not, Favette!—we shall meet as we part!"

Richelieu took up his Dresden saucer of cherries once more with a burst of laughter.

"*Voilà un drôle!*—this fellow takes things seriously. What fools there are in this world! It will be a charming little story for Versailles. Dieu! how Louis will laugh when I tell it him! I fear though, ma chérie, that the 'friend of your childhood' will make you lose your reputation by his impolitic epithets!"

"When one has nothing, one can lose nothing—eh, ma chère?" laughed Marie Camargo. "Monsieur le Duc, she does not hear us——"

"No, *l'infidèle!*" cried Richelieu. "Mademoiselle! I see plainly you love this rude lover of bygone days better than you do us!—is it not the truth!"

"Chut! nobody asks for truths in a polite age!" laughed Thargélie Dumarsais, shaking off unwelcome memories once for all, and looking down at the King's diamond gleaming in the light—the diamond that prophesied to her the triumph of the King's love.

"Naturally," added La Camargo. "My friend, I shall die with envy of your glorious jewel. *Dieu! comme il brille!*"

"DEADLY DASH."
A STORY TOLD ON THE OFF DAY.

On the off-day after the Derby everybody, except the great winners, is, it will be generally admitted, the resigned prey to a certain gentle sadness, not to say melancholy, that will only dissipate itself under a prolonged regimen of S. and B., Seidlitz well dashed with Amontillado, or certain heavenly West Indian decoctions;— this indisposition, I would suggest, we should call, delicately and dubiously, Epsomitis. It will serve to describe innumerable forms and degrees of the reactionary malady.

There is the severest shape of all, "dead money," that covers four figures, dropped irretrievably, and lost to the "milkers;" lost always *you* say because of a cough, or because of a close finish, or because of a something dark, or because of a strain in the practising gallops, or because of a couple of brutes that cannoned just at the start; and never, of course, because the horse you had fancied was sheerly and simply only fit for a plater. There is the second severe form, when you awake with a cheerful expectation of a summons for driving "at twelve miles an hour" (as if that wasn't moderate and discreet!), and for thereby smashing a greengrocer's cart into the middle of next week, and running a waggonette into an omnibus, as you came back from the Downs, of which you have no more remembrance than that there was a crash, and a smash, and a woman's screams, and a man's "d—n the swells!" and a *tintamarre* of roaring conductor and bellowing greengrocer, and infuriated females, through which you dashed somehow with a cheer—more shame for you—and a most inappropriate *l'Africaine* chorus from the men on your drag. There is the milder form, which is only the rueful recollection of seeing, in a wild ecstasy, the chesnut with the white blaze sweep with his superb stride to the front, and of having, in your moment of rapturous gratitude to the red and blue, rushed, unintentionally, during the discussion of Fortnum and Mason's hamper, into a promise to take Euphrosyne Brown to Baden in August, where you know very well she will cost you more than all your sums netted through Gladiateur. There are slenderer touches of the malady, which give you, over your breakfast coffee, a certain dolorous meditation as to how you could have been such a fool as to have placed all your trust in Danebury, or to have put in a hole through Spring Cottage just what your yacht costs for three months; which makes you wonder why on earth you took that lot of actresses on to the hill, and threw money enough away on them in those wages of idiotcy (or wages of sin, as your uncle the dean would translate it), of cashmeres, eau de Cologne, gloves, and bracelets, to have purchased those two weight carriers offered you at 600*l.* the pair, and dirt cheap at that; or which makes you only dully and headachily conscious that you drank champagne up on the box-seat as if you were a young fellow from Eton, and now pay for the juvenile folly, as you know you deserve to do, when that beautiful white Burgundy at your club, or your own cool perfect claret at home, seems to stare you in the face and ask, "Why *did* you crack all those bottles of Dry on the Downs?"

There are symptoms and varieties innumerable of the malady that I propose shall be known henceforward as Epsomitis; therefore, the off-day finds everybody more or less slightly done up and mournful. Twenty-four hours and the Oaks, if properly prepared for by a strictly medicinal course of *brûles-gueules*, as the Chasseurs say, smoked perseveringly, will bring all patients round on the Friday; but during the twenty-four hours a sense that all on and off the course is vanity and vexation of spirit will generally and somnolently predominate in the universal and fashionable disease of Epsomitis.

One off-day, after the magnificent victory of Monarque's unrivalled son, an acquaintance of mine, suffering considerably from these symptoms, sought my philosophy and my prescriptions. A very sharp irritant for Epsomitis may be administered in the form of "I told you so! It's all your own fault!" But this species of blister and douche bath combined is rarely given unless the patient be mad enough to let his wife, if he unluckily have one, learn what ails him. As far as I was concerned, I was much too sympathetic with the sufferer to be down upon him with the triumphant reminder that I had cautioned him all along not to place his trust in Russley. I, instead, prescribed him cool wines, and led him on to talk of other people's misfortunes, the very best way to get reconciled with your own. We talked of old times, of old memories, of old acquaintance, in the twilight, between Derby and Oaks. We got a little melancholy; too much champagne is always productive on the morrow of a gentle sentimental tinge, and a man is always inclined to look on the world as a desert when he has the conviction that he himself has been made a fool in it. Among other names, that of Deadly Dash came up between us. What had become of him? I did not know; he did. He told me; and I will tell it here, for the story is of the past now.

"Deadly Dash! What a shot he was! Never missed," said my friend, whose own gun is known well enough at Hornsey-wood House; therewith falling into a reverie, tinged with a Jacques-like gloom of Epsomitis in its severest form, from which he awoke to tell me slowly, between long draughts of iced drinks, what I write now. I alter his tale in nothing, save in filling in with words the gaps and blanks that he made, all-eloquent in his halting oratory, by meditative, plaintive, moralising puffs from his tonic, the *brûle-gueule*, and an occasional appeal to my imagination in the customary formula of "Oh, bother!—*you* understand—all the rest of it, you know," which, though it tells everything over claret, is not so clear a mode of relation in type. For all else here the story is as he gave it to me.

"Deadly Dash!" It was a fatal sounding sobriquet, and had a fatal fascination for many, for me as well as the rest, when I was in my salad days and joined the old —th, amongst whose Light Dragoons it was so signally and ominously famous. The nickname had a wide significance; "*he always kills*," was said with twofold truth, in twofold meaning of Dash; in a *barrière* duel he would wheel lightly, aim carelessly, and send the ball straight as any arrow through heart or lung, just as he fancied, in the neatest style anybody could dream of; and in an intrigue he took just the same measures, and hit as invariably with the selfsame skill and the self-same indifference. "He always kills," applied equally to either kind of affair, and got him his sobriquet, which he received with as laughing an equanimity as a riding man gets the Gilt Vase, or a "lover of the leash" the Ravensworth Stakes, or the Puppy Cup and Goblet. He was proud of it, and had only one regret, that he lived in the dead days of the duel, and could only go out when he was on French soil. In dare-devilry of every sort he out-Heroded Herod, and distanced any who were mad enough to try the pace with him in that steeple-chase commonly called "going to the bad." It was a miracle how often he used to reach the stage of "*complete ruin*" that the Prince de Soubise once sighed for as an unattainable paradise; and picked himself up again, without a hair turned, as one may say, and started off with as fresh a pace as though nothing had knocked him over. Other men got his speed sometimes; but nobody could ever equal his stay. For an "out and out goer" there was nobody like Deadly Dash; and though only a Captain of Horse, with few "expectations," he did what Dukes daren't have done, and lived at a faster rate than all the elder sons in the kingdom put together. Dash had the best bow and the brightest wits, the lightest morals and the heaviest debts of any *sabreur* in the Service; very unscrupulous fellows were staggered at *his* devil-me-care vices; and as for reputation,—"a deuced pleasant fellow, Dash," they used to say at the Curragh, in the Guards' Club, at Thatched House anniversary dinners, in North Indian cantonments, in Brighton barrack-rooms, or in any of the many places where Deadly Dash was a household word; "a very pleasant fellow; no end 'fit' always, best fun in life over the olives when you get him in the humour; shoot you dead though next morning, if he want, and you be handy for him in a neat snug little Bad; make some devil of a *mot* on you too afterwards, just as pleasantly at if he were offering you a Lopez to smoke!"

Now, that was just the sort of celebrity that made me mad to see the owner of it; there wasn't a living being, except that year's favourite out of the Whitewall establishment, that I was half so eager to look at, or so reverent when I thought of, as "the Killer." I was very young then. I had gone through a classic course of yellow covers from Jeffs' and Rolandi's, and I had a vague impression that a man who had had a dozen *barrière* affairs abroad, and been *"enfant"* to every lovely *lionne* of his day, must of necessity be like the heroes of Delphine Demirep's novels, who had each of them always a "je ne sais quoi de farouche et de fier dans ses grands yeux noirs, et toute la révélation d'une ame usée, mais dominée par des passions encore inépuisables, écrite sur son sombre et pale visage," &c., &c., in the Demirep's most telling style.

I don't know quite what I expected to see in the Killer, but I think it was a sort of compound of Monte Cristo, Mephistopheles, and Murat mixed in one; what I did see was a slight delicate man, with a face as fair and soft as a girl's, the gentlest possible manners, and a laugh like music. Deadly Dash had led a life as bad as he could lead, had lit his cigar without a tremor in the wrist, on many grey mornings, while his adversary lay dying hard among the red rank grasses, had gamed so deep twenty-four hours at a stretch that the most reckless *galérie* in Europe held their breath to watch his play; had had a tongue of silver for his intrigues and a nerve of steel for his *vendetta;* had lived in reckless rioting and drunk deep; but the Demirep would not have had him at any price in her romance; he looked so simply and quietly thorough-bred, he was so utterly guiltless of all her orthodox traits. The gentlest of mortals was Deadly Dash; when you first heard his sweet silvery voice, and his laughter as light and airy as a woman's, you would never believe how often abroad there a dead man had been left to get stiff and cold among the clotted herbage, while the Killer went out of the town by the early express, smoking and reading the "Charivari," and sipping some cold Curaçoa punch out of his flask.

"Of course!" growled a man to me once in the Guards' smoking-room, an order of the Scots Fusiliers to Montreal having turned him misanthrope. "Did Mephistopheles ever come out in full harness, with horns and tail complete, eh? Not such a fool. He looked like a gentleman, and talked like a wit. Would the most dunder-headed Cain in Christendom, I should be glad to know, be such an ass as to go about town with the brand on his forehead, when he could turn down Bond-street any day and get a dash of the ladies' pearl powder? Who ever *shows* anything now, my good fellow? Not that Dash 'paints,' to give the deuce his due—except himself a little blacker even than he is; he don't cant; he couldn't cant; not to save his life, I believe. But as to his bewitching you, almost as bad as he does the women, I know all about that. I used to swear by him till——"

"Till what?"

"Till he cut a brother of mine out with Rachel, and shot him in the woods of Chantilly for flaring-up rough at the rivalry. Charlie was rather a good fellow, and Dash and I didn't speak after that, you see. Great bore; bosh too, perhaps. Dash brews the best Curaçoa punch in Europe, and if he name you the winning mount for the Granby, you may let the talent damn you as they like. Still you know, as he killed Charlie——" and the Guardsman stuck a great cheroot in his mouth, in doubt as to whether, after all, it wasn't humbug, and an uncalled-for sacrifice, rather than scenic and sentimental, to drop an expert at Curaçoa brew, and a sure prophet for Croxton Park, just because, in a legitimate fashion, he had potted your brother and relieved your entail;—on the whole, a friendly act rather than otherwise? "Keep clear of the Killer, though, young one," he added, as he sauntered out. "He's like that cheetah cub of Berkeley's; soft as silk, you know, *patte de velours*, and what d'ye call 'em, and all the rest of it, but deucedly deadly to deal with."

I did know: it was the eternal refrain that was heard on all sides; from the wily Jews through whose meshes he slipped; the unhappy duns who were done by him; the beauties who were bewitched by him; the hosts and husbands who, having him down for the pheasants, found him poach other preserves than those of the cover-sides; the women who had their characters shattered by a silvery sneer from a voice that was as soft, in its murderous slander, as in its equally murderous wooing; and all the rest, who, in some shape or another, owed ruin to that Apollo Apollyon—Deadly Dash. Ruin which at last became so wide and so deep, that even vice began to look virtuous when his name was mentioned (vice always does when she thinks you are really cleared out), and men of his own corps and his own club began to get shy of having the Killer's arm linked in theirs too often down Pall Mall, for its wrist was terribly steady in either Hazard, whether of the yard of green table or the twenty yards of green turf.

At last the crisis came: the Killer killed one too many; a Russian Prince in the Bois de Vincennes, in a quarrel about a pretty wretched little chorus-singer of the Café Alcazar, who took their fancies both at once. The *mondes* thought it terribly wicked, not the deed, you know, but the audacity of a cavalry man's having potted a Very Serene High Mightiness. In a Duke, all these crimes and crim-cons, though as scarlet, would have been held but the crimson gold-dotted fruit adorning the strawberry-leaves; Deadly Dash, a Light Dragoon, whose name was signed to plenty of "floating little bills," could not bid high enough to purchase his pardon from Society, which says to its sinners with austere front of virtue, "Oblivion cannot be hired—unless," adds Society, dropping to mellowest murmur her whisper, "unless you can give us a premium!" So Dash, with a certain irresistible though private pressure upon him from the Horse Guards—sent in his papers to sell. What had been done so often could not now be done again; the first steeplechaser in the Service could not at last even save his stake, but was finally, irretrievably, struck out.

Certainly the fellow was a bad fellow, and deserved his crash, so far; he had no scruples, and no conscience; he spared neither woman nor man; of remorse he had never felt a twinge, and if you were in his path he would pick you off some way or other as indifferently as if you were one of the pigeons at Hornsey. And yet, he had been kind to me, though I was a young one; with his own variable Free Lance sort of liberality, the man would give his last sou to get you out of any difficulty, and would carry off your mistress, or beggar you at chicken-hazard, with the self-same pleasant air the next day: and I could not help being sorry that things had come to this pass with him. He shot so superbly! Put him where you would, in a warm corner while the bouquets of pheasants were told off; in a punt, while a square half-mile of wild ducks whirred up from the marshes; in a dark forest alley in Transylvania, while the great boar rushed down through the twilight, foaming blood and roaring fury; in a still Indian night with the only target here and there a dusky head diving amidst the jhow jungle three hundred yards away: put him where you would, he was such a magnificent shot! The sins of a Frankenstein should not have lost such a marksman as Deadly Dash to the Service.

But the authorities thought otherwise; they were not open to the fact, that the man who had been out in more *barrière* affairs, and had won more Grand Military stakes than any other, should, by all laws of war-policy, have had his blackest transgressions forgiven him, till he could have been turned to account against Ghoorkas, Maories, or Caffres. The authorities instead, made him send in his papers, not knowing the grand knack of turning a scamp into a hero—a process that requires some genius and some clairvoyance in the manipulator—and Deadly Dash, with his lightest and airiest laugh, steamed down channel one late autumn night, marked, disgraced, and outlawed, for creditors by the score were after him, knowing very well that he and his old gay lawless life, and his own wild pleasant world, and his old lands yonder in the green heart of the grass countries that had gone rood by rood to the Hebrews, were all divorced for ever, with a great gulf between them that could never close.

So he dropped out of the Service, out of the country, out of remembrance, out of regret; nobody said a De Profundis over him, and some men breathed the freer. We can rarely be sure of any who will be sorry to miss us; but we can always be certain of some to be glad we are gone. And in the Killer's case these last were legion. Here and there were one or two who owed him a wayward, inconstant bizarre, fit of generosity; but there were on the other hand hundreds who owed him nothing less than entire ruin.

So Deadly Dash went with nobody to regret him and nobody to think of him for a second, after the nine hours' wonder in the clubs and the mess-rooms that his levanting "under a cloud" occasioned; and so the old sobriquet that had used to have so signal a notoriety, dropped out of men's mouths and was forgotten. Where he was gone no one knew; and, to be sure, no one asked. Metaphorically, he was gone to the devil; and when a man takes that little tour, if he furnish talk for a day he has had very distinguished and lengthened obsequies as friendship goes in this world. Now and then, in the course of half a dozen years, I remembered him, when I looked up at the head of a Royal over my mantelpiece, with thirteen points, that he had stalked once in Ayrshire and given to me; but nobody else gave a thought to the Killer. Time passed, and whether he had been killed fighting in Chili or Bolivia, shot himself at Homburg, become Mussulman and entered the Sultan's army, gone to fight with the Kabyles and Bedouins, turned brigand for the Neapolitan Bourbons, or sunk downward by the old well-worn stage, so sadly and so often travelled, into an adventurer living by the skill of his écarté and the dread surety of his shot, we did not know; we did not care. When Society has given a man the sack, it matters uncommonly little whether he has given himself a shroud.

Seven or eight years after the name of Deadly Dash had ceased to be heard among cavalry men, and quoted on all things "horsey," whether of the flat or of the ridge and furrow, I was in the Confederate States, on leave for a six months' tour there. It was after Lee's raid across the border and the days of Gettysburgh. I had run the blockade in a fast-built clipper, and pushed on at once into the heart of Virginia, to be in the full heat of whatever should come on the cards; cutting the cities rather, and keeping as much as I could to the camps and the woods, for I wanted to see the real thing in the rough. In my relish for adventure, however, I was a trifle, as it proved, too foolhardy.

Starting alone one day to cross the thirty miles or so that parted me from the encampment of some Virginian Horse, with no other companions than a very weedy-looking steel grey and a brace of revolvers,

I fairly "lost tracks," and had not a notion of my way out of a wilderness of morass and forest, all glowing with the scarlet and the green of the Indian summer. Here and there were beautiful wild pools and lakes shut in by dense vegetation, so dense, that at noon it was dark as twilight, and great table-lands of rock jutted out black and rugged in places; but chiefly as far as was to be seen stretched the deep entangled woodland, with nothing else to break it, brooding quietly over square leagues of swamp. The orioles were singing their sweetest, wildest music overhead; sign of war there was none, save, to be sure, now and then when I came on a black, arid circle, where a few charred timbers showed where a hut had been burnt down and deserted, or my horse shied and snorted uneasily, and half stumbled over some shapeless log on the ground—a log that when you looked closer was the swollen shattered body of a man who had died hard, with the grass wrenched up in his fingers that the ants had eaten bare, and the hollows of his eyes staring open where the carrion birds had plucked the eyeballs out. And near *him* there were sure to be, half sunk in swamp, or cleaned to skeletons by the eagles and hawks, five, or ten, or twenty more, lying nameless and unburied there, where they had fallen in some scuffle with pickets, or some stray cavalry skirmish, to be told off as "missing," and to be thought of no more. These groups I came upon more than once rotting among the rich Virginian soil, while the scarlet and purple weight of blossoming boughs swayed above, and the bright insect life fluttered humming around them; they were the only highway marks through the wooded wilderness.

So lonely was it mile after mile, and so little notion had I of either the way in or the way out, that the *hallali* of a boar-hunt, or the sweet mellow tongues of the hounds when they have found in the coverts at home, were never brighter music to me than the sharp crack of rifles and the long sullen roll of musketry as they suddenly broke the silence, while I rode along, firing from the west that lay on my left. The grey, used to powder, pointed his ears and quickened his pace. Though a weedy, fiddle-headed beast, his speed was not bad, and I rattled him over the ground, crashing through under-growth and wading through pools, with all my blood up at the tune of those ringing cheery shots; the roar growing louder and louder with every moment, and the sulphur scent of the smoke borne stronger and stronger down on the wind, till the horse broke *pêle-mêle* through the network of parasites; dashed downward along a slope of dank herbage, slipping at every step, and with his hind-legs tucked under him; and shot, like a run-in for a race, on to a green plateau, where the skirmish was going on in hot earnest.

A glance told me how the land lay. A handful of Southern troopers held their own with tremendous difficulty against three divisions of Federal infantry, whom they had unexpectedly encountered, as the latter were marching across the plateau with some batteries of foot artillery,—the odds were probably scarcely less than five to one. The Southerners were fighting magnificently, as firm in their close square of four hundred as the Consular Guard at Marengo, but so surrounded by the Northern host, that they looked like a little island circled round by raging breakers. Glancing down on the plain as my horse scoured and slid along the incline, the nucleus of Southerners looked hopelessly lost amidst the belching fire and pressing columns of the enemy. The whole was surrounded and hidden by the whirling clouds of dust and smoke that swirled above in a white heavy mist; but through this the sabres flashed, the horses' heads reared, maddened and foam-covered, like so many bas-reliefs of Bucephalus, the lean rifle-barrels glittered, and for a moment I saw the Southern leader, steady as a rock in the centre, hewing like a trooper right and left, and with a grey heron's feather floating from his sombrero, a signal that seemed as well known and as closely followed as the snowy plume of Murat.

To have looked on at this and not have taken a share in it, one would have been a stone, not a man, and much less a cavalry-man; I need not tell you that I smashed the grey across the plateau, hurled him into the thick of the mêlée, dashed *somehow* through the Federal ranks, and was near the grey plume and fighting for the Old Dominion before you could have shouted a stave of "Dixie." I was a "non-combatant," I was a "neutral"—delicate Anglo-euphemism for coward, friend to neither and traitor to both!—I was on a tour of observation, and had no business to fire a shot for one or the other perhaps, that I forgot all that, and with the bridle in my teeth and a pistol in each hand, I rode down to give one blow the more for the weak side.

How superbly that Grey Feather fought!—keeping his men well up round him, though saddle after saddle was emptied, and horse after horse tore riderless out of the ranks, or reeled over on their heads, spurting blood, he sat like a statue, he fought like a Titan, his sabre seemed flashing unceasingly in the air, so often was it raised to come down again like lightning through a sword-arm, or lay open a skull to the brains; the shots ploughed up the earth round him, and rattled like hail through the air, a score of balls were aimed at him alone, a score of sabres crossed his own; but he was cool as St. Lawrence ice, and laid the men dead in struggling heaps under his charger's hoofs: only to fight near the man was a glorious intoxication; you seemed to "breathe blood" till you got drunk with it.

The four hundred had been mowed down to two; I did as good work as I could, having wrenched a sword out of some dead trooper's hand; but I was only one, and the Northerners counted by thousands. Come out of it alive I never expected to do; but I vow it was the happiest day of my life—the pace was so splendidly fast! The Grey Feather at last glanced anxiously around; his men stuck like death to him, ready to be hewed down one by one, and die game; his teeth were set tight, and his eyes had a flash in them like steel. "Charge! and cut through!" he shouted, his voice rolling out like a clarion, giving an order that it seemed could be followed by nothing short of supernatural aid. The Southrons thought otherwise; they only heard to obey; they closed up as steadily, as though they were a squadron on parade, despite the great gaps between them of dying chargers, and of heaped-up killed and wounded, that broke their ranks like so much piled stones and timber; they halted a moment, the murderous fire raking them right and left, front and rear; then, with that dense mass of troops round them, they charged; shivered the first line that wedged them in; pierced by sheer force of impetus the columns that opened fire in their path; wrenched themselves through as through the steel jaws of a trap, and swept out on to the green level of the open plateau, with a wild rallying Virginian shout that rings in my ears now!

I have been in a good many hot things in my time; but I never knew anything that for pace and long odds could be anything near to that.

I had kept with them through the charge with no other scratch than a shoulder-cut; and I had been close to their chief through it all. When we were clean out on the plains beyond pursuit—for the Union-men had not a squadron of cavalry, though their guns at long range belched a storm in our wake—he turned in his saddle without checking his mare's thundering gallop, and levelled his rifle that was slung at his side. "I'll have the General, anyhow," he said, quietly taking aim—still without checking his speed—at the knot of staff-officers that now were scarce more than specks in a blurred mass of mist. He fired; and the centre figure in that indistinct and fast-vanishing group fell from the saddle, while the yell of fury that the wind faintly floated nearer told us that the shot had been deadly. The Grey Feather laughed, a careless airy laugh of triumph, while he swept on at topmost pace; a little more, and we should dive down into the dark aisles of grand forest trees and cavernous ravines of timber roads, safe from all pursuit; a second, and we should reach the green core of the safe and silent woods, the cool shelter of mountain-backed lakes, the sure refuge of tangled coverts. It was a guinea to a shilling that we gained it; it was all but won; a moment's straight run-in, and we should have it! But that moment was not to be ours.

Out of the narrow cleft of a valley on the left, all screened with hanging tumbled foliage, and dark as death, there poured suddenly across our front a dense body of Federal troopers and Horse Artillery, two thousand strong at the least, full gallop, to join the main army. We were surrounded in a second, in a second overpowered by sheer strength of numbers; only two hundred of us, many sorely wounded, and on mounts that were jaded and ridden out of all pace, let us fight as we would, what could we do against fresh and picked soldiers, swarming down on us like a swarm of hornets, while in our rear was the main body through which we had just cut our way? That the little desperate band "died hard," I need not say; but the vast weight of the fresh squadrons pressed our little knot in as if between the jaws of a trap, crushing it like grain between two iron weights. The Grey Feather fought like all the Knights of the Round Table merged in one, till he streamed with blood from head to foot, and his sabre was hacked and bent like an ash-stick, as did a man near him, a tall superb Virginian, handsome as any Vandyke or Velasquez picture. At last both the Grey Feather and he went down, not by death—it would not come to them—but literally hurled out of their stirrup-leathers by crowding scores who poured on them, hamstrung or shot their horses, and made them themselves prisoners—not, however, till the assailants lay heaped ten deep about their slaughtered chargers. For myself, a blow from a sabre, a second afterwards, felled me like so much wood. I saw a whirling blaze of sun, a confused circling eddy of dizzy colour, forked flames, and flashes of light, and I knew no more, till I opened my eyes in a dark, square, unhealthy wooden chamber, with a dreamy but settled conviction that I was dead, and in the family vault, far away under the green old elms of Warwickshire, with the rooks cawing above my head.

As the delusion dissipated and the mists cleared, I saw through the uncertain light a face that was strangely but vaguely familiar to me, connected somehow with incoherent memories of life at home, and yet unknown to me. It was bronzed deeply, bearded, with flakes of grey among the fairness of the hair, much aged, much worn, scarred and stained just now with the blood of undressed wounds and the dust of the combat, for there was no one merciful enough there to bring a stoup of water; it was rougher, darker, sterner, and yet, with it all, nobler, too, than the face that I had known. I lay and stared blankly at it: it was the face of the Southern Leader of the morning, who sat now, on a pile of straw, looking wearily out to the dying sun, one amongst a group of twenty, prisoners all, like myself. I moved, and he turned his eyes on me; they had laid me down there as a "gone 'coon," and were amazed to see me come to life again. As our eyes met I knew him—he was Deadly Dash.

The old name left my lips with a shout as strong as a half-killed man can give. It seemed so strange to meet him there, captives together in the Unionists' hands! It struck him with a sharp shock. England and he had been divorced so long. I saw the blood leap to his forehead, and the light into his glance; then, with a single stride, he reached the straw I lay on, holding my hands in his, looking on me with the kindly eyes that had used to make me like the Killer, and greeting me with a warmth that was only damped and darkened by regret that my battle done for fair Virginia had laid me low, a prisoner with himself, and that we should meet thus, in so sharp an hour of adversity, with nothing before us but the Capitol, the Carroll prison, or worse. Yet thus we did meet once more, and I knew at last what had been the fate of Deadly Dash, whom England had outlawed as a scoundrel, and the New World had found a hero.

Though suffering almost equally himself, he tended me with the kindliest sympathy; he came out of his own care to ponder how possible it might be to get me eventual freedom as a tourist and a mere accidental sharer in the fray; he was interested to hear all that I would tell him of my own affairs and of his old friends in England, but of himself he would not speak; he simply said he had been fighting for the Confederacy ever since the war had begun; and I saw that he strove in vain to shake off a deep heart-broken gloom that seemed to have settled on him, doubtless, as I thought, from the cruel defeat of the noon, and the hopeless captivity into which he, the most restless and the most daring soldier that ever saw service, was now flung.

I noticed, too, that every now and then while he sat beside me, talking low—for there were sentinels both in and out the rude outhouse of the farm that had been turned into our temporary prison—his eyes wandered to the gallant Virginian who had been felled down with himself, and who, covered like himself with blood and dust, and with his broken left arm hanging shattered, lay on the bare earth in a far-off corner motionless and silent, with his lips pressed tight under their long black moustaches, and such a mute unutterable agony in his eyes as I never saw in any human face, though I have seen deaths enough in the field and the sick-ward. The rest of the Confederate captives were more ordinary men (although from none was a single word of lament ever wrenched); but this superb Virginian excited my interest, and I asked his name, in that sort of languid curiosity at passing things which comes with weakness, of the Killer, whose glance so incessantly wandered towards him.

"Stuart Lane," he answered, curtly, and added no more; but if I ever saw in this world hatred, passionate, ungovernable, and intense, I saw it in the Killer's look as his glance flashed once more on to the motionless form of the handsomest, bravest, and most dauntless officer of his gallant regiment that he had seen cut to pieces there on that accursed plateau.

"A major of yours?" I asked him. "Ah, I thought so; he fought magnificently. How wretched he looks, though he is too proud to show it!"

"He is thinking of—of his bride. He married three weeks ago."

The words were simple enough, and spoken very quietly; but there was an unsteadiness, as of great effort, over them; and the heel of his heavy spurred jack-boot crashed into the dry mud with a grinding crush, as though it trod terrible memories down. Was it a woman who was between these two comrades in arms and companions in adversity? I wondered if it were so, even in that moment of keen and heavy anxiety for us all, as I looked at the face that bent very kindly over the straw to which a shot in the knee and a deep though not dangerous shoulder-wound bound me. It was very different to the face of eight or nine years before—browner, harder, graver far; and yet there was a look as if "sorrow had passed by there," and swept the old heartlessness and gay callousness away, burning them out in its fires.

Silence fell over us in that wretched outshed where we were huddled together. I was hot with incipient fever, and growing light-headed enough, though I knew what passed before me, to speak to Dash once or twice in a dreamy idea that we were in the Shires watching the run-in for the "Soldiers' Blue Riband." The minutes dragged very drearily as the day wore itself away. There were the sullen monotonous tramp of the sentinels to and fro, and, from without, the neighing of horses, the bugle calls, the roll of the drums, the challenge of outposts—all the varied, endless sounds of a camp; for the farm-house in whose shed we were thrown was the head-quarters *pro tem.* of the Federal General who commanded the Divisions that had cost the Killer's handful of Horse so fearfully dear. We were prisoners, and escape was impossible. All arms of course had been removed from us; most, like myself, were too disabled by wounds to have been able to avail ourselves of escape had it been possible; and the guard was doubled both in and out the shed; there was nothing before any of us but the certainty of imprisonment in all its horrors in some far-off fortress or obscure gaol. There was the possible chance that, since certain officers on whom the Northerners set great store had lately fallen into Southern hands, an exchange might be effected: yet, on the other side, graver apprehensions still existed, since we knew that the General into whose camp we had been brought had proclaimed his deliberate purpose of shooting the three next Secessionist officers who fell into his power, in requital for three of his own officers who had been shot, or were said to have been shot, by a Southern raider. We knew very well that, the threat made, it would be executed; and each of us, as the sun sank gradually down through the hot skies that were purple and stormy after the burning day, knew, too, that it might never rise again to greet our sight. None of us would have heeded whether a ball would hit or miss us in the open, in a fair fight, in a man-to-man struggle; but the boldest and most careless amidst us felt it very bitter to die like dogs, to die as prisoners.

Even Deadly Dash, coolest, most hardened, most devil-may-care of soldiers and of sinners, sat with his gaze fastened on the slowly sinking light in the west with the shadow of a great pain upon his face, while every now and then his glance wandered to Stuart Lane, and a quick, irrepressible shudder shook him whenever it did so. The Virginian never moved; no sign of any sort escaped him; but the passionate misery that looked out of his eyes I never saw equalled, except, perhaps, in the eyes of a stag that I once shot in Wallachia, and that looked up with just such a look before it died. He was thinking, no doubt, of the woman he loved—wooed amidst danger, won amidst calamity, scarcely possessed ere lost for ever;—thinking of her proud beauty, of her bridal caress, that would never again touch his lips, of her fair life that would perish with the destruction of his.

Exhaustion from the loss of blood made everything pass dreamily, and yet with extraordinary clearness, before me. I felt in a wakening dream, and had no sense whatever of actual existence, and yet the whole scene was so intensely vital and vivid to me, that it seemed burned into my very brain itself. It was like the phantasmagoria of delirium, utterly impalpable, but yet intensely real. I had no power to act or resist, but I seemed to have ten times redoubled power to see and hear and feel; I was aware of all that passed with a hundred-fold more susceptibility to it than I ever felt in health. I remember a total impossibility that came on me to decide whether I was dreaming or was actually awake. Twilight fell, night came; there was a change of sentries, and a light, set up in a bottle, shed a glittering, feeble, yellow gleam over the interior of the shed, on the dark Rembrandt faces of the Southerners and on the steel of the guards' bayonets. And I recollect that the Killer, who sat by the tossed straw on which they had flung me, laughed the old, low, sweet, half-insolent laugh that I had known so well in early days. "*Il faut souffrir pour être beau!* We are picturesque, at any rate, quite Salvatoresque! Little Dickey would make a good thing of us if he could paint us now. He is alive, I suppose?"

I answered him I believe in the affirmative; but the name of that little Bohemian of the Brush, who had used to be our butt and *protégé* in England, added a haze the more to my senses. By this time I had difficulty to hold together the thread of how, and when, and why I had thus met again the face that looked out on me so strangely familiarly in the dull, sickly trembling of the feeble light of this black noisome shed in the heart of Federal Divisions.

Through that haze I heard the challenge of the

sentries; I saw a soldier prod with his bayonet a young lad who had fainted from hemorrhage, and whom he swore at for shamming. I was conscious of the entrance of a group of officers whom I knew afterwards to be the Northern General and his staff, who came to look at their captives. I knew, but only dreamily still, that these men were the holders of our fate, and would decide on it then and there. I felt a listless indifference, utter and opium-like, as to what became of me, and I remember that Stuart Lane, and Dash himself, rose together, and stood looking with a serene and haughty disdain down on the conquerors who held their lives in the balance—without a trace of pain upon their faces now. I remember how like they looked to stags that turn at bay; like the stags, outnumbered, hunted down, with the blood of open wounds and the dust of the long chase on them; but, like the deer, too, uncowed, and game to the finish.

Very soon their doom was given. Seven were to be sent back with a flag of truce to be exchanged for the seven Federal officers they wanted out of the Southerners' hands, ten were to be transmitted to the prisons of the North,—three were to be shot at day-dawn in the reprisal before named. The chances of life and of death were to be drawn for by lottery, and at once.

Not a sound escaped the Virginians, and not a muscle of their English Leader's face moved: the prisoners, to a man, heard impassively, with a grave and silent dignity, that they were to throw the die in hazard, with death for the croupier and life for the stake.

The General and his staff waited to amuse themselves with personally watching the turns of this new

Rouge et Noir; gambling in lives was a little refreshing change that sultry, dreary, dun-coloured night, camped amongst burnt-out farms and wasted corn-lands.

Slips of paper with "exchange," "death," and "imprisonment" written on them in the numbers needed were made ready, rolled up, and tossed into an empty canteen; each man was required to come forward and draw, I alone excepted because I was an officer of the British Army. I remember passionately arguing that they had no right to exempt me, since I had been in the fray, and had killed three men on my own hook, and would have killed thirty more had I had the chance; but I was perhaps incoherent in the fever that was fast seizing all my limbs from the rack of undressed wounds; at any rate, the Northerners took no heed save to force me into silence, and the drawing began. As long as I live I shall see that night in remembrance with hideous distinctness: the low blackened shed with its fœtid odours from the cattle lately foddered there; the yellow light flaring dully here and there; the glisten of the cruel rifles; the heaps of straw and hay soaked with clotted blood; the group of Union Officers standing near the doorway; and the war-worn indomitable faces of the Southerners, with the fairer head and slighter form of their English Chief standing out slightly in front of all.

The Conscription of Death commenced; a Federal private took the paper from each man as he drew it, and read the word of destiny aloud. Not one amongst them faltered or paused one moment; each went,—even those most exhausted, most in agony,—with a calm and steady step, as they would have marched up to take the Flag of the Stars and Bars from Lee or

Longstreet. Not one waited a second's breath before he plunged his hand into the fatal lottery.

Deadly Dash was the first called: there was not one shadow of anxiety upon his face; it was calm without effort, careless without bravado, simply, entirely indifferent. They took his paper and read the words of safety and of life—"Exchange." Then, for one instant, a glory of hope flashed like the sun into his eyes—to die the next; die utterly.

Three followed him, and they all drew the fiat for detention; the fifth called was Stuart Lane.

Let him have suffered as he would, he gave no sign of it now; he approached with his firm, bold cavalry step, and his head haughtily lifted; the proud, fiery, dauntless, Cavalier of ideal and of romance. Without a tremor in his wrist he drew his paper out and gave it.

One word alone fell distinct on the silence like the hiss of a shot through the night—"*Death!*"

He bowed his head slightly as if in assent, and stepped backward—still without a sign.

His English chief gave him one look—it was that of merciless exultation, of brutal joy, of dark, Cain-like, murderous hate; but it passed, passed quickly: Dash's head sank on his chest, and on his face there was the shadow, I think, of a terrible struggle—the shadow, I know, of a great remorse. He strove with his longing greed for this man's destruction; he knew that he thirsted *to see him die.*

The Virginian stood erect and silent: a single night and the strong and gallant life, the ardent passions, the chivalrous courage to do and dare, and the love that was in its first fond hours, would all be quenched in him as though they had never been; but he was a soldier, and he gave no sign that his death-warrant was not as dear to him as his bridal-night had been. Even his conquerors cast one glance of admiration on him; it was only his leader who felt for him no pang of reverence and pity.

The lottery continued; the hazard was played out; life and death were scattered at reckless chance amidst the twenty who were the playthings of that awful gaming; all had been done in perfect silence on the part of the condemned; not one seemed to think or to feel for himself, and in those who were sent out to their grave not a grudge lingered against their comrades of happier fortune. Deadly Dash, whose fate was release, alone stood with his head sunk, thoughtful and weary.

The three condemned to execution were remanded to separate and solitary confinement, treated already as felons for that one short night which alone remained to them. As his guards removed him, Stuart Lane paused slightly, and signed to his chief to approach him; he held out his hand to Dash, and his voice was very low, though it came to my ear where they stood beside me: "We were rivals once, but we may be friends *now*. As you have loved her, be pitiful to her when you tell her of my death,—God knows it may be hers! As you have loved her, feel what it is to die without one last look on her face!"

Then, and then only, his bronze cheek grew white as a woman's, and his whole frame shook with one great silent sob; his guard forced him on, and his listener had made him no promise, no farewell; neither had he taken his hand. He had heard in silence, with a dark and evil gloom alone upon him.

The Federal General sharply summoned him from his musing, as the chief of those to be exchanged on the morrow under a white flag of parley; there were matters to be stated to and to be arranged with him.

"I will only see you alone, General," he answered, curtly.

The Northerner stared startled, and casting a glance over the redoubtable leader of horse, whose grey feather had become known and dreaded, thought of possible assassination. Deadly Dash laughed his old light, ironic, contemptuous laugh.

"A wounded unarmed man can scarcely kill you! Have as many of your staff about you as you please, but let none of my Virginians be present at our interview."

The Northerners thought he intended to desert to them, or betray some movement of importance, and assented; and he went out with them from the cattle-shed into the hot, stormy night, and the Southerners who were condemned to death and detention looked after him with a long, wistful, dog-like look. They had been with him in so many spirit-stirring days and nights of peril, and they knew that never would they meet again. He had not given one of them a word of adieu; he had killed too many to be touched by his soldiers' loss. Who could expect pity from Deadly Dash?

An hour passed; I was removed under a guard to a somewhat better lodging in the granary, where a surgeon hastily dressed my wounds, and left me on a rough pallet with a jug of water at my side, and the sentinel for my only watcher, bidding me "sleep." Sleep! I could not have slept for my ransom. Though life had hardened me, and made me sometimes, as I fear, callous enough, I could not forget those who were to die when the sun rose; specially, I could not forget that gallant Virginian to whom life was so precious, yet who gave himself with so calm a fortitude to his fate. The rivalry, I thought, must be deep and cruel, to make the man from whom he had won what they both loved turn from him in hatred, even in such extremity as his. On the brink of a comrade's grave, feud might surely have been forgotten?

All that had just passed was reeling deliriously through my brain, and I was panting in the sheer irritation and exhaustion of gunshot wounds, when through the gloom Dash entered the granary, closely guarded, but allowed to be with me on account of our common country. Never was I more thankful to see a familiar face from home than to see his through the long watches of that burning, heavy, interminable night. He refused to rest; he sat by me, tending me as gently as a woman, though he was suffering acutely himself from the injuries received in the course of the day; he watched me unweariedly, though often and often his gaze and his thoughts wandered far from me, as he looked out through the open granary door, past the form of the sentinel, out to the starry solemn skies, the deep woods, and the dark silent land over which the stars were brooding, large and clear.

Was he thinking of the Virginian whose life would die out for ever with the fading of those stars, or of the woman whom he had lost, whose love was the doomed soldier's, and would never be his own, though the grave closed over his rival with the morrow's sun?

Dreamily, half unconsciously, in the excitement of fever, I asked him of her of whom I knew nothing:

"Did you love that woman so well?"

His eyes were still fixed on the distant darkening skies, and he answered quietly, as though rather to his own thoughts than my words: "Yes; I love her—as I never loved in that old life in England; as we never love but once, I think."

"And she?"

"And she—has but one thought in the world—*him*."

His voice, as he answered, now grated with dull, dragging misery over the words.

"Had she so much beauty that she touched you like this?"

He smiled slightly, a faint, mournful smile, unutterably sad.

"Yes; she is very lovely, but her beauty is the least rare charm. She is a woman for whom a man would live his greatest, and if he cannot live for her—may—die."

The utterance was very slow, and seemed to lie on me like a hand on my lips compelling me to silence; he had forgotten all, except his memory of her, and where he sat with his eyes fixed outward on the drifting clouds that floated across the stars, I saw his lips quiver once, and I heard him murmur half aloud: "My darling! My darling! You will know how I loved you *then*——"

And the silence was never broken between us, but he sat motionless thus all the hours through, looking out at the deep still woods, and the serene and lustrous skies, till the first beams of the sun shone over the hills in the east, and I shuddered, where I lay, at its light;—for I knew it was the signal of death.

Then he arose, and bent towards me, and the kindly eyes of old looked down on mine.

"Dear old fellow, the General expects me at dawn. I must leave you just now; say good-bye."

His hand closed on mine, he looked on me one moment longer, a little lingeringly, a little wistfully, then he turned and went out with his guard; went out into the young day that was just breaking on the world.

I watched his shadow as it faded, and I saw that the sun had risen wholly; and I thought of those who were to die with the morning light.

All was very calm for awhile; then the beat of a drum rolled through the quiet of the dawn, and the measured tramp of armed men sounded audibly; my heart stood still, my lips felt parched—I knew the errand of that column marching so slowly across the parched turf. A little while longer yet, and I heard the sharp ring of the ramrods being withdrawn, and the dull echo of the charge being rammed down: with a single leap, as though the bullets were through me, I sprang, weak as I was, from my wretched pallet, and staggered to the open doorway, leaning there against the entrance, powerless and spell-bound. I saw the file of soldiers loading; I saw the empty coffin-shells; I saw three men standing bound, their forms distinct against the clear, bright haze of morning, and the fresh foliage of the woods. Two of them were Virginians, but the third was not Stuart Lane.

With a great cry I sprang forward, but the guards seized my arms and held me, helpless as a woman, in their gripe. He whom we had called Deadly Dash heard, and looked up and smiled. His face was tranquil and full of light, as though the pure peace of the day shone there.

The gripe of the sentinels held me as if in fetters of iron; the world seemed to rock and reel under me, a sea of blood seemed eddying before my eyes; the young day was dawning, and murder was done in its early hours, and I was held there to look on—its witness, yet powerless to arrest it! I heard the formula—so hideous then!—"Make ready!"—"Present!"—"Fire!" I saw the long line of steel tubes belch out their smoke and flame. I heard the sullen echo of the report roll down from the mountains above. When the mist cleared away, the three figures stood no longer clear against the sunlight; they had fallen.

With the mad violence of desperation, I wrenched myself from my guards, and staggered to him where he lay; he was not quite dead yet; the balls had passed through his lungs, but he breathed still; his eyes were unclosed, and the gleam of a last farewell came in them. He smiled slightly, faintly, once more.

"She will know how I loved her now. Tell her I died for her," he said, softly, while his gaze looked upwards to the golden sun-rays rising in the east.

And with these words life passed away, the smile still lingering gently on his lips;—and I knew no more, for I fell like a man stunned down by him where he was stretched beside the grave that they had hewn for him ere he was yet dead.

I knew when I saw him there, as well as I knew by detail long after, that he had offered his life for Stuart Lane's, and that it had been accepted; the Virginian, ignorant of the sacrifice made for him, had been sent to the Southern lines during the night, told by the Northerners that he was pardoned on his parole to return in his stead a distinguished Federal officer lately captured by him. He knew nothing, dreamt nothing, of the exchange by which his life was given back to the woman who loved him, when his English Leader died in his place as the sun rose over the fresh summer world, never again to rise for those whose death-shot rang sullen and shrill through its silence.

So Deadly Dash died, and his grave is nameless and unknown there under the shadow of the great Virginian forests. He was outlawed, condemned, exiled, and the world would see no good in him; sins were on him heavily, and vices lay darkly at his door; but when I think of that grave in the South, where the grass grows so rankly now, and only the wild deer pauses, I doubt if there was not that in him which may well shame the best amongst us. We never knew him justly till he perished there.

And my friend who told me this said no more, but took up his *brûle-gueule* regretfully. The story is given as he gave it, and the States could whisper from the depths of their silent woods many tales of sacrifice as generous, of fortitude as great. That when he had related it he was something ashamed of having felt it so much, is true; and you must refer the unusual weakness, as he did, to the fact that he told it on the off-day of the Derby, after having put a cracker on Wild Charley. A sufficient apology for any number of frailties!

THE END.

PRINTING OFFICE OF THE PUBLISHER.